# PROTEST & PROGRESS

In my judgment, *Protest and Progress* is the most important book ever published on race relations in the Adventist church. It is essential reading for anyone desiring a well-informed perspective on the racial issues that continue to challenge the Adventist church. It combines first-rate scholarship with the kind of insight that could only come from the author's deep personal roots and decades of leadership in the Black Adventist experience. Dr. Rock guides the reader through four definitive episodes in the quest for more just, equitable, and mission-effective church structures in a racially-divided nation, telling much that has never been told in print before, with an abundance of documentation, much of it never before made public. He then deploys his expertise in theology and sociology of religion to chart a way forward. Even those inclined to take issue with aspects of Dr. Rock's proposal will find their knowledge expanded and perceptions sharpened by a careful reading of his analysis. Lucid, candid, provocative, yet redemptive, *Protest and Progress* is an exceptionally rare and invaluable gem given the church by one who has long loved it and served it with high distinction.

*Douglas Morgan, Professor of History*
*Washington Adventist University*

*Protest and Progress* offers a challenging and thoughtful look at four major twentieth-century protests that are still, to some extent, the hew and cry of a long-neglected people group for inclusion into the full life of the Seventh-day Adventist Church. As such, the book is a major contribution to the understanding of race relations, past and present, within the context of the Seventh-day Adventist Church in North America.

*Rosa Maria Taylor Banks, Retired General Conference Associate*
*Secretary and Former North American Division*
*Director of Human Relations*

This is one of the most important books that I have read in a long while. Written with unswerving honesty, it traces the struggles of African-American Seventh-day Adventists for justice and equality. I found much to admire and applaud, but much that made me sad. Dr. Rock makes a powerful case for the continuance of Regional conferences. Highly recommended, indispensable for administrators and Seminary students.

*William G. Johnsson, former editor*
**Adventist Review** *and* **Adventist World**

In this well written, carefully documented, provocative, historical and informative work, Dr. Calvin Rock takes readers behind the scenes into the causes for, decision-making surrounding, and factors resulting from the struggles of Black Seventh-day Adventists. *Protest and Progress* is a valuable tool which provides current leaders, from all hues, members of the Seventh-day Adventist Church, readers, and researchers profoundly significant data behind the realities that are both historical and lived experiences.... His perspective is valid and germane not just because he is related to some of the major players but also because he himself was in the room and/or at the table for some of the pertinent issues presented. This eyewitness outlook adds credibility to the work as does the fact that he was and is regarded as a respected, informed and credible leader of the church.

**Bertram Melbourne, Professor of Biblical Language and Literature**
**Former Interim Dean and Associate Dean**
**Howard University School of Divinity**

Calvin Rock has deepened my understanding of race relations in the Adventist Church. When the subject of Regional Conferences comes up I now have a better understanding of their origin and continued need for their existence. Will there be a time when they are no longer needed? Maybe. But Dr. Rock's history and insights are informative to both sides of the issue.

**Larry R. Moore, President, Southwestern Union Conference**
**Seventh-day Adventist Church**

For anyone seeking a deeper understanding of the intersections between race, culture, and mission among Seventh-day Adventists in North America, Calvin Rock's *Protest and Progress* is a valuable read....The author presents, in an accessible way, how the perspectives of the legendary leaders of the "colored work," the "Negro work," the "black work" and ultimately the "African-American work" positively impacted the growth and culture of the Seventh-day Adventist Church in North America. For anyone wishing to go beyond surface pronouncements around unity, reconciliation, justice, and mission, this work will prove incisive and illuminating. The thoughtful reader will leave this book asking himself or herself, "Where do I go from here?"

**Leslie Pollard, President**
**Oakwood University**

Once in a while, words from the printed page reach up and grab you—not a vice-like grip that jolts and jostles but more of an embrace welcoming you to something real. Like *Protest and Progress*. Here early Rock-solid personal experience greets you and preambles a long look at race and rights in the reach for leadership among Blacks and Whites within Seventh-day Adventism in America. No dry theory here. The author was strategically there for half a century amid fray and interplay not as spectator but participant. We owe him and Providence for keeping us closer to reality.

*Mervyn A. Warren (Retired), Interim President/Provost/Dean of Religion, Oakwood University*

Calvin Rock's book traces segments of the journey of the Seventh-day Adventist Church from the perspective of Black Adventists in its founding nation, the United States. It appears at a most timely point in human history. It comes after thousands of years of so-called improvements in human relations which purportedly have led to increased acceptance between racial and ethnic groups. Yet, while many gains have been realized, society and the Church continue to face challenges of immense magnitude in regard to full inclusion for all people, particularly in leadership, worldwide. Dr. Rock's vivid portrayal of what he calls the "push" for legitimate involvement of Black Adventists in the full array of church affairs is compelling for those from whom it evokes memories for reflection and healing; and for those whose personal experiences are different, it provides insights for greater understanding. This work calls for general civility among people groups and for the intentional elimination of racial and ethnic competition in support of all people in the Church's opportunities for ministry and service. Perhaps it points to a Seventh-day Adventist Church that is defined by the love of which its equality testifies.

*Ella Smith Simmons, General Vice President*
*General Conference of Seventh-day Adventists*

An uncommon blend of scholar and church leader, Rock is uniquely qualified to write this book, having been an eyewitness to much of the story that he articulates lucidly and clearly.… Drawing from primary more often than secondary sources, Rock leaves few stones unturned in his investigation, resulting in a book that fills some important gaps in African-American and Seventh-day Adventist denominational history. Readers will find much in this compelling book that will challenge and stretch them, which should not be surprising given that conversations about race are inherently complex and difficult.

*R. Clifford Jones, President*
*Lake Region Conference of Seventh-day Adventists*

Dr. Rock's book is the perfect antidote for the collective amnesia of the Seventh-day Adventist church when it comes to racism and the church's reluctance to confront the antithesis of the gospel of Jesus Christ. It should be mandatory reading for every Seventh-day Adventist member and leader.

*Craig R. Jackson, Dean, Loma Linda University*
*School of Allied Health Professions*

Calvin B. Rock skillfully traces the steps of Black Adventism from its modest origins to its burgeoning impact today. He adeptly chronicles major movements in Adventist history which address issues facing the Black Adventist community, and ultimately clarifies the need for specific, relevant ministry from the Black perspective. All who read this work will walk away with a clearer understanding of the positive imprint of Black Adventism on the global church as collectively we "march to Zion."

*Carlton P. Byrd, Pastor, Evangelist*
*Breath of Life Television Speaker/Director*

Calvin Rock's analysis is crystal clear and his pointed presentation of the current and oft repeated discussion by both Black and White Seventh-day Adventists to de-legitimize Regional conferences is more than fairly dealt with, chronicling their beginning, contribution to the world church in soul winning, training of Black Adventist leaders, educational advancement, and financial contribution to the world church's budget. This is a must read for anyone curiously interested or seriously concerned with these issues and more. I highly recommend it.

*Ricardo Graham, President*
*Pacific Union Conference of Seventh-day Adventists*

Dr. Rock has captured a historical as well as personal perspective of the Black Adventist journey within the church structure. This important work provides context and understanding of the current racial and ethnic issues that face the church. These issues are relevant both to the church and to society in general.

*Larry Blackmer, Vice President for Education*
*North American Division, Seventh-day Adventist Church*

*Protest and Progress* bears out truth, with a light that will never dim. It is a historical work of history, protest, and progress. Its clear tone resonates with a sense of justice and urgency that transports the struggles of the past into lessons for the struggles of the present. This book is a legacy of service to Africans, African Americans, Anglo Americans, Asian Americans, South Americans, and every leader of the global community with a free mind, who can appreciate what it means to protest and progress; not only in the past, but the present and the future. May each reader be inspired.

*Delbert W. Baker, Vice Chancellor/President*
*Adventist University of Africa, Nairobi, Kenya*

Both historians and general readers will be interested in Rock's description of key protest movements in the spectacular growth of Black Adventism. He is particularly effective in describing developments in which he was a participant, such as the campaign for extending "Regional" organization to the union conference level. As he looks to the future, he offers a defense of the continuing relevance of Regional conferences. Even those who disagree with Dr. Rock's conclusions will be intrigued, provoked, and enlightened by this book.

*Eric Anderson, Professor of History*
*Pacific Union College*

# PROTEST & PROGRESS

## BLACK SEVENTH-DAY ADVENTIST LEADERSHIP AND THE PUSH FOR PARITY

### Calvin B. Rock

Andrews University Press

Andrews University Press
Sutherland House
8360 W. Campus Circle Dr.
Berrien Springs, MI 49104–1700
Telephone: 269–471–6134
Fax: 269–471–6224
Email: aupo@andrews.edu
Website: http://universitypress.andrews.edu

Copyright © 2018 by Andrews University Press

All rights reserved. No part of this book may be used or reproduced in any manner or translated into other languages without written permission from the publisher except in the case of brief quotations embodied in critical articles and reviews.

ISBN: 978–1–940980–22–5

Printed in the United States of America
22  21  20  19  18     2  3  4  5  6

Library of Congress Cataloging-in-Publication Data

Names: Rock, Calvin B., author.
Title: Protest and progress : Black Seventh-day Adventist leadership and the push for parity / Calvin B. Rock.
Description: Berrien Springs : Andrews University Press, 2018. | Includes bibliographical references and index.
Identifiers: LCCN 2017048998 | ISBN 9781940980225 (pbk. : alk. paper)
Subjects: LCSH: African American Seventh-day Adventists. | Christian leadership—Seventh-day Adventists.
Classification: LCC BX6153.2 .R63 2018 | DDC 286.7/3208996073—dc23
LC record available at https://lccn.loc.gov/2017048998

|  |  |
|---:|:---|
| Project Director | Ronald Alan Knott |
| Project Editor | Deborah L. Everhart |
| Text Editing | Benjamin Baker, Ronald Alan Knott, Gerald Wheeler |
| Editorial Assistance | Jonathan Gardner, Jasmine Logan, Keldie Paroschi |
| Documentation | Bryan Banos, William E. Dudgeon III, Sikhululekile Hlatshwayo Daco |
| Cover and Text Design | Max Gordienko |
| Image Processing | Pheonix M. Hardin |
| Proofreading | Deborah L. Everhart, Samuel Pagán De Jesús |
| Indexing | Natanael Abriol, Timothy Arena, L. S. Baker, Jr. |

Typeset: 10.5/14 Minion Pro

*To my wife Clara*
*without whose recall, research, and encouragement*
*this book could not have been*

# CONTENTS

Preface  xiii

Introduction  1

## PART ONE: THE PROTEST MOVEMENTS

1  The Push for Social and Administrative Participation, 1889–1928  13

2  The Push for Colored Conferences, 1929–1944  29

3  The Push for Black Unions, 1969–1980  97

4  The Push for Equitable Retirement Security, 1998–2000  149

## PART TWO: THE CHALLENGE AHEAD

1  The Question  163

2  Theoretical Replies  167

3  Replies of Practical Reasoning  217

4  Conclusion  225

## PART THREE: APPENDICES

Name Index  307

Subject Index  313

# PREFACE

*Protest and Progress* has two related goals. The first focuses on the four major twentieth-century endeavors of Black Seventh-day Adventist leadership to achieve parity within the whole body of believers and to maximize its witness beyond the church. The second examines the reasons for the continuation of Regional conferences, the most significant structural change for which Black leadership appealed.

However, before plunging into the history of Black Seventh-day Adventist social protest, a bit of personal background will help the reader to understand the writer's motives and, in fact, the need for this discussion.

My maternal grandmother, Etta Littlejohn Bradford (1881–1945), was a mulatto born in Vicksburg, Mississippi. In 1895 she accepted Adventism on the decks of the missionary boat *Morning Star,* built by Edson White, one of the sons of James and Ellen White. He had sailed the vessel from Lake Michigan where it was built down the Mississippi River into the Deep South. There along its shores he and the Southern Missionary Society taught literacy and religion to the children of the recently freed slaves.[1]

When what is now Oakwood University opened its doors as the Oakwood Industrial Training School on November 16, 1896, my grandmother Etta enrolled as one of the original sixteen students.[2] After leaving Oakwood, she studied nursing at Melrose Sanitarium in the Boston area, where for a short time she attended the church's prophet, Ellen White, as a chambermaid (nurse's assistant) and assisted White on some of her travels.

Following her graduation from Melrose, Etta married Robert Lee Bradford (1879–1957), a ministerial graduate of Oakwood. The Bradfords would have eight children in

ETTA LITTLEJOHN BRADFORD (1881–1945), author's maternal grandmother and among the earliest Black converts to Adventism. Courtesy of the author.

all, the fourth being my mother, Eva (1912–2009). The couple was successful in rearing their children in the ways of the Lord. In fact, through his efforts and example, Robert influenced his father, Robert Lafayette Bradford; son, Charles E. Bradford; and two grandsons, Robert Douglas and myself, to become Adventist pastors. In addition, two of Robert and Etta's granddaughters and one great granddaughter became ministers' wives.

While the genealogical roots on the maternal side of my family trace back to American slavery and their acceptance of Adventism three decades after Emancipation, the story differs on the paternal branch of the family tree. My father and his parents were immigrants to the United States from the Caribbean. Emily Bovell Rock, my paternal grandmother, reached New York City from her native Barbados aboard the ship *Vasari* at age thirty-eight on December 8, 1922; my paternal grandfather, George Benjamin Rock, arrived at age forty-two aboard the same vessel on January 9, 1924. Neither joined the Seventh-day Adventist Church, never severing the ties they had forged with the Anglican church on the island known as "Little England."

However, during the early years of their stay in the United States, three of their five children did connect with Adventism: my aunts Itena and Ermie, and my father, George (1910–1996), who at age seventeen arrived in New York City from Barbados by way of Trinidad on December 2, 1925, on the passenger ship *Vauban*. He was introduced to Adventism through his marriage to my mother, Eva Bradford.

ROBERT LEE BRADFORD (1879–1957), ministerial graduate from Oakwood, with his Philadelphia congregation. Courtesy of the author.

My parents were living in Harlem when I was born in a hospital in Brooklyn, New York, on July 4, 1930. It was a heady time in Harlem, America's "Black Metropolis." On one hand, "The Great Depression" was just beginning; but on the other, the Harlem Renaissance, Black America's memorable explosion of intellect and art which had begun in the 1920s, was still in celebration mode. All was not well in my family, though. My father, for reasons having to do with his visa that I have never understood, returned to Barbados shortly before my second birthday. I never saw or heard from him until he and my mother were reunited thirty-two years later. And so, it was just the three of us: my mother, my sister Etta (nine months younger), and me.

I do not recall any attempts by anyone on either side of my family to educate me in matters of race during my early years. What I do remember is the belief I had as a youngster that Harlem, where I had been born, was the greatest place in the world. The Harlem Ephesus Seventh-day Adventist Church, where I attended Sabbath School, and Harlem Academy, where I attended through grade five, were staffed with caring and protective men and women.

I did notice, however, at a very young age that when the Black boxer Joe Louis fought, people in the crowded brownstone apartments throughout our Harlem neighborhood would await the outcome with great anticipation. When Louis won, especially when the opponent was White, they exploded with parades and danced in exhilaration.

I also observed that, with one noticeable exception, when our church members went on outings to local recreation parks where other racial groups had gathered, we cautiously avoided contact, and there was never any disturbance. The single exception occurred one Sunday morning when I went with a number of our Ephesus Church teenage boys to a nearby park to watch them play ball. As we entered the park, a much larger group of White teenagers attacked

EVA BRADFORD-ROCK (1912–2009), author's mother and fourth child of Robert Lee and Etta Littlejohn Bradford. Courtesy of the author.

them and a bloody fist-fight ensued. It ended when we frantically retreated to safety. Although I was not hurt, I remember well the feeling of being helplessly overwhelmed by superior force and victimized, in the true sense of the word, by those who did so for seemingly no other reason than a sense of racial entitlement.

In September 1941 when I was eleven, my family migrated from what seemed to be the all-Black world of Harlem to the multi-ethnic society of Los Angeles. My younger sister, Wanda, was added to our family several years later. It was during my first several years on the West Coast, the World War II years of 1941 to 1945, that my racial perceptions and attitudes took on a definitive hue and they were decidedly negative, not so much from personal experience but from what I encountered in print. I was both fascinated and flabbergasted by the constant reports and photographs in newspapers of Blacks (including soldiers returning from the War) being not just discriminated against, but also beaten, stoned, and lynched by such groups as the Ku Klux Klan without fear of punishment. The Black newspaper chains, particularly the Associated Negro Press (ANP), actively reported such events during the 1940s, and I was then, as now, an avid reader of the news (Appendix 1).

Parents of the few Black students, scattered among the predominately White elementary church schools in the Los Angeles area, often told horror stories of racial discrimination in those institutions. This was true as well for those of Black students who, having completed our Black eighth-grade Adventist school, had enrolled in the one available Adventist school with twelve grades, the predominately White Linwood Academy.

I also heard that the White-administered Adventist colleges in the country enrolled Negro students on a strict quota basis. Those fortunate enough to be admitted could room only with other Blacks, were restricted to a separate table in the school's dining room, and were forbidden, under the threat of expulsion, to date across "the color line."

In addition, what I saw at camp meetings and special convocations, youth federations, and similar events was White leadership almost exclusively. White pastors preached and prayed. If Black pastors participated at all, it was to present quartet music or, as was the case with one or two who had strong lungs and engaging personalities, directing song service. Furthermore, I observed that they did so with a degree of enthusiasm and pride that even then, in my early teens, I could not understand given their seemingly lesser status.

By age thirteen, as the result of what I had read, heard, seen, and, to a lesser degree, experienced was that I could not bring myself to repeat the phrase "one-nation indivisible with liberty and justice for all" from the Pledge of Allegiance, nor sing the words: "We are not divided, all one body we" from "Onward Christian Soldiers." Although I said nothing to anyone about my feelings, I often wondered how any honest person, Black or White, could express what I regarded as such categorical untruths—and especially on the holy Sabbath day.

My negative regard for America's "liberty and justice for all" pledge received stark confirmation the summer of my eighteenth birthday, when I rode a Trailways bus from Los Angeles to Huntsville, Alabama, for my freshman year at Oakwood College. Shortly after the bus entered the state of Texas, the driver pulled over to the shoulder of the road and demanded that I move from my seat near the front to the back of the bus. I refused, muttering something to the effect that I had paid my money like everybody else. There was a momentary standoff as I sat surprised, bewildered, embarrassed, and frankly angry as the driver stood hovering over me. Looking up at him, I wondered just how I would protect myself if he tried to physically force me to the back of the bus. When he saw that I had no intention of budging, he turned toward the exit, swung open the door, and menacingly proclaimed, "If you don't move, I'm going to get the police!"

It was then that the full reality hit me. I was the only Negro (we were not called African-American as of yet) on the bus and we were parked on a lonely road in an isolated township near what I suspected was a hostile population with a biased judge. Then I imagined myself spending my freshman year locked up in a lonely Texas jail. As I thought about my mother and the anxiety she would feel, I bit my lip, swallowed my dignity, and in full view of the nearly full busload of quietly gazing Whites, gathered my luggage and walked toward the rear of the bus—not all the way but far enough to comply.

My remaining three and a half years as a college student in and around the Huntsville community during the late 1940s and early 50s produced no such dramatic incident, yet "Separate but Equal" cast its dark and intimidating pall whenever we left the Oakwood campus. Los Angeles was not perfect, but I always felt relieved when on the return home the bus or train sped into the welcoming sunshine of California. At least, I felt I had a fighting chance there.

In well over half a century of service in the Seventh-day Adventist Church, I have often felt uncomfortable repeating the lofty declarations of equality in the Pledge of Allegiance and "Onward, Christian Soldiers." But the genuine acceptance I experienced with White colleagues and constituents during the final three and a half decades of my ministry has made doing so possible.

The earliest portion of this latter service (1967–1970) involved a stint as the associate ministerial secretary for the Southern Union Conference. As the second Black (preceded by associate secretary Warren Banfield) to be elected to union level service in this territory (containing the eight states with the most haunting record of race crimes in the nation), I was at times apprehensive but always sincere about enhancing fellowship. My time in the field—preaching and consulting at churches, camp meetings, and workers' meetings—never disappointed.

My experience at the office was not as remarkable. While there were a number of persons serving there who went out of their way to support and include me (one of whom, thankfully, was the treasurer), there were others whose reactions revealed what I sensed as tepid concern for bridge-building opportunities in this region of North America. But, again, those were testy years for the nation, particularly the time of Martin Luther King's assassination (1968) and the spate of riots that followed. It was possible, during those times, to ascribe fear and uncertainty rather than racial animus to arms-length colleagues.

My fourteen-year presidency at what was then Oakwood College (1971–1985) presented no such challenge or need for explanation. That is because my Caucasian colleagues (presidents) of the other General Conference and North American Division schools of higher education were friendly, inclusive, and, without knowing it, very confirming of the tenets of brotherhood.

Each of the three General Conference presidents (of whom all were White), with whom I served while a General Conference vice president (1985–2002), demonstrated genuine concern for racial concord. The first, Neal C. Wilson (1979–1990), made heroic efforts to include African Americans in various facets of denominational service. The second, Robert S. Folkenberg (1990–1999), worked to truly integrate Black and White service units. And the third, Jan Paulsen (1999–2010), demonstrated his belief in racial equality by his support for the election of an African, Matthew Bediako, as the General Conference's first Black secretary, and of Ella Simmons, as the first Black female vice president. And my fellow vice presidents (a total of nine through the years) were almost without exception also very culturally sensitive.

There could not have been a more affirming relationship pattern than those that I sustained during my eleven years of chairing the boards of Loma Linda University and Hospital (1991-2002). The respect and cooperation I received was broad and consistent. What problems I did encounter—and there was one major attempt to disparage—I judged to be politically rather than racially motivated. Even after a decade and a half since leaving that responsibility, I am humbled by the acknowledgements afforded there by the faculty, staff, and administration. On a number of occasions I did hear painful stories about or from Black faculty and students in the Loma Linda environment, so I knew that there were issues even in that "blue zone" of rich Adventist culture. However, I had observed enough, experienced enough, and perhaps matured enough not to let such accounts sour my attitudes and relationships.

Other factors vital to sustaining my faith in the church's mission and programs were: (1) recognizing its racial sins as contrary to its fundamental beliefs; (2) maintaining a sense of loyalty to the organization that provided my salary; and (3) finding ways to enhance the Black community while at the same time fulfilling wider assignments.[3]

I wish, in this vein, to correct an unfortunate view regarding this latter point. That is, the rather common belief in the Black Adventist community is that those Blacks who dare to speak out against inequality often find themselves elected to either national or international positions to "keep them quiet." I have found, however, that far from being shunned or faced with conspiratorial efforts to quiet them, Adventist Blacks who address racism within the church firmly yet fairly are, in the main, respected by the majority leadership.

Further, I have found that Blacks who serve in the church's national and international offices, while not favoring any one particular group, are uniquely positioned to speak, vote, counsel, publish, recommend, and appoint in ways helpful to their ethnic brothers and sisters. My many years of chairing groups such as the Church Manual Committee, the church's Constitution and By-laws Committee, the Theological Education Committee, the International Education Committee, and the boards of Christian Record Services, Inc., Griggs University, Loma Linda University and Hospital, and Oakwood University, plus membership on a vast number of other committees and boards, afforded numerous opportunities in this regard. Most Black Adventists whom their community regards as being "hushed" by such appointments are actually positioned to be more helpful than before, but they do so without fanfare and notice. I count it an honor to have been able to contribute to the stature of African-American Seventh-day Adventism in this manner. That contribution finds particular satisfaction in the services of Delbert Baker, Rosa Banks, Garland Dulan, Thompson Kay, Leslie Pollard, and Ella Simmons, all of whose ministries to the wider Adventist community I was able, by God's grace, to influence directly.

So, to the question of whether those belonging to a discriminated minority can faithfully serve their majority-administered church while maintaining their ethnic dignity, I answer with a resounding Yes! This is a central theme in *Protest and Progress*. Perhaps what most qualifies me to write this work is the rich bounty of recall and witness handed down by front-line protest participants in both my wife's and my lineage. I also count it a high privilege, having been born just sixty-eight years after the end of American slavery, to have seen and known so many of the key players in the drama of the twentieth-century Black Adventist leadership protests that this work examines. Some of those honored players in that drama include J. L. Moran, J. G. Thomas, Eva B. Dykes, J. H. Wagner, Sr., W. W. Fordham, Jacob Justiss, Valerie Justiss-Vance, F. L. Peterson, H. D. Singleton, Georgia Harris, Willie Lee, E. E. Cleveland, and Owen A. Troy, Sr., to name a few. Memories of them and their colleagues, and the stories I heard them tell about their immediate predecessors, naturally color my feelings about their exploits. But on the whole I think that I have in the first part of this study treated the events objectively. I make no such claim regarding the second part. It is confessedly my personal conclusion regarding an emotional topic about which an informed understanding is generally lacking, yet is absolutely essential for the fulfillment of the church's mission.

Finally, I wish to acknowledge the archivists at the General Conference of Seventh-day Adventists and the Oakwood University Library for their help in locating materials; James Lewis and the Office for Regional Conference Ministry for valuable statistical information; Benjamin Baker for fact verification and editorial assistance; and Alvin Kibble for his personal encouragement and financial arrangements critical to the development of this project.

Calvin B. Rock
Las Vegas, Nevada
January 2018

## Notes

1. Ronald D. Graybill's *Mission to Black America: The True Story of J. Edson White and the Riverboat Morning Star*, a book sharing Edson White's *Morning Star* adventures, has been made available for free online by the General Conference Archives (http://documents.adventistarchives.org/Books/MTBA1971.pdf).

2. Read about the founding of Oakwood and its charter students in Mervyn A. Warren's *Oakwood! A Vision Splendid Continues, 1896–2010* (https://archive.org/details/oakwoodvision18962010warr), 8–24.

3. Here are some examples of how I attempted to enhance the Black community: (1) Serving as a founding member of the Atlanta-based Human Relations Council, an Adventist interracial group of lay and clergy established in 1969 to promote racial harmony in that area; (2) working as member of the steering committee of ten that spearheaded the push for Black Unions within the North American Division of Seventh-day Adventists during the decades of the 1970s and 1980s; (3) assisting in founding "Operation Reach Back: The Association of Black SDA Professionals" (1994) and continuing as its chair while serving as an officer of the General Conference; (4) responding in print to editorials and articles that misrepresented or disparaged Black culture and/or achievements; and (5) producing articles, papers, sermons, and books intended to inform church members and others in ways that both support Black growth and development and, in general, enhance the church's racial understanding and harmony.

# INTRODUCTION

Protest, when carried out in a manner that commands not just attention but also respect, is an important mechanism in any people's growth as they overcome the social burdens imposed by a more dominant group and achieve a more equitable status. Black Seventh-day Adventists' advance from where the dawn of the twentieth century found them to where they are now is to a great extent the result of such activity.

Black leadership engaged in four major protest movements:

1. The push for social and administrative participation (structural integration): 1889–1928
2. The push for Colored conferences (structural accommodation): 1929–1944
3. The push for Black Unions (modified structural autonomy): 1969–1980
4. The push for equitable retirement security: 1998–2000

As these pages will show, these movements differed in their immediate results. The first sought relevant administrative presence within existing local conference structures. The second (in lieu of the denial of the first) created a modified or parallel structural arrangement originally labeled "Colored conferences." The third (in the wake of that success) attempted a modified self-determination through the grouping of Black local conferences into union conference structures. The fourth, a fiscal component inherent in all of the former three, was a vigorously contested desire of the Black conferences to establish their own system of retiree benefits.

While contemporary circumstances shaped each movement and caused them to differ in various ways as they sought particular ends, each shared the same ultimate goal—that of human dignity and the fulfillment of gospel mission. *Protest and Progress* speaks to how Black Adventists achieved those ends and how, to an extent not often realized, they were linked across the years. It will do so by examining the protest strategies of each movement. While this study will not mention every change agent (not all are even known, for that matter), those whose services I do highlight speak eloquently for their "comrades-at-arms" whose unrecorded sacrifices were critical to where Black Adventists are today.

It is important in this regard to note that while *Protest and Progress* necessarily identifies various Black leaders who braved criticism and misunderstanding in their quest for justice, White leadership also had those, both clergy and lay, who contributed heroically to the struggle. They included Ellen White (1827–1915), the church prophet who wrote forcefully against slavery and for equality both within and outside the church;[1] John Byington (1798–1887), the first General Conference president during the years of 1863–1865 who was an active Abolitionist;[2] Uriah Smith (1832–1903), the first General Conference Secretary and early church author and editor;[3] and James White (1821–1881), husband of Ellen White, early church organizational leader, and first editor of the official church paper, the *Review and Herald*).[4]

ELLEN G. WHITE (1827–1915), church prophet and crusader for human rights.

Smith attacked the religious leaders of his day for their role in the suffering of America's indentured slaves, condemning them for what he said was the "white-washed villainy" of the many pulpits where support of slavery gave evidence of "the dragonic spirit of the nation . . ."[5]

James White, prior to the Emancipation Proclamation, used the pages of the *Review and Herald* to attack as "laggards" those who did not endorse freedom for slaves, and, while admitting his position to be radical, compared President Abraham Lincoln to the Pharaoh of ancient Hebrew slavery.[6] In the same vein, in an article titled "The Nation" in 1862, James White wrote:

> For the past ten years the *Review* has taught that the United States of America were a subject of prophecy, and that slavery is pointed out in the prophetic word as the darkest and most damning sin upon this nation. It has taught that Heaven has wrath in store for the nation which it would drink to the very dregs, as due punishment for the sin of slavery. And the anti-slavery teachings of several of our publications based upon certain prophecies have been such that their circulation has been positively forbidden in the slave States. Those of our people who voted at all at the last Presidential election, to a man voted for Abraham Lincoln. We know of not one man among Seventh-day Adventists who has the least sympathy for secession.[7]

On another occasion, commenting on freed slaves who, while serving in the Union Army, pursued former slave owners into the swamps of North Carolina, he wrote: "What could be more appropriate than that the slaves themselves should be the instruments used to punish the merciless tyrants who have so long ground them to the dust."[8]

Yet another of the church's pioneer leaders who spoke forcefully against racial injustice was Joseph Bates (1792–1872), who is listed (along with James and Ellen White) as one of the triumvirate who founded the Seventh-day Adventist Church.[9] But while these and other early leaders were socially liberal, their successors were not. They were not only socially conservative, but they also saw to it that church policies and practices conformed to the racially restrictive ideology of the time. As a result, the church began the twentieth century not only as theologically conservative, but also socially conservative as established by both social custom and government law—most notably the nation's "Separate but Equal" mandate of 1896.

JOHN BYINGTON (1798–1887), first General Conference president and active abolitionist. Courtesy of the Ellen G. White Estate.

On the broader scene, the country, still clawing its way out of slavery and recovering from the devastation of the Civil War, was overtly racist. The Confederate South, smarting from the war's defeat, now inflicted cruel vengeance upon its four million freed but impoverished Black population. That they were able to do so with impunity largely resulted from president Rutherford B. Hayes's (1877–1881) fulfillment of his promise to remove the occupying Union troops from the South if he received the region's vote. Meanwhile, the victorious North, wearied of the struggle and anxious to heal the wounds of war, was actively accommodating to restrictive political strategies and civil law.

Equally responsible for the nation's prevailing social atmosphere was the position of conservative religionists, both South and North. As has been repeatedly demonstrated, without proper hermeneutics, theological conservatism is the sure parent of social conservatism and its demonstrated reluctance to change—that is, to engage fresh ideas such as righting societal wrongs.[10] Not surprisingly, as its numbers grew, Adventism also became highly conservative. At its worse, the church consciously endorsed the popular theological views of racial inferiority and, at best, truly believed that fixing injustices was not the work of the church and that social evils could wait for their resolution at the Second Coming.

JAMES WHITE (1821–1881), church cofounder and crusader against slavery. Courtesy of the Ellen G. White Estate.

Church prophet Ellen G. White, however, vigorously warned against such attitudes and their resultant practices. But her cautions and denunciations were no more effective than were those of the Hebrew prophets who railed against injustice in their times. Still, many White members regarded Black believers as true brothers and sisters and were greatly disturbed by the prevailing conditions.

However, given the social climate both within and without the denomination, Adventists, for the most part, shied away from challenging the status quo. Some failed to act because of the obvious futility of bending society toward a more just structure. Others did so fearing the cultural hostility toward an embryonic church already marginalized because of its Sabbath views. A number, disappointed and exasperated, left the church never to return.

So it was that the Seventh-day Adventist Church entered the twentieth century in lock-step with the rest of conservative Christianity in its twin theories of Black racial inferiority and toleration of social evil. For some, the former belief found its root in Noah's curse on his grandson Canaan (Gen. 9:25–27) and Paul's New Testament insistence that Onesimus, the runaway slave, return to his master, Philemon (Philem. 10–21).

Proponents of these theories believed that they found support for them in the fact that Jesus never openly addressed the bitter inequities imposed by Rome and that while Paul affirmed that God had, indeed, "made from one blood every nation of men," He had at the same time "determined . . . the boundaries of their dwellings" (Acts 17:26). In addition, the apostle appeared to mandate unswerving obedience to government laws (Rom. 13:1–6).

Thus, under the pressure of America's "Separate but Equal" decree, and with ill-formed understandings of both scriptural social codes and the counsel of Ellen White, Black Seventh-day Adventists found themselves sadly conflicted. On the positive side, the church provided them a clear vision of both history and the future through biblical prophecy. They found assurance of salvation through the symbols of the heavenly and earthly sanctuaries. And the doctrine of the Second Coming offered the glad hope of the soon return of Christ and eternal life in the world to come. Meanwhile, however, the church's restrictive social policies and practices (i.e., denial of representation within existing structures; refusal of access to churches, hospitals, and schools; and the denomination's unfair distribution of material resources) caused constant pain and shame.

History records that during the fourth and fifth decades of the century, landmark legislation (i.e., the Voting Rights Act of 1944, the laws affecting interstate commerce in 1946, housing in 1947, labor in 1953, and the repeal of the "Separate But Equal" doctrine in 1954) brought gradual change to the nation. Sadly, however, history also reminds us that transformation within the church came only after existing laws had begun to alter secular society and most of the other churches, even the conservative ones, had already initiated social reform.

In addition, history will likewise show that such shifts resulted not so much because of convictions regarding racial equality and a willingness to stand up for justice, but because of various catalyst or "trigger events" that appeared to force the church into action. That is not to say that there were not many brave, socially convicted White believers who expressed themselves during those middle decades of the twentieth century—there were. It is rather that Adventists, the people of prophecy, were during these trying circumstances less than prophetic in social (especially racial) matters.

Fortunately, beginning in 1950, there emerged a series of General Conference presidents whose actions countered prevailing social attitudes and assisted in moving the church beyond the policies of "Separate but Equal." The first was J. L. McElhany (1880–1959), whose presidency (1936–1950) pre-dated the Civil Rights Movement, but who, realizing the need for special structure in the Black sector, took the lead in obtaining arrangements that resulted in Regional conferences. W. H. Branson (1887–1961) served as denominational president from 1950 to 1954. He wrote a groundbreaking letter dated December 15, 1953, to all North American Division union and local conference presidents and chairpersons of hospitals and college boards urging them to implement non-discriminatory admissions policies. While the letter mentioned nothing about hiring, according to Branson the very thought of being admitted to the church's hospitals and schools and attending its churches without fear of rejection resulted in "many tears" by the Black members with whom he had verbally unveiled his plans (Appendix 2).

W. H. BRANSON (1887–1961), General Conference president and spokesperson for desegregated facilities. Courtesy of the General Conference Archives.

We see the unbridled appreciation of Black leadership for Branson's statement in a letter dated November 5, 1953, from C. E. Moseley (1906–2001), then secretary of the Negro Department (Appendix 3), and in another dated October 13, 1954, from O. A. Troy, Sr. (1899–1962), then Associate Secretary of the Religious Liberty Department of the General Conference of Seventh-day Adventists (Appendix 4).

The third president was R. R. Figuhr (1896–1983), General Conference leader from 1954 to 1966.

His report to the General Conference session in 1958 included the following statement on "oneness":

> We are a universal church. We could not be otherwise. The divine mandate, to proclaim the gospel to every nation and people, makes us such. Consistent with this fact, we believe, is the universal brotherhood of man and that God "hath made of one blood all nations . . . to dwell on all the face of the earth," as the Scriptures say. We therefore deplore, as contrary to the spirit of the gospel, any effort to depreciate as inferior any nation or people, believing that all alike are precious in God's sight. We believe in the oneness that there is in Christ and as set forth by the apostle Paul, "There is neither Jew nor Greek, there is neither bond nor free, there is neither male nor female: for ye are all one in Christ Jesus" (Galatians 3:28).[11]

The fourth president was Figuhr's immediate successor, Robert H. Pierson (1911–1989), whose tenure (1966–1979) spanned thirteen of the tumultuous years that followed the assassinations of John and Robert Kennedy and Martin Luther King, Jr. The fifth was N. C. Wilson (1920–2010), world leader from 1979 to 1990. Wilson, many of whose activities I will present in later chapters, was especially effective in formulating policies and procedures that would benefit Black Adventists.

As for the Black Adventist leaders themselves, we should note two distinctive types of protest activity. The first is "positional," that is, involving the administrative platform from which the leader spoke. The second is "territorial," having to do with the primary field of practice or application. As such, Black Adventist leaders' efforts mirror those of Martin Luther King, Jr., and Adam Clayton Powell, Jr., both Baptist ministers, who are widely regarded as the two most effective Black clergy change agents of the twentieth century.

Powell, after several years of effective Harlem-based protests as a pastor, ran for and was elected to political office. In 1941 he became New York City's first Black council representative, and then in 1945 won a seat in the U.S. House of Representatives where he served, with two interruptions, until 1970. He made his primary protests within the context of the political system. King, choosing to retain his identity with his local parish, remained outside the organized political system.

For Black Adventist leaders, "the system" is the set of organized conference structures having regulatory powers over their functions (e.g., the union, division, and General Conference). The "local parish" comprises the local congregation or church district in which a pastor functions.

The second distinction that we may draw can best be viewed in light of what W. E. Burghardt Du Bois labeled the "twoness" of African-American citizenship.[12] Du Bois's theory is that Black Americans, being culturally unassimilated into America's melting pot, must live a double existence—one within the Black community itself and the other in the broader society. Thus, Black leadership finds itself called to a dual focus. As a result, it must vigorously address the disadvantages encountered in both arenas, that of mainstream society and the Black community. Given this reality, it is not surprising that Black activists have often concentrated on one aspect to the seeming exclusion of the other and that their difference of emphasis has, at times, as we shall see later, produced visible tensions within their ranks.

One reason that Black clergy were so prominent in protest during these decades is that they alone held what limited access their community had to the church's White decision-makers. While denied part of standard committees and counsels, responsible Black leaders did at times receive visits from their superiors or invitations to special meetings to discuss the conduct of Black churches in their areas.

The second reason is that, at the turn of the twentieth century and through most of its decades, clergymen (there were few clergywomen) typically functioned as both political and religious leaders of the Black community. In fact, in the earlier days of slavery itself, those slaves recognized as spiritual leaders led both violent and non-violent forms of protest. The non-violent kind found expression in such activities as work slowdowns and sabotage and the Underground Railroad. The violent kind manifested itself in bloody revolts such as those sparked by Gabriel Prosser (Virginia, 1800) who, inspired by Judges 15, proclaimed himself the Black Sampson; Denmark Vesey (South Carolina, 1822) who, motivated by the exploits of Moses's successor (Josh. 6:20, 21), saw himself as the Black Joshua; and the most celebrated of them all, Nat Turner (Virginia, 1830), for whom Luke 12:37–40 served as a blueprint for insurrection. We should also note that while the dynamics discussed above assured Black clergy recognition as primary spokespersons for twentieth-century protest and progress, their endeavors were at each point supported and in some cases eclipsed by the attitudes and actions of Black laity.

The heroic efforts of the Washington, D.C.-based "Committee for the Advancement of World-Wide Work among Colored Seventh-day Adventists" led by Joseph Dodson (chairman) and Valerie Justiss-Vance (secretary) during the middle to late 1940s is one example. Another is the work of the Laymen's Leadership Conference directed by Frank Hale, Jr., and Mylas Martin during the decades of the 1950s through the 1970s. Without their social protest, progress within the church would not have been nearly as rapid or successful.

Part one of this book, "The Protest Movements," recounts the circumstances and dynamics of the four primary protests engaged by Black leadership through the end of the twentieth century. Part two, "The Challenge Ahead," seeks to inform the debate regarding the continued presence of Black Adventism's primary and most enduring protest endeavor, Regional conferences. It will speak in favor of diversity of operations. However, as I hope will be apparent, it is a diversity mandated by genuine minority needs and legitimated by policies and procedures connecting them in loyal, productive, relationship within the wider system.

## A WORD ON NOTES AND USAGE

Endnotes are supplied so that the reader may review the sources. In light of the vast resources now available on the web, I have occasionally tried to provide links to free materials. My aim is not for absolute scholarly detail, but to provide enough information for convenient further investigation. For events in which I was an eyewitness, sources will often not be cited. The Appendices at the back of the book feature many invaluable documents in their entirety.

This book employs the terms "Black," "Negro," "Colored," and "African American" without regard to specific periods of general societal usage. It will, however, by the language of various documents, remind the reader of the way White culture labeled the descendants of slavery during the various decades following Emancipation. The only official change of designation by the Seventh-day Adventist church was that voted in October 26, 1944: "That wherever in the Constitution or By-Laws the term 'Negro' is used, this be changed to 'Colored.'"[13]

I will alternate with the terms "Regional conference," "Black conference," and "Colored conference." I will primarily use the first term, since it is the official designation for the historic and current nine Black-administered conferences with a mostly Black membership: Allegheny East, Allegheny West, Central States, Lake Region, Northeastern, South Atlantic, South Central, Southeastern, and Southwestern. They were named "Regional" because when organized their territories covered regions of the country rather than one or two States, as did the then exclusively White-administered conferences.

For purposes of clarity, *Adventist Review* will be used throughout this work to refer to the church's official periodical, previously titled *Review and Herald*.

**Notes**

1. *Seventh-day Adventist Encyclopedia,* rev. ed. (Washington, DC: Review and Herald, 1996), 873–881; see Ellen G. White, *The Southern Work* (Washington, DC: Review and Herald, 1966). Here is a new comprehensive compilation of Ellen G. White's statements on Black people, a work of almost 1,500 pages: http://www.blacksdahistory.org/files/125793452.pdf.

2. *Seventh-day Adventist Encyclopedia,* rev. ed., 267.

3. Ibid., 618.

4. Ibid., 890–899.

5. Uriah Smith, "The Degeneracy of the United States," *Advent Review and Sabbath Herald* (June 17, 1862), 22.

6. Ibid., 7.

7. James White, "The Nation," *Review and Herald* (August 12, 1862); cited in Arthur L. White, *Ellen G. White: The Progressive Years, 1862–1876,* vol. 2 (Hagerstown, MD.: Review and Herald, 1985), 41.

8. James White, "Justice Awaking," *Advent Review and Sabbath Herald,* vol. 23, no. 9 (January 26, 1864), 68.

9. F. D. Nichol, *The Seventh-day Adventist Encyclopedia* (Washington, DC.: Review and Herald, 1966), 107.

10. My usage of "social conservatism" describes the stance of persons protecting policies and practices seen as favoring the socially advantaged—individuals usually associated with right-wing political views.

11. Minutes of the Seventh-day Adventist General Conference Session, June/July 1958.

12. W. E. Burghardt Du Bois, *The Souls of Black Folk* (New York: The New American Library, 1969), 45.

13. Minutes of the General Conference Committee, October 26, 1944.

# PART ONE

# THE PROTEST MOVEMENTS

# 1
## THE PUSH FOR SOCIAL AND ADMINISTRATIVE PARTICIPATION, 1889–1928

The first and earliest twentieth-century Black Adventist protest is best understood in light of the courageous ministry of Charles Marshall Kinney (1855–1951), often labeled as the "Father of Black Seventh-day Adventism."

Kinney was born a slave on a plantation to Andrew and Lucy Kinney in Richmond, Virginia. After emancipation his family migrated to Reno, Nevada. There, in the summer of 1878 at the age of twenty-three, he was one of hundreds who attended evangelistic meetings in Reno conducted by J. N. Loughborough at which Ellen White was also a featured speaker. Attracted and won over by the message, Kinney became a Seventh-day Adventist on September 28, 1878. Records indicate that he attended Healdsburg College (now Pacific Union College) from 1883 to 1885. His official ministerial work began when S. N. Haskell, president of the California Conference, sent him to "labor among his own people" in Kansas in the spring of 1885.[1]

Kinney's initial years of ministry were spent as a colporteur—selling religious literature, giving Bible studies, and preaching in Black neighborhoods in Topeka, Emporia, and other towns in eastern Kansas. The only prejudice Kinney experienced in these early years of ministry was of the denominational kind by Black ministers of other Protestant faiths. But that would change with his next assignment in St. Louis, Missouri, where he went in the winter of 1888 to 1889.[2]

At the time, St. Louis had an Adventist congregation of approximately fifty members, almost certainly all White. However, Kinney's successful efforts among the Blacks of the city soon altered the composition, causing, as might be expected, especially at that date, a negative reaction within the membership. Noting the change, Dan T. Jones (1855–1901), General Conference secretary, wrote of "a large and increasing interest among the colored people" of "a very fine class" who had been won by Kinney and were attending the Adventist church.³ Later, in affirmation of Kinney's work, he wrote:

> I have always felt deeply for the colored people, knowing that even now they labor under many disadvantages. I have a sympathy for the race and have always had. I early imbibed the abolitionist sentiments . . . I now want to see the race rise to an equal position with others in this nation. But the only way it can be accomplished is by education and refinement. The members of the white race who neglect these sink to a lower level. . . . You are doing a noble work.⁴

The White members of the St. Louis congregation, however, had no such lofty sentiments: they did not overcome their feelings. Kinney left St. Louis disappointed and dejected by the way the White members in the St. Louis Church treated the fledgling Black converts.

CHARLES M. KINNEY (1855–1951), first Black clergy protestor. Courtesy of the Southern Union Conference.

In commenting further on the situation, Dan T. Jones observed to Kinney (who had moved on to Louisville, Kentucky) that there was a challenge as to "the attitude of some of the white people [at the St. Louis Church] toward the colored people," and that as a result "the colored folks there generally would prefer an organization to themselves."⁵ Whether Jones saw this as pointing to colored conferences is not clear, but his comments were remarkably practical and progressive, given the racial climate of the time.

Ellen White visited the St. Louis Church on the last Monday of March

1890 after Kinney's departure. She immediately grasped the appalling racism manifested there, and in fact received a vision as she knelt to pray before addressing the congregation. Her recount of what happened is recorded in "Our Duty to the Colored People," her landmark address to General Conference leaders on March 21, 1891. She also commented to her son Edson, somewhat later, that in encountering the racial situation at the St. Louis Church, "we had some experiences at St. Louis that I can never think of without a feeling of dread."[6]

At the Nashville, Tennessee, camp meeting, on the Wednesday before his ordination on October 2, 1889, Kinney (the first Black to be so honored) issued his first public appeal on behalf of his people (Appendix 5). Reacting to the unkind treatment that the few Blacks in attendance received, he publicly addressed the situation at that convocation—and his people's plight in general within the church—in a twelve-point proposal.

The pastoral Kinney prefaced his remarks by stating that "I would be extremely glad if there were no necessity to carry them out" and that "this question [of segregation] is one of great embarrassment and humiliation, and not only to me, but to my people also." He also issued a passionate statement on the power of the gospel, declaring himself a prisoner of hope and the "Third Angel's message as having the power in it to eliminate or remove this race prejudice upon the part of those who get hold of the truth."

With that established, Kinney presented twelve points that, among other things, called for:

- an end of second-class status for Blacks in church assemblies;
- a separate meeting structure in cases in which the two races could not assemble together "without limitation";
- education by the General Conference of worthy Colored individuals to engage in various branches of ministry; and
- the same relationship (when formed) of Colored conferences to the General Conference that White conferences had.

Throughout his statement, Kinney made clear that his concern was a dual one: the discouraging and negative effect that prejudice had on the Colored believers and potential adherents, and what he labeled as the "obstacle" that Colored presence presented in White gatherings to White gospel witness.[7]

His very balanced approach is reflected in notes written across the top of the speech he prepared for his 1891 report to the General Conference.

They read, "Gratitude for what has been done," "Statistics not known," "Difficulties—stigma, reproach, race prejudice"—"Is it time?"[8]

The question "Is it time?" was followed by two scriptural references. The first was Psalm 69:9: "Because zeal for Your house has eaten me up, and the reproaches of those who reproach You have fallen on me." The second was Ezekiel 22:29–30: "The people of the land have used oppressions, committed robbery, and mistreated the poor and needy; and they wrongfully oppress the stranger. So I sought for a man among them who would make a wall, and stand in the gap before Me on behalf of the land, that I should not destroy it."

A particularly noteworthy aspect of Kinney's approach is that though he conceived Colored conferences five-and-a-half decades before their inception. He continued to express the belief that the gospel of Christ can erase all racial divisions and he could labor with the hope that its empowering influence would make these units unnecessary.

## LEWIS C. SHEAFE

A second leading Black minister in the push for full inclusion in church functions during this period was Lewis C. Sheafe (1859–1938).[9] As described by George Knight in Douglas Morgan's monumental work on Sheafe's life, "Sheafe was the first world-class preacher/leader in the African-American segment of Adventism."[10] John Harvey Kellogg, a contemporary of Sheafe's, described him as "an orator, a wonderfully able man... a more liberally educated and cultivated man and can deliver a more forcible address than any other Seventh-day Adventist minister. We have not a white minister that can begin to stand beside him."[11]

Sheafe was born in Baltimore, Maryland, to free Blacks Joseph and Louise Sheafe on November 16, 1859.[12] He relocated with his mother and brother to Boston, Massachusetts, in 1864, where he spent most of his childhood. After a conversion experience in 1875, he decided to enter the ministry and attended Wayland Seminary in Washington, D.C., from 1885 to 1887. Upon graduating he began pastoring a Baptist Church in Alexandria, Virginia, and was recognized as having a strong bent for social activism.

Sheafe became an Adventist as a result of influences while he was a patient at the Battle Creek Sanitarium in 1896. Soon after his baptism he accepted the call to ministry and soon earned the reputation of a personable and popular Seventh-day Adventist pastor.

Like Kinney a decade before him, however, Sheafe was not in the ministry long before he found himself severely disturbed by the racial practices in the church. In Morgan's words:

> By 1899 Sheafe's three years in the Adventist community had been a perplexing mixture of joy and disillusionment, of idealistic aspiration frustrated by lack of resources and slowness of progress. Was there, after all, a future for him in Adventism? The uncertainties pressed him to the point of seeking counsel from a woman he had never met, who lived on the other side of the world in Australia, but whom he, with his Adventist brothers and sisters, had come to regard as "a special servant of the Lord."[13]

In pouring out his heartfelt concerns to Ellen White, Sheafe wrote: "My heart leaped for joy as I thought of the possible help to come to my people through the third [angel's] message." But, he continued, "for warmth I've found coldness, for freedom bondage, and for confidence distrust. . . . The caste feeling in this country is strong, it grows worse each year—it is tolerated in all the denominations; it seems that every man's hand is against us . . . the Negro is despised by the very people who make such professions."[14]

Like Kinney, Sheafe firmly believed that the Adventist message gave promise of fostering true brotherhood. 'My people hail it with delight," he remarked, but "then they say 'We will measure the depth and purity of the Christianity of SDA by their attitude toward the Negro.'" He then posed a question that Black Adventist leaders would grapple with for decades to come: "Is there a place in this message for the Negro with the white man?"[15] He even questioned Ellen White regarding the wisdom of separate schools, churches, and organizations for Blacks. However, remarkably, in spite of his disappointments Sheafe continued to press his White brethren for full acceptance and inclusion, as had Kinney.

Sheafe also addressed other church leaders, including J. H. Kellogg, A. T. Jones, and A. G. Daniells, regarding the church's racial posture. Meanwhile, he kept very busy fulfilling preaching assignments in both the North and South, all the while valiantly tackling the "color line" both inside and outside the church.

In 1902 General Conference president A. G. Daniells assigned Sheafe and White minister J. S. Washburn (1863–1955) to hold evangelistic meetings in Washington, with the hope of establishing one Black congregation and one White congregation in the capital.[16] Sheafe's tent meetings were attended by thousands of people, garnering considerable coverage from the secular news media, and resulted in seventy-five new members joining what was christened First Seventh-day Adventist Church, the very first Adventist congregation in the city. However, the congregation divided on September 22 when forty of its White members—roughly half the congregation—departed to form the Second Seventh-day Adventist Church. Sticking to his conviction that integration best mirrored the gospel, Sheafe remained pastor of the racially-integrated First Church.

His attitudes, as will be noted in Chapter 2, changed markedly, but at this early point in his Adventist journey Sheafe, like Kinney and most other Black leaders, though realizing little progress in the removal of the segregated patterns in the church, continued to protest and work in quest of their removal.

## JAMES H. HOWARD (1861–1936)

The hope of full inclusion in the social and administrative affairs of the church, held by Pastors Kinney, Sheafe, and most other Black clergy of this era, were forcefully expressed in the communications of Washington, D.C. layman, James H. Howard, M.D. graduate of Howard University and government federal clerk. In his letter to Ellen White on March 23, 1902, in referencing the dissolution of what had begun as a racially inclusive Seventh-day Adventist congregation in the nation's capital, Howard, the first lay-leader on record to become publicly involved, stated:

JAMES H. HOWARD (1861–1936), a lay physician who sought for social justice in the church. Courtesy of the Office of U.S. Customs and Passports.

Now, after more than a decade of standing in the name of Christ against the tide of racial oppression that surged throughout the nation in the 1890s, indications that the Adventists too were capitulating caused corresponding damage to the church's witness... people outside the church, of both races (even some who are interested in the truth), are surprised, disappointed and even becoming hardened against the cause because a worldly spirit and prejudice against the colored people have arisen in the Adventist Church.

> The colored people . . . prefer and hope for union for the truth's sake, not because they seek affiliation with the opposite race. They are confident that if the spirit of separation prevail, great harm will be done to the cause here. And they pray the Lord will show their brethren their error. . . .[17]

And Howard did not stop there. He pressed his concern for a racially inclusive church to Daniells as well, stating:

> I tell you plainly, Brother Daniells, with all respect, that you and your committee are grievously wrong in your cause and policy on the race question . . . you are wrong at a time when the world is growing worse in this respect and so much needs your wise and corrective influence. . . . The compromising plea of expediency, policy, the demands of the world and doing the thing that good may come, is too weak and unworthy of our cause. . . . It would seem that while the people of the world will disregard each other more and more because of national differences, the people of the Savior would be the more careful not to seem to justify the others in their wicked discriminations.
>
> It is difficult to see why it is necessary to make a race line in the Adventist denomination in the face of the fact that the truth involves a positive protest against any such thing in the church. . . . Such a policy not only discredits the body of people who profess to be getting ready to meet the Lord at his coming and be translated, but it deceives the world as the true standard of righteousness, seduces and perverts the conscience and heart of the church and renders obtuse its spiritual discernment.
>
> I plead not for any fanatical affiliation of the races. That is not desired by either party. But in the name of Heaven, the message and righteousness I plead for a pure and correct standard and practice in this denomination, or church, which professes to be the last.[18]

Meanwhile, as Kinney conjectured would happen, the number of Black churches in the United States steadily increased during the next several years. Whereas by the end of 1889 there was just one recognized Black congregation (Edgefield Junction, Tennessee), by 1909 there were approximately sixty Black churches and companies (primarily in the South) listing slightly more than 900 members.

In 1909, a group of Black pastors presented to church leadership a unified appeal for participation and representation in the organized body. The document, titled "An Appeal in Behalf of the Work among Colored People," was signed by twelve of the leading Black ministers and sent to the General

Conference Committee. In "An Appeal" the ministers tactfully sounded an alarm that the race question would not go away—would only grow larger if unaddressed. The final paragraph expressed their wish for the upcoming General Conference session held later that year in Washington, D.C. It read:

> We therefore, earnestly pray that the General Conference will at this time formulate some plans that will make for the more systematic and diligent spread of the third Angel's Message among the ten million Negroes in this country. We stand ready to heartily co-operate with our white Brethren in any plan which may be devised for a more efficient work among this people.[19]

Their efforts were recognized at a session business meeting on May 28, 1909, by a response from Daniells, the General Conference president. He pointed out that the church had created the North American Foreign Department four years earlier focusing on the work among German, Swedish, Danish, and Norwegian groups and the need to do more among the Colored population. Without mentioning "The Appeal," Daniells gave a compelling rationale for establishing the new department:

> Now we have come to the place where we feel that a far greater effort, a more systematic effort, a more concerted effort, shall be put forth in behalf, of this part of our population. We have a number of our colored brethren with us at this Conference. . . . We have met with them in their councils; they have counseled with us, and we with them, and they came to us with a request that we establish this department, the Negro Department. . . . [T]he members of the General Conference Committee who have taken the matter under consideration have agreed to it, and now it is recommended in the constitution: I believe that this is a step in the right direction, that it will help us to organize the work in behalf of these people, that it will help us to systematize our efforts, in raising money and in expending it so that we can have one solid, systematized, concerted effort to push this important branch of the work. I believe that under this direct effort we shall see the work in behalf of the colored people of this country go forward with greater success than we have ever seen before.[20]

Several of the Black ministers in attendance spoke in support of Daniells's presentation. Among them were J. K. Humphrey (1877–1952) of New York City, who remarked that he had been advocating the idea since 1905, and W. H. Green (1871–1928), later to be the first Black leader of the Negro Department, who admitted that he had not been in favor of the idea until he had actually seen the needs in the field.[21]

The proposal for a Negro Department was discussed again at the meeting on June 1. Several Black leaders addressed the issue as follows:

A sampling of their remarks bear quoting, in order that one may get a feel for the proceedings and sentiment.

Sydney Scott (1874–1934), a minister from Texas:

> The relations between the races in the South are becoming wider and wider. Seventh-day Adventists are not responsible for it, neither am I responsible for it. The conditions are to be met, and they have to be met in a common-sense way. I hope that this department work will meet the condition, and yet I have had some doubts about it. It is in my mind a question of representation. The relation between the colored and the white man in the South is becoming a serious question. In the South our people are losing confidence in the white man. It is just as well to handle this question without gloves. If this departmental work is carried out on a plan that will give a just representation to the negro churches, then I say "Amen" to the plan. If it will be one-sided, then I say "No" in the loudest tone.[22]

T. H. Branch (1856–1924), the first Black Adventist to serve as a missionary to Africa:

> I am glad to say I believe with all my soul that this is the right thing in the right place at the right time. I have been in this truth for sixteen years. I worked hard before I went to Africa seven years ago, and today I will agree with you that of all the work we have done in this country, with the assistance of the white brethren there are not over a thousand colored people in the truth to-day. Our hands have been tied. Now this department will loosen our hands so we can work for our own people, and if you do not pass it, you will tie up our feet as well as our hands. . . .
>
> I believe that if the colored people would step aside, not away from the white brethren, and with peace and harmony on both sides work directly for their people, we should have numbers of people in the truth in a short time, like the Germans and other nationalities.[23]

W. H. Green (1871–1928), first Black secretary of the General Conference Negro Department. Courtesy of the General Conference Archives.

J. K. Humphrey, pastor in Harlem, New York:

> Of the eleven millions of colored people in the United States, three and one-half millions are in the North and seven and a half millions are in the South. Among them scarcely anything is being done. As I studied the situation, I found that the other nationalities were getting along first-rate; and as we hear their reports, we find the work is growing. It encourages you to listen to these reports of how the work is going among the Germans, Danes, Scandinavians, and others; but when it comes to the Negroes, do you hear anything? . . .
>
> I pray that this department that has been proposed, not because of color (while that may be one of the indirect reasons) but primarily to foster the work among the Negro people, may be created. Let us take away the color basis; we should not look at it that way. God does not look at it that way. I believe that the Negro has a soul, and that God desires he should be saved. And I feel that a better step could not have been taken than to put this work on a departmental basis, in order that more efficiency may be given to this work throughout the country, and a greater work be done in the future than in the past.[24]

W. H. Green:

> We have solemnly subscribed our names to this paper ["An Appeal"], and have sent it in to you, without any request having come from you. I believe the department ought to be maintained, and we pledge our support to it. I want to say one thing more, and that is this: I notice that almost every man under the heavens seems to be proud of the fact that he belongs to his race. If there is one thing I have never been ashamed of, it is that I am a Negro.[25]

David E. Blake (1877–1917) a pastor, later to become a physician:

> I believe one of the very best things that could ever be done for the advancement of this work is the step that has been taken. I believe it is of God. We have prayed since we have been on this ground that the Lord would bring something about that would cause an advancement of our work among the colored people of the South.[26]

The resolution on the table for a creation of the "North American Negro Department of the General Conference" was unanimously adopted at the business session on June 1, 1909.

For the first nine years of its operation, the new department was directed by a succession of three Caucasian ministers: J. W. Christian (1909–1910), A. J. Haysmer (1910–1914), and C. B. Stephenson (1914–1918). They were concerned and diligent in their efforts but this, of course, was not what the Black leaders had mind. They concluded, however, that these appointments, though not adequate, were part of a positive step, and the best that could be had at the time. They nevertheless sought change.

They did so by reminding church leaders of the obvious difficulties of White directors in coordinating their evangelistic programs, counseling their churches, and providing representation in formal councils regarding the work in Black communities. If they were to have a separate supervisory unit for their function, it should be, they felt, one of their own. To be refused a place at the table in the existing system and provided White leaders to represent them in the newly-formed structural accommodation was simply not palatable. Their voices were heard, and in the early part of 1918, W. H. Green, a former lawyer respected by his peers and trusted by White church leaders, was appointed at the age of forty-seven as the first Black to head the Negro Department.[27]

Black leadership, along with an expanding laity that by then had reached 3,500, regarded Green's appointment as a signal triumph. One of their own now officially represented them. His efforts, they assumed, would be pivotal in the struggle for more relevant evangelistic planning along with equal treatment within the body of believers.

But they were mistaken. The presence of the director did fulfill a measure of practical benefits including a "foot in the door" sense of belonging. However, it fell short of gaining inclusion in administrative affairs. Black church employees still found themselves excluded from critical discussions and decision-making. The result was that they remained trapped in a second-class status, being systematically denied parity in matters of employee education, equal salaries and benefits, church budgeting, enhanced service opportunities, and even basic facilities, such as cafeterias.

A word should be said here about the calcifying segregationist attitudes toward Blacks in Adventism. Unfortunately, a statement by no less than the church prophet, Ellen White, would seem to confirm the church's social conservatism. As mentioned earlier, in 1891, White had gone against the grain of prevailing racial attitudes: "You have no license from God to exclude the colored people from your places of worship. Treat them as Christ's property, which they are, just as much as yourselves. They should hold membership in the church with the White brethren. Every effort should be made to wipe out the terrible wrong which has been done them."[28]

And in that same year, speaking to the delegates at the 1891 General Conference session, this brave woman in seeming reply to Kinney's question, "Is it time?" stated:

> I know that which I now speak will bring me into conflict. This I do not covet, for the conflict has seemed to be continuous of late years; but I do not mean to live or die a coward, leaving my work undone. I must follow in my Master's footsteps. It has become fashionable to look down upon the poor, and upon the colored race in particular. But Jesus, the Master, was poor, and He sympathizes with the poor, the discarded, the oppressed, and declares that every insult shown to them is as if shown to Himself.[29]

However, four years later in 1895, in what seemed to be a reversal of position and a concession to prevailing racial attitudes, she advised: "In regard to white and colored people worshipping in the same building, this cannot be followed as a general custom with profit to either party—especially in the South. The best thing will be to provide the colored people who accept the truth, with places of worship of their own, in which they can carry on their services by themselves. . . . Let them understand that this plan is to be followed until the Lord shows us a better way."[30]

Unfortunately, the church for decades reacted to this statement, given as common-sense caution against actions that would jeopardize gospel proclamation, as if it were perpetual principle. The "better way" became synonymous with the Second Advent.

During the middle 1920s, A. W. Spalding (1877–1953), well-known White Adventist educator and author, characterized Ellen White's commonsense statement above as conforming, or yielding, to public opinion that the gospel not be hindered. But in less than logical language and seeming defense of the church's reluctance to act against injustice, even when it reasonably might have done so, he explained this position as based "not on principle" but on what he termed "the principle of policy." In spite of its dubious formulation, many Adventist members, especially where segregation was the custom, obeyed it as a fundamental, Bible-based teaching of the church.[31]

This then was the mindset that governed the church's social practices at the time of Green's appointment and beyond. Blacks were eager to have primary participation in the governance of the fledgling but rapidly growing Black membership that had doubled during the first two years of Green's service. But they had neither voice nor vote in the determination of salaries, the transfer of pastors from church to church and state to state, the approval or denial of building purchases and construction, or the hiring and firing of ministers and teachers, even though they were the most affected by such decisions.

Meanwhile, Green, the director of the office established to advise, not administer, the Black workers around the nation (administration was still handled by White conference leadership), was fighting a losing battle to keep up with his increasingly impossible assignment. Green—referred to in private by the Black pastorate as "Cross-Country Green" because of his extremely heavy travel schedule—died October 31, 1928, at age 57 after ten years on the job. Black Adventism believed that he had literally worked himself to death. The official report of his death given in the *Adventist Review* read in part, "He always labored unsparingly, and came home at the close of an itinerary very tired and worn. Without warning he passed away."[32]

Green's later obituary in the *Advent Review*, prepared by G. E. Peters, J. K. Humphrey, and A. E. Webb, gave a fuller account of his last days:

> After attending the Fall Council at Springfield, Mass., Elder Green paid his last visit to his home church, Hartford Avenue, Detroit, October 6, and preached a very touching sermon and assisted in the ordinances of the Lord's house. He remained home until the twelfth of the month, attending to official affairs and making a visit to Holly, Mich., to see his two daughters, who are students in the Adelphian Academy at that place. He left home the night of the twelfth to serve the church in Omaha, Nebr., the next Sabbath. After leaving Omaha, he visited Kansas City, Mo.; Wichita, Kans.; Oklahoma City, Okla., Fort Worth, San Antonio, and Houston, Texas, from which place he journeyed to the Florida camp meeting, stopping a few hours in New Orleans, La. The night of the twenty seventh of October he started from Orlando, Fla., for his home in Detroit, intending to leave early enough to meet his appointment in Milwaukee, Wis., November 3.
>
> On his way to Detroit he traveled in a roundabout way, using his railroad passes to save the amount of fares to the cause he so much loved. Having missed his train in Atlanta, Ga., he was forced to spend most of the day Monday in that city, arriving in Detroit about 10 p.m. Tuesday. He was suffering with a severe cold and retired shortly expressing in weary tones the desire to rest and sleep until morning, because he had not been in bed for four nights. He soon seemed to be sleeping quite naturally. His wife was awaked about two o'clock by a peculiar noise he was making, and thinking he was troubled with dreams, tried to arouse him, but soon realized that he was beyond human help. No word was spoken by him, neither did he show any signs of consciousness. He passed quietly into eternity with his work on earth done.[33]

Green's untimely demise, believed by Black Adventists as a case of "death from exhaustion," confirmed for them the inadequacy of the department as constituted and the futility of any further attempts to achieve an active role in administering the burgeoning Black membership.

The fact that he had to work out of his home in Detroit, Michigan, and not, as did other General Conference leaders, from facilities in Washington, D.C., 526 miles away, contributed to this belief. We should note that immediately after Green's death the General Conference Committee, at its 1929 autumn session, voted that in the future the Negro Department leader would "locate in Washington, having his headquarters at the General Conference office" (Appendix 6).

It was under these conditions that after almost three decades of frustration, early twentieth-century Black leadership, enthused by the rapid growth of Black membership but restricted by national law and the church's simplistic view of the prophet's social rationale, abandoned its quest for participation within the current conference structure and began its second major protest endeavor—the push for structural accommodation.

### Notes

1. S. N. Haskell, "The Cause on the Pacific Coast," *Advent Review*, vol. 72, no. 35 (May 19, 1885), 320.

2. Perhaps the most extensive discussion of Kinney's time in St. Louis is in Benjamin Baker's 2011 Howard University PhD dissertation, "'I Do Not Mean to Live a Coward or Die a Coward:' An Examination of Ellen G. White's Lifelong Relationship to Black People," 323–331.

3. Dan T. Jones to C. M. Kinney, April 30, 1890, Secretariat Incoming Letters, RG 21, General Conference Archives.

4. Ron Graybill, "Charles M. Kinny—Founder of Black Adventism," *Review and Herald* 30 (13 January 1977): 7.

5. Ibid., 1.

6. E. G. White to James Edson White, March 1, 1904, Letter 105, 1904 (https://egwwritings.org/?ref=en_Lt105-1904.2&para=7991.8).

7. All material quoted in the section on Kinney at the 1889 camp meeting can be found in Appendix 5.

8. Ron Graybill, "Charles M. Kinny—Founder of Black Adventism," *Review and Herald* 30 (13 January 1977): 6–8.

9. Douglas Morgan has established a website dedicated to the life and ministry of Lewis C. Sheafe (http://www.lcsheafe.net).

10. Douglas Morgan, *Lewis C. Sheafe: Apostle to Black America* (Hagerstown, MD: Review and Herald Publishing Association, 2010), 11.

11. J. H. Kellogg to E. G. White, December 19, 1900; quoted in Morgan, *Lewis C. Sheafe*, 18.

12. This section draws from Douglas Morgan's excellent timeline of Sheafe's life at http://www.lcsheafe.net/timeline.html

13. Morgan, *Lewis C. Sheafe*, 150.

14. Ibid., 150–151.

15. Ibid., 151.

16. A recent treatment of this period in Washington, D.C., and A. G. Daniells and race in general, can be found in Benjamin McArthur's *A. G. Daniells: Shaper of Twentieth-Century Adventism* (Nampa, ID: Pacific Press Publishing Association, 2015), 215–246.

17. Morgan, *Lewis C. Sheafe*, 198, 199.

18. Ibid., 264, 265.

19. "An Appeal in Behalf of the Work among the Colored People," undated, Box A825, File A. G. Daniells, General Conference Archives.

20. "Twenty-Sixth Meeting," *General Conference Bulletin*, May 30, 1909, 209–210 (http://documents.adventistarchives.org/Periodicals/GCSessionBulletins/GCB1909-14.pdf).

21. Ibid., 210–211.

22. Thirty-Fourth Meeting, *General Conference Bulletin*, June 2, 1909, 286 (http://documents.adventistarchives.org/Periodicals/GCSessionBulletins/GCB1909-17.pdf).

23. Ibid., 286.

24. Ibid., 287.

25. Ibid.

26. Ibid., 287–288.

27. *Seventh-day Adventist Encyclopedia*, rev. ed. (Washington, DC: Review and Herald, 1996), 1063.

28. Ellen G. White, *Southern Work* (Washington, DC: Review and Herald, 1966), 15.

29. Ibid., 10, 11.

30. Ellen G. White, *Testimonies for the Church* (Boise, ID: Pacific Press, 1948), 1:202.

31. Ron Graybrill, "Charles M. Kinny—Founder of Black Adventism," *Review and Herald Magazine* (Jan. 13, 1977), 6–7.

32. J. L. McElhany, "North American Division, *Adventist Review*, vVol. 107, no. 24 (June 1, 1930): 45.

33. G. E. Peters, J. K. Humphrey, A. E. Webb, "Elder W. H. Green," *Adventist Review*, vol. 105, no. 52 (December 27, 1928), 21.

# 2
## THE PUSH FOR COLORED CONFERENCES, 1929–1944

The push for Colored conferences, or accommodation within the organizational structure, formally began near the end of the third decade of the twentieth century, a period initiated by the "Red Summer" race riots of 1919, so named because of the particularly bloody race riots in a number of cities, including Chicago, Illinois; Washington, D.C.; Charleston, South Carolina; Knoxville and Nashville, Tennessee; Longview, Texas; and Omaha, Nebraska.

Several factors contributed to these and other violent conflicts during the first few years of the centuries' third decade. One was the armed resistance in the Black community spearheaded by the resolve of Black soldiers returning from service in World War I. After their experience abroad, they now determined to resist the kind of abuses they had endured in America. Having been willing to die for democracy on foreign shores, they now returned home ready to fight and die here for their freedom as well. And many did get lynched while still in their uniforms as White America sought to put Negroes back in their place—especially those "spoiled" in France.

Another factor was the newfound capacity of recently migrated Blacks from the South to do what it had previously been almost impossible to do about lynching and other indignities—fight back. During the decade between 1910 and 1920, more than 500,000 Blacks fled the social, political, and physical oppression in the South to the crowded industrial centers of the North. Through the pages of *Crisis,* the official news magazine of the National Association for the Advancement of Colored People (NAACP),

W. E. B. Du Bois, who had derisively labeled America as the "land of the thieves and the home of the slaves," had as far back as 1911 "encouraged Blacks to fight back. 'If we are to die,' he angrily wrote after a Pennsylvania mob lynched a Negro in 1911, 'in God's name let us not perish like bales of hay.'"[1]

A third factor was the deepening frustration of Black Americans with the difficult conditions of their overpopulated neighborhoods. Having escaped the terrors of the oppressive South, they now found themselves trapped in the harsh life of the insensitive North. They soon discovered that the weather was too cold, crime too frequent, jobs too few, and their income too low. They soon experienced the different, but equally humiliating, attitudes among many Whites in the North. The Southern White attitude generally seemed to say: "We don't care how close you get [you can cook our food and nurse our babies], just don't get too big." In the North it was: "We don't care how big you get, just don't get too close!"

Most of Black America in the 1920s, even before the onslaught of the Great Depression, suffered from either the overt racism of the still angry South, whose senators killed the Dyer Anti-lynching Bill with three successive filibusters in 1922, 1923, and 1924, or the cold indifference of the crassly materialistic North, where 40 percent of the lynching and most of the rioting was taking place.[2]

As was typical, the Seventh-day Adventist church was not merely guarded in its response to the era's racial tensions and disparities; it functioned in strict obedience to the patently discriminatory laws of the land, believing that it should leave issues of civil and social justice exclusively to civic authorities. In consequence, Black Adventists found themselves locked out of worship in White churches, denied admittance to White hospitals and schools, shut out of policy-making/leadership positions within the church structure, and generally embarrassed in the Black community because of Adventism's radical withdrawal from social protest (Appendix 7).

Jacob Justiss (1919–1978), noted Black scholar and preacher, commented on the situation as follows:

> When the membership naturally complained of these conditions, the [Black] ministers responded in the accepted role of the Negro ministry—that of race leader. Robert Bradford and Thomas Allison protested. Elder Shaefe [sic] reacted . . . Elder J. K. Humphrey responded . . . the Manns set up an economic base for the fast-growing membership. The ministry as a whole presented memorials to the General Conference protesting that the Negro constituency was not receiving equal treatment in the existing conference system.[3]

Given such realities, it is not surprising that in 1929 the Black Adventist leadership in the United States, convinced that current administrative arrangements would not be adjusted to meet the needs of their people, petitioned for an arrangement that they thought would provide greater relevance to their personal needs and evangelistic endeavors: Colored conferences.

## THE EARLY ATTEMPT FOR COLORED CONFERENCES

While various individuals had urged the formation of Colored conferences in prior years, the first recorded evidence of a united approach for structural accommodations appears in the minutes of the General Conference Committee (GCC), March 3, 1929. The lead item on the agenda that day is titled "Council for Colored Workers" and reads in part:

> The chairman called attention to the proposal to hold a special council with certain colored workers prior to the Spring Meeting of the Committee, and it was
> 
> VOTED, That a meeting be called for 10 A.M., April 24, at the General Conference office in Takoma Park, and that the conferences concerned be invited to send the following colored workers, with the understanding that the conferences provide for the transportation of these workers . . .
> 
> FURTHER VOTED, That in arranging for this meeting with these workers, we assure them of our cordial attitude, and our desire to frankly and freely discuss their problems with them, at the same time *advising them not to attempt to hold any preliminary meetings for the discussion of these questions.*[4] (emphasis supplied)

The minutes of the March 3 meeting do not mention Colored conferences directly. However, GC leadership's prohibition of caucusing in advance, and subsequent GCC minutes stating as much, all make it safe to say that creating Colored conferences was precisely what Black leaders had in mind, and that White administrators knew it.[5] The Black leaders were cordially received and heard at the April 24 meeting and were delighted by the decision to pass their request along to the up-coming General Conference Committee session.

The regularly called Spring Meeting took place five days later, April 29, 1929, and formally addressed the request of the Colored leadership. The minutes state that the session began with a quartet number by F. L. Peterson, T. H. Allison, R. L. Bradford, and J. G. Dasent (all Colored) and then prayer by J. F. Huenergardt (associate secretary of the Bureau of Home

Missions). After these preliminaries, the meeting then considered the item titled: "Recommendation from the Council with Colored Workers." The critical elements of the report stated:

> Whereas, In a council with leading colored workers from various sections of the United States a request having been presented by these colored brethren reading as follows:
>
> "That the General Conference in Spring Council, at Washington, D. C., consider the organization of Negro conferences in the following unions: Atlantic, Columbia, Lake, Central and Pacific, that will function in all of their departments exactly as the white conferences now function, and be united to the entire body in the usual organized way," . . .
>
> And whereas, We recognize that such a fundamental change in our plan of operation is of far-reaching and fundamental importance; . . .
>
> We recommend, That the Spring Council be asked to appoint a well-selected commission, with colored representatives, to gather information and to give study to definite plans for the future of the colored work, such commission to report to the Autumn council.[6]

Thus, for the first time, the denomination officially placed the Colored church leadership's desire for Colored conferences before the church's decision-makers. The session politely heard the request and appointed a small committee to organize a larger group for in-depth study and to report back to the full body with appropriate recommendations at the Autumn Council in September-October of that same year.

The larger study group, labeled the "Commission on Negro Work," consisted of twenty-two individuals, including eight Colored pastors: G. E. Peters, J. G. Dasent, J. K. Humphrey, J. M. Campbell, T. H. Allison, P. G. Rogers, and representatives not named in the minutes from both the Southeastern and Southern unions. The commission presented its report at the Autumn Council later that year on September 26, 1929.

Its recommendations, remembered as "The 1929 Resolution," comprised four full pages of suggestions for the betterment of the Colored work. They included such plans as giving Colored church employees representation on local conference committees and, with the exception of the Southeastern, Southern, and Southwestern Unions, their union committees as well. Further, they recommended that both the local conferences and unions of those latter areas establish Negro committees comprised of the White leadership of those conferences along with one or two Colored representatives. Other recommendations involved Christian education, the colporteur and medical ministries, and finances. Curiously, the report made absolutely no mention of Colored conferences.⁷

As smoothly as the church handled and worded the process of appeal, it is clear from unofficial reports that White leadership, in general, regarded the Colored conference request, at best, as the well-meaning hopes of unprepared visionaries, and, at worst, a push for power by a few overly-ambitious malcontents. We find evidence of this attitude expressed in the subsequent testimony of several Colored leaders, including F. L. Peterson (1893–1969), who was elected secretary of the Negro Department in 1930, the very next year. Peterson later revealed that after the adoption of the commission's recommendations, church leaders privately instructed him and other advocates for Colored conferences never to mention the subject again. Thus, ironically, Black leaders had been warned not to caucus about their desires *before* they met with White leadership and were told *after* the denial never to bring it up again.⁸

Subsequently, the recommendations of the 1929 resolution met with reactions ranging from indifference to outright resistance in most places. After twelve years of disappointed observation on these matters, G. E. Peters (1883–1965), then serving for the second time as secretary of the Negro Department, reflected upon the disappointment of Black leaders at the General Conference Autumn Council of 1941:

G. E. PETERS (1883–1965), secretary of the General Conference Negro Department. Courtesy of the General Conference Archives.

Brother Chairman, this plan has been carried out in full in certain Union Conferences; but carried out only in part in other union territory. The Union Conferences that are now operating the plan in its completeness are the Southern and the Southwestern Union. . . .

Thirty-one years have passed since the department was first organized, with the employment of a full time General Secretary. As has been already stated, we numbered then only 900, but some one had a vision and the vision brought results. We now number 15,000 and the advancement merits a full time secretary in each union conference to spend his entire time in the duties outlined by the Autumn Council of 1929.

With my plea for the perfecting and strengthening of the department, I would also suggest that the Negro Advisory Committee be called together in 1942 and every two years thereafter. Sufficient time should be given to discuss plans and recommendations for the development of the colored work with its own peculiar problems . . .

In closing, Brother Chairman, I ask for continued confidence in the consecrated ability of Negro leaders. Give us a fair chance of greater responsibility with our own people, and I assure you there will be yet greater results in the building up of the work of God as related to the Great Advent Movement; where all races should stand together united and true, for the completing of the task committed to us by our Lord and Saviour Jesus Christ.[9]

Unfortunately, the plaintive cry of Peters and other dedicated Black ministers for implementation of the 1929 resolution failed to bring about what they deemed as satisfactory results and thoughts of Colored conferences again began to re-emerge. However, without the needed votes in appropriate committees to advance the initiative, they were completely stymied. In consequence, Black leaders had to rely upon the limited clout of the Negro Department to deal with matters of racial injustice as well as public ministry.

## CATALYSTS OF CHANGE

Events both without and within the church in the interim—between the first and failed protest for Colored conferences in 1929–1930 and the protest which succeeded in 1943–1944—were critical to their beginning. In the broader society this was accented by (1) the century's second massive migration of Blacks (the first was during World War I) who left the South for munitions jobs as World War II began and expanded; (2) efforts of Black activists such as A. Philip Randolph and first president of the N.A.A.C.P. Walter White, who, on June 18, 1941, met with President Franklin Roosevelt and threatened the government with the international embarrassment of a mass march on Washington unless Blacks were equally hired; (3) President Roosevelt's signing Executive Order 8802, on June 25, 1941, establishing the Fair Employment Practices Committee; (4) the opening of an N.A.A.C.P. advocacy bureau in the nation's capital in 1942; and (5) the establishment in 1943 of the Congress of Racial Equality and its use of nonviolent direct action tactics to integrate public establishments.

As a result of these and other such developments in the public sector, the national mood by the mid-1940s was generally disposed to accommodating units of organizational (political) authority within the Black community itself. For many, that was preferable to continually attempting to ward off encroachments imposed by integration. Meanwhile, there were protest events within the Adventist community that were no less significant for shifting attitudes and changing decisions regarding the status of its Black membership. Several of the more effective deserve mention.

## The Claude Barnett Revelations

Claude Barnett (1889–1967), celebrated Black journalist, was the founder of the Associated Negro Press (ANP), the nation's largest Black news chain during most of its existence (1919–1964). The ANP distributed news releases from its Chicago headquarters to most of the Black newspapers in the United States, including ones in New York, Philadelphia, Baltimore, Norfolk, Atlanta, Houston, Kansas City, and Oklahoma City. In addition, through the World News Service (WNS), it provided news releases in English or in French to more than one hundred African newspapers.

Barnett was, throughout his career, keenly sensitive to the racial struggles endured by the Black community in the United States. Such weekly publications were, as much as anything else, Black America's official voice of public protest against racial oppression. His papers, archived in the Chicago Historical Society, consist of thousands of articles and letters involving racial challenges to every major societal sector, including organized religion.[10] Barnett regularly monitored and addressed racial issues in a wide number of religious bodies, including Catholic, Congregationalist, Disciples of Christ, Episcopalian, Jewish, Lutheran, Methodist, Presbyterian, Seventh-day Adventist, Spiritualist, and Unitarian denominations.

CLAUDE BARNETT (1889–1967), celebrated founder of the Associated Negro Press. Courtesy of the Oakwood University Archives.

During the middle 1930s, Barnett became aware of racial problems within the Adventist denomination. Records indicate that Black leaders and laity informed him of troubling incidents, though most, fearing reprisals, refused to reveal their identity.

One leader who did not shy away from friendship with Barnett was Owen A. Troy, Sr. (1899–1962). It is not clear how much of the church's inner workings he shared with Barnett, but surviving correspondence reveals a warm and collegial relationship between the two. Their letters cover Troy's years of graduate studies at the University of Chicago (MA) and the University of Southern California (ThD, 1952), through various pastorates, and during his service as the associate secretary of the General Conference Sabbath School Department (1959–1962).

What is clear is that, through various contacts, Barnett became aware of the situation within Adventism and for several years worried church leadership by threatening exposure of the denomination's troubling racial practices. Several times he actually published embarrassing accounts of certain incidents. The fact that his office was in Chicago, Illinois, gave him ready familiarity with racial incidents at nearby Emmanuel Missionary College (EMC; now Andrews University) in Berrien Springs, Michigan.

OWEN A. TROY, SR. (1899–1962), first person in the church to earn a doctorate of theology, and a social activist. Courtesy of the General Conference Archives.

On December, 31, 1938, Barnett wrote to H. J. Klooster (1896–1963), then president of EMC, inquiring about various allegations of racial inequities. These included the school's policy of seating Colored students at separate tables in the dining hall, and its agreement with certain Black leaders that Colored students "go South" to Oakwood Junior College in Huntsville, Alabama, before being accepted into any of the majority White colleges in the United States for their upper division studies. Barnett closed his letter to Klooster by asking:

How can your denomination fulfill its world-wide mission program which I have seen outlined in your Harvest Ingathering pamphlet and close your school to a minority group such as the Negro race? . . . We get at different periods articles from the Humphrey and other schismatic groups, which we have refused to publish, but when we see both white and colored entering into a sort of Munich accord to barter the race's rights, we must let the news break. But can your denomination afford this uncomplimentary publicity which undoubtedly will affect your collection of funds, both in your Negro constituency and among liberal white people?[11]

Barnett's records reveal that the source of his information regarding what he coined the "Munich accord"[12] was Georgia R. Harris, a young adult Adventist living in Indianapolis, Indiana, not a student at EMC, who stated that she spoke for a broad spectrum of Colored youth around the country.

Harris had written a letter to Klooster on December 1 in which she made several claims about conditions at the college. Klooster replied in a letter to Harris dated December 11 in which he disputed some of Harris's claims, as well as its generally negative tone, and gave a straightforward explanation of certain school policies. After all, he reasoned, they (sixteen Black students at that time) were afforded their full "rights and privileges," and that continued agitation would be detrimental to opening the doors of further progress (Appendix 8). Harris apparently supplied both documents to Barnett.

Armed with the information, Barnett had written his letter to Klooster and almost immediately went to press with a news story on EMC racial matters. Some form of that story appeared in the January 7, 1939, *The New York Amsterdam News* seen throughout the country and picked up by other news agencies. It was headlined: "7th Day Adventist Jim Crow Called 'Uncle Tom' Sellout." The subheading read: "College Head Defends Bias; Clergyman and Educator Named As Condoning Segregation." What followed was a scathing rebuke of the school's racial policies:

> Defending segregation as practiced in the dining hall of Emanuel Missionary college, Berrien Springs, H. J. Klooster, president of that well-known denominational school, last week disclosed the origin of his policy, involving T. H. Allison, Chicago clergyman, pastor of the Shiloh Tabernacle, and J. L. Moran, president of Oakwood Jr. college, Huntsville, Ala. . . .
>
> Negro constitutents [sic] had protested against recently adopted policies which assign to young Negro men a Jim-crow in the daily dormitory worship and to all colored students Jim-crow tables in the only dining hall operated by the college. . . . College authorities, however, resolutely

re-affirmed the new policy and threatened to bar Negro students from the school entirely if protests continue. . . .[13]

It should be noted that Klooster had specifically denied any separation of any kind among students except at the dining tables and had explained that at some length. Three weeks later, another article appeared with the headline: "Chicago Adventists Deplore Jim Crow at SDA College: White Head of School Refuses to Comment on Situation, as Does Chicago Clergyman, Pressed for Interview." Apparently, Barnett had not received or been denied a reply for further comment from Klooster. In the article, Barnett cited famed author Arna Bontemps, then a Seventh-day Adventist, as follows:

> In some quarters race relations seem to improve with time. In others they tend to grow worse. No effort has been spared to consolidate gains, however, and segregation and kindred evils, even in so small a group as Seventh-day Adventists, should not be passed unnoticed . . . I sympathize with the Negro students at Emanuel.[14]

The article also quotes Troy:

> It is extremely unfortunate that our youth have to submit to the soul-embittering effects of prejudice and segregation. While not seeking to defend either the reported discrimination practiced at our Michigan denominational college or the dictatorial agreement entered into by the Oakwood Junior College president and Northern white college presidents, I can say from experience that these evils will be corrected when brought to the attention of our world conference officials at Washington.[15]

Extensive correspondence among several parties[16] shows that Oakwood's president, J. L. Moran (1894–1972), inundated with criticism from Colored believers around the country, rather angrily asked Barnett where he got his information. Barnett refused to tell him, and it was not until almost four weeks later that Georgia Harris, learning of Moran's extreme displeasure and veiled threat to take legal action against Barnett, wrote a letter to Moran confirming her role in the protest (Appendix 9).

Both Allison and Moran disputed Klooster's interpretation of their conversations with the presidents of the denomination's northern colleges in a letter to Klooster, who had not been at the meeting when the so-called "Munich accord" was discussed. In his reply, Klooster acknowledged that he had, indeed, not been present in those meetings, but that his view had been acquired from his own subsequent personal conversations with Moran. He also maintained that it made sense for Colored students to support Oakwood

Junior College before doing upper division work elsewhere. Nevertheless, he apologized to Moran and Allison for any misunderstanding and confusion his statements to Harris may have caused. Given the widespread condemnation that Moran, in particular, endured, he was probably very grateful for Klooster's sympathetic words (Appendix 10).

My own observations as a former Oakwood president (during a much more prosperous time) are that while I understand how the appearance of such an arrangement was potentially disastrous, the idea of trying to build enrollment at a struggling Black junior college during the early 1930s with a plan of acceptance for upper division studies at the church's better endowed senior colleges would have been very appealing. J. L. Moran, my high school principal at Pine Forge Academy (1946–1947), was no "Uncle Tom." As the first Black president of Oakwood (1932–1945) and principal of Pine Forge (1946–1948), he was a truly transformational leader in both institutions' climb to respectability. Barnett's implied conclusions regarding Moran's racial clarity were, it appears, questionable. However, Barnett's sincerity and dedication with regard to investigating racial injustice within the Adventist Church and the Christian community, in general, were not.

Barnett's February 1939 letter to F. L. Peterson, then secretary of the Negro Department, typifies the strength of his resolve:

> As you possibly know, our press service is furnished to 70 newspapers in this country. We have reporters and correspondents in the principal cities and sections of the United States, as well as a number of foreign countries, thus keeping our ears close to the ground for the latest news. . . . Unfortunately, several reports have come to our office in recent months in respect to segregation that is practiced within S.D.A. circles. . . .
>
> We, on the outside in the newspaper world, have wished that such a world-wide organization as yours had some sort of policy which would serve to assist us in interpreting news that comes to us. This E.M.C. matter is no longer just a denomination problem. All race matters become larger than their denominations. . . .
>
> Confidentially, I would like to tell you that reports have come to my office that the N.A.A.C.P. is about to take action in this case. You can readily see that if this matter is not corrected, it will have its effect in other parts of the state of Michigan and other northern states. When each action is taken, it will fall our duty to pass this on to our chain of newspapers.[17]

Barnett was highly instrumental in raising racial concern in the Adventist community not only among church members, but also with the general public. One must consider his releases as a "shot across the bow," if not a direct hit to the Adventist ship of state—a clear indicator to North American church leadership of the gathering clouds of racial unrest brewing within its borders. As his April 24, 1948, letter to General Conference president J. L. McElhany reveals, his vigilance regarding the church's racial posture continued even after administration had taken the bold step in proposing Colored conferences. His communication to McElhany about comments upholding racial segregation said to have been made by Carlyle B. Haynes (1887–1958) at the Beverly Road Seventh-day Adventist Church on April 3, 1948, as later reported by the *Atlanta Constitution,* is very telling.

Haynes, who had served as the president of the Greater New York Conference (1922–1926), the South American Division (1926–1930), and the Michigan Conference (1934–1940), as well as director of the Seventh-day Adventist War Service Commission (1940 until his retirement in 1955), was arguably one of the most eminent Adventist authors of his time. He penned forty-five books, several translated into other languages, most notably: *God Sent A Man, The Divine Art of Preaching, Living Evangelism, The Return of Jesus, Christianity at the Crossroads, Our Times and Their Meaning* (perhaps the most widely read), and *The Other Side of Death.*[18]

What distinguished Haynes in the Black community was not his prolific authorship. It was his often expressed fondness for the musical ability of Black Adventists and his ardent anticipation of going over to the "Colored side of heaven" to hear them sing, a rather common notion of White Christians during the early twentieth century.

Upon receiving a copy of the Atlanta newspaper's account of Haynes's remarks seeming to confirm the church's position on racial segregation, Barnett, in his usual courteous but probing style, addressed McElhany as follows:

> The following article appeared in *The Atlanta Constitution* of April 3, 1948, and reads as follows:
> "Adventist Upholds Racial Segregation"
> "Doctrines of the universal fatherhood of God and brotherhood of man have no place in the Christian church and are 'altogether untrue,'" Carlyle B. Haynes, of Washington, D. C., told a congregation here Friday at the Beverly Road Seventh-day Adventist Church.
> "Haynes upheld racial segregation, maintaining it was 'originated by God and set forth in the Bible as the divine way for the nations and races to get on together.'"

Since/above statements are so definitely contrary to the views held by most leading denominations and since they are both un-Christian and un-democratic, I am asking that you verify this account before I turn it over to one of our columnists for publication and comment.

Unlike the other prominent denominations, we do not have in our files any statements and pronouncements setting forth your views and teachings in respect to segregation, anti-lynching or Fair Employment legislation for the benefit of minority groups. . . . If we had such information here in our office, in a case like this we would know your stand and thereby be able to take issue with the individual rather than the denomination.

Kindly supply us with the following information for our files from your published writings of [sic] from your creed. If your creed and teachings do not set forth your belief and teaching along this line, could your committee give us a statement along these lines?

1) What is your belief and teaching relative to the Fatherhood of God and the brotherhood of man?

2) What is your denomination's teaching realtive [sic] to segregation and discrimination against persons on account of color or race.

The following information is also needed?

1) Do Negro American students attend your colleges in Washington, D. C.?

2) Are Negro Americans received as patients at your Sanitarium at Washington, D. C.?

3) Do you employ any Negroes in your publishing house?

4) Are Negroes of your own denominational connection permitted to dine in your dining hall at your headquarters?

Last year I visited a number of your mission fields in West Africa. I appreciate the excellent work that you are conducting there. Also I met some of the Negro American missionaries who are over there.

Knowing of your world-wide work as favorably as I do, naturally such statements as appeared in the *Atlanta Constitution* surprise me and certainly will counteract your work among the darker races and at the same time tend to make mockery out of your teaching of the Coming of Christ who shall establish His kingdom made up of all nations and peoples of the earth.[19]

The pointed questions in Barnett's letter again suggest that at least some individuals within the church membership saw the use of the public press as a safe and effective way to protest racial indignities.

The answer to Barnett's second question regarding the church's official statement spelling out its position regarding segregation was that it did not have one. In fact, it did not officially address the issue until 1961, making it one of the last of recognized American denominations to publicly declare its position on the matter, following the Presbyterian Church USA (1956), Evangelical United Brethren (1956), United Church of Christ (1956), The Methodist Church (1956), The Church of the Brethren (1956), the Lutheran Church-Missouri Synod (1956), American Baptist Convention (1957), American Unitarian Association (1957), Disciples of Christ (1957), The Catholic Church (1958), and the Union of American Hebrew Congregations (1959).[20]

## The Lucille Byard Affair

While Barnett's various revelations alerted the church hierarchy to the growing danger and potential damage of unwanted publicity, it was the Byard affair of late 1943 that served as the primary catalyst to bring about needed change in the church.[21]

Lucille Byard (1877–1943), a 66-year-old Black Seventh-day Adventist woman residing in Jamaica, Long Island, New York, had developed liver cancer with a chronic case of cachexia ("the wasting syndrome") by the summer of 1943. She and her husband James wanted her to be treated in an Adventist facility for obvious reasons, and were impressed that the Washington Sanitarium and Hospital in Takoma Park, Maryland, was the best option. The Byards asked Jeter E. Cox, Sr. (1885–1961), Black pastor of the nearby Bethel Seventh-day Adventist Church in Brooklyn and former employee of the Columbia Union (where the Sanitarium was located), to write a letter of introduction to the Washington Sanitarium, arranging for Lucy Byard to be admitted there. Cox agreed, making arrangements and confirming with the Sanitarium that Byard would be admitted on September 21, 1943. The Byards apparently could not afford the expenses, and so the Bethel Church assumed her medical bills. Most significantly, the staff of the Sanitarium did not know that Byard was Black when they confirmed her admission to their facility.

It is important to note that in 1943 the Washington Sanitarium was just that, a sanitarium. In the early 1940s the Sanitarium was moving more toward the acute care hospital model instead of the traditional Battle Creek lifestyle and retreat center. However, it still adopted a more holistic approach to health and wellness, with a central social component. Sanitarium patients would socialize together indoors in the dining room and other meetings, and out of doors on the sanitarium grounds in the seasons when the weather was pleasant, all as part of their treatment. Because of this social aspect, the Sanitarium did not admit Blacks in 1943, although earlier it had, on rare occasions, admitted them to an isolated section of the facility to be treated by physicians during off-hours.

There are two extant accounts of what occurred when the Byards arrived at the Washington Sanitarium on that fateful day—one from James Byard and the other from Robert Hare (1890-1965), the medical director of the Sanitarium. Byard wrote the following to G. E. Peters, then secretary of the Colored Department, six days after the episode.

> We, after much effort, arrived in Washington by rail and went directly to the Sanitarium. I went to the office and informed them that I was Mr. James Byard, of Jamaica, Long Island, and that Elder Cox had made reservations for my sick wife. The attendant acknowledged my reservation, went out and spoke to my wife and proceeded upstairs. He returned shortly and called me into the office, and told me that he regretted to say this, but it was against the law of the State of Maryland to admit colored people into the Sanitarium.
>
> I, of course, was stunned, for my wife had been looking forward with much anticipation to going to this particular Sanitarium, because she felt that she would be among her own people. There would be an understanding among them that she could not expect in an outside hospital. In fact her hopes were so high that her health was much better than it had been for days, and she even suffered the tiresome and painful train ride because of the expected destination. I warned the attendant of my wife's condition, and reminded him that she needed immediate attention; also that I was not acquainted with any hospital in Washington, D.C., hoping that he might examine her and find out her critical state, but to no avail. I was utterly confused and tried to get in touch with you, but was unsuccessful. The attendant recommended me to Freedman's Hospital, and assured me that she would be accepted there. He called a taxi, told the driver the hospital to take us to, and my wife and I were driven away.[22]

Robert Hare's account to GC president McElhany, and treasurer and Washington Sanitarium Board chair W. E. Nelson (1883-1953), on November 15, 1943—after the episode had created an uproar in the Black Adventist community—was somewhat different:

> On September 21, a telegram was received at 11:00 P.M., stating that Mrs. Byard would arrive on the 7:05 train Wednesday morning—Elder Cox asking that she be met. As we do not have special means of meeting patients they took a taxicab and arrived at the Sanitarium between 9:00 and 10:00. Mr. Baker called me immediately and told me of the fact that Mrs. Byard was a colored person. In view of the fact that we had carried on our correspondence, not knowing that she was colored, I advised that we receive her into the institution giving her a private room and arrange for her meals to be sent on trays, and plan for her examination and diagnosis by our physicians

in off hours, hoping that Mrs. Byard would see the fairness of this in view of our misunderstanding and the social sentiment that exists in Maryland. As an alternative Mr. Baker and I suggested the idea that she might go to Freedman's Hospital in Washington and have diagnostic work done which she desired. I did not come to the office to meet Mrs. Byard at the time, feeling that in all probability she would elect to take the private room. When I finished my rounds I came back to my office and inquired what she had decided to do. I learned then that she and her husband had refused to accept our offer of a private room and had gone to Freedman's Hospital.[23]

Contrary to the common narrative, Lucy Byard did not die on the way to Freedman's Hospital, or even shortly after. She died more than a month later on October 30, 1943, in Freedman's Hospital, her immediate cause of death being cachexia from liver cancer.[24]

There was an immediate uproar in the Black Adventist community over the egregious episode even before Byard's death. Indignant Black laypersons ignored all lines of communication and expressed their displeasure to the highest church official: GC president J. L. McElhany. First Jamaica Seventh-day Adventist Church, Byard's home congregation, wrote a letter to McElhany on October 25, signed by sixteen members including James Byard, five days before Byard's death:

> Dear Elder Mc Elhany:
>
> We, the membere [sic] of the First Jamaica S.D.A. church of Jamaica, Long Island, who are acquainted with the way Sister Byard was treated at the Washington Sanitarium, do hereby resent such treatments which was [sic] shown our beloved sick sister.
>
> We would like to make the following suggestions to you, as our leader and representative who made contact for her going there; It seems that since they were expecting her down as a patient, knowing she was a SEVENTH DAY [sic] ADVENTIST and after seeing her condition on arrival there (VERY ILL, AN AGED WOMAN AND WEARY FROM TRAVELING) [sic] Regardless to any thing else we feel that she should have been accepted in said institution. But by being inhumanly turned away and in no condition to travel back to New York had to seek immediate medical attention in a worldly institution.
>
> This of course is a disadvantage to her husband and loved ones unnessarily [sic]. Realizing there are many good worldly institutions here in our own community. WE FEEL THAT ALL UNNECESSARY EXPENSE SHOULD BE CHARGED TO THIS INSTITUTION AND A BILL OF SAME PRESENTED TO THEM. TO BE PAID ON DEMAND.

If not paid immediately, action should be taken in the form of a law suit for damages.[25]

Never before had Black laypeople threatened a sitting General Conference president with a lawsuit against one of the church's institutions. Two days before Christmas, the Sharon Seventh-day Adventist Church, a congregation in Byard's home borough of Jamaica, Long Island, sent a written protest to McElhany on December 23, 1943:

> We, the undersigned members of the Sharon S.D.A. Seventh-day Adventist church, hereby protest the treatment that was shown our late beloved sister Lucy Byard of the Jamaica S.D.A. Church of Jamaica, New York, at the Washington Sanitarium September 22, 1943.
> 
> We as a people are standing for better treatment and conditions for Colored Seventh-Day [sic] Adventist throughout this last warning message to a prejudice, wicked and dying world.[26]

Not sensing the magnitude of the Byard infraction, on Sabbath morning, October 16, just weeks after Byard was turned away from the Washington Sanitarium, GC vice president and president of the North American Division W. G. Turner (1885–1978), who was White, delivered the sermon at Ephesus Seventh-day Adventist Church, the largest Black congregation in the Washington, D.C., area. His text was from 1 Peter 4:12–13: "Beloved, think it not strange concerning the fiery trial which is to try you, as though some strange thing happened to you; but rejoice to the extent that you partake of Christ's sufferings." Turner had—in the words of Jacob Justiss, who later became pastor of Ephesus—"hardly sat down" when, incensed by Turner's temerity, James O. Montgomery, went to the front and said:

> Yes, I think it very strange that there is an Adventist college [Washington Missionary College, now Washington Adventist University] nearby to which I cannot send my children. Yes, I think it is strange! A denominational cafeteria in which I cannot be served, and now this incident—I think it mighty strange! I am not prepared to hear you say "Servants obey your masters," meaning the General Conference our master.[27]

The unfortunate circumstances of Byard's death, the misplaced emphasis of Pastor Turner's attempt at damage control, and the activism of Black New York and D.C. laypeople evoked a new level of Black Adventist protest intensity throughout the country.

## The Committee for the Advancement of World-Wide Work among Seventh-day Adventists

One immediate consequence of the tragic mistreatment of Mrs. Byard and of Pastor Turner's "strange" sermon was the emergence in the Washington, D.C., area of a large and very effective protest committee of laity. A person close to the scene wrote of its organization:

> The group . . . met . . . in the back room of Dodson's Book Store [in Washington] that was destined to be the first office of the Allegheny Conference. They passed the hat to help on the telephone bill and began calling various persons to apprize them of their actions, viz; J. G. Dasent, New Orleans, Arna Bontemps, Nashville, Tennessee, O. A. Troy, Pasadena, California, and L. H. Bland, Baltimore.
>
> These agreed to have their names placed on a letter head. Because several persons outside the United States were contacted the committee named itself "The National Association [it was later changed from National to Committee] for the Advancement of World-Wide Work Among Colored Seventh-Day Adventists."[28]

The Committee is widely regarded as the first organized protest of Black American Adventists laypersons. Among its members were a number of highly educated and articulate Black female believers living in the nation's capital. Included were Helen Sugland, public school teacher; Willie Dodson, principal of the Washington, D.C., Junior High School; Lula Bell Cox, instructor and critic teacher in the D.C. school system; Valerie Justiss-Vance, soon to be the second Black Seventh-day Adventist to receive a Ph.D.; and Alma J. Scott, president of Howard University Alumni.

Perhaps the most prominent woman Committee member was Eva B. Dykes (1893–1986), niece of James H. Howard.[29] The first Black woman in America to complete the requirements for the PhD degree (Radcliffe, 1921), Dykes was soft spoken yet a plain-spoken activist for full integration in earlier years. However, she is listed as being active in the mid-1940s movement leading to the formation of Regional conferences. She is also remembered for creating a national stir within the Black higher education system one year after the Byard incident by giving up her prominent position as a well-known professor at Howard University to teach at what was then the little-known Oakwood Junior College. Her participation in the protest that was organized on that day in October 1943 in the back room of Dodson's store had a wide and lingering influence.[30]

The broad circulation of protest materials, including missives to top Adventist church leaders by this blue-ribbon group of academicians, government employees, and other professionals, jolted the church system and awakened White church leadership to new and potentially very divisive currents in the church.

The committee's signature document, "Shall the Four Freedoms Function among Seventh-day Adventists?" had as its thesis the inability of the policy of White Adventists in responsible positions to stand "the acid test of the judgment" (Appendix 11). Their eight-page statement supporting this assertion is a classic expression of the disenchantment generally experienced in Black America at that time. Its central indictments of the Seventh-day Adventist Church were that:

- The policy in the educational and medical programs is discriminatory and un-Christlike.
- The policy in the administrative sphere is discriminatory and un-Christlike.
- The policy used in the area of employment is unfair, partial, and un-Christlike.
- The policy in spiritual matters is too one-sided and narrow.

To these observations the Committee added a number of detailed recommendations for both short and long term remedies to the church's racial ills.

Eva B. Dykes (1893–1986), the first Black woman in America to complete the requirements for the PhD degree.

Most observers believe that these three developments—the Claude Barnett revelations, the Lucy Byard affair, and the work of the Committee for the Advancement of the World-Wide Work among Seventh-day Adventists, along with the swelling tide of less prominent incidents in Adventist churches and schools—were, as stated earlier, even more critical to changing the church leadership's posture toward Black believers' concerns than were the external events in the interval between 1929 and 1944.

## Additional Factors

Several more developments from 1929 to 1943, which led to the major shift in the stance of White leaders vis-à-vis the Black work, must be mentioned. Mirroring African Americans on the national scale, during this period Black Adventism also matured greatly. By the mid-1940s there were more than 20,000 Black Adventists in the United States. Leading them was a very capable corps of ministers that was a force to be reckoned with, comprised of those who had built up the work in the lean years and had mastered the dynamics of the local church and the conference, union, division, and General Conference structure.

The early 1940s ushered in the era of the Civil Rights Movement in the nation, a time when Whites realized that some concessions would have to be made to Blacks. America was a decade removed from the overthrow of "Separate but Equal" in 1954. Increasingly weary of Black America's push for full inclusion, Whites were now generally disposed to supporting units of organizational (political) authority within the Black community itself, as opposed to integration in White communities and institutions. Ironically, this period would be headlined by a Seventh-day Adventist named Irene Morgan, who refused to give up her seat on a bus in Virginia in 1946, and ultimately won the U.S. Supreme Court case *Morgan v. Virginia* that struck down racial segregation on commercial interstate buses.[31]

## COLORED CONFERENCES ORGANIZED

Leadership's reversal of attitude and opinion was starkly and surprisingly revealed at the 1943 Autumn Council in Takoma Park, Maryland. General Conference president J. L. McElhany announced that "during the time of the Council the officers and the union conference presidents had been giving some study to the question of the future development of our colored work." He then recommended that the General Conference Committee make arrangements for a meeting on "the future development of our colored work in North America" at the next Spring Meeting in 1944. Importantly, McElhany included that "there shall be a number of representatives of our colored work invited to attend."[32]

The GCC took several actions as to the composition of the members of "the future of the colored work" meeting. On January 13, 1944, it voted that the "Union Colored Secretaries" and a specified number of

Black representatives from each union be invited to the group.³³ On March 9, 1944, it voted "That each union conference that has a colored constituency be asked to select one layman from its membership to sit with the group in Chicago..."³⁴ There were several votes for certain individuals to join the special committee. Just before the beginning of Spring Meeting, it was voted that the presidents of the conferences in North America should be invited to attend.³⁵

The committee discussing the future of the Colored work in North America met on April 8 at the Stevens Hotel in Chicago, Illinois, the venue of the historic 1944 Spring Meeting. The meetings began with an eight-paragraph speech by McElhany, in which he summarized the closely-guarded discussions during the preceding six months involving General Conference and Union Conference leadership on the subject of the Colored work.³⁶

It was clear that White leadership, stung by rising racial tensions (particularly those sparked by the recent Lucy Byard affair) but more generally and genuinely, the rapid growth of Black churches, had concluded that the time had come to organize Colored conferences. McElhany's concluding challenge made this very clear. He put it this way:

> Should we continue to operate on the status quo?... We want you brethren to express yourselves; Whether we continue as we are or has the time come when we ought to proceed to organize conferences? If we should decide to organize conferences I do not feel that it could cover every Union in the North American field.... We don't want to undertake anything that will make us ashamed; I have known conferences to be organized with only 800 members which proved to be successful.³⁷

A. Wellington Clarke, one of the more outspoken Blacks present, responded first: "Is there," he asked, "a necessity for change or are you brethren forcing this upon us?" To which McElhany replied, "No, this is nothing that has been forced upon the brethren.... We are anxious that the Lord will lead us in developing a plan that will be for the best interest of developing the work."³⁸ Several prominent White leaders, including E. D. Dick (GC secretary) and L. H. Christian (GC vice president) added supportive comments to McElhany's statement, and the April 8, 1944, morning session ended.

It was the second day of the meeting, April 9, 1944, that the Black leaders coalesced around the White leadership's encouragement to move ahead with the organization of Colored conferences. Minutes of that session indicate that some Black leaders present there did not agree with the idea. One was T. M. Fountain (1899–1989), a Black minister, who concluded a passionate speech in favor of the "status quo" by declaring:

> In regard to the colored conferences: I want to say here that the laymen's movement was born in Washington [D.C.]. Some of these same laymen told me that they were not in favor with colored conferences.... If there are those in favor with the conferences they are very few. I can't believe that anyone would like to be a president. I don't believe a word of it. None of our churches are in favor of pulling out.... I don't believe anyone is in favor of the colored conferences here in this place.... We don't want colored conferences.[39]

G. E. Peters, at that time secretary of the Negro Department, followed Fountain's speech by asking what Fountain wanted. Repeating a term used by McElhany in his comments the day before, Fountain replied, "That we maintain the status quo." Then, without hesitation, he moved the continuation of the "status quo," a motion seconded by E. S. Dillett.[40]

At that point the term "status quo" took on a life of its own. For those who opposed Colored conferences, it meant continuing the quest for needed administrative authority within White-led conferences. That those in favor of establishing separate units administered by themselves viewed the expression as having a distinctly different (and pejorative) connotation, however, was shown in Owen A. Troy Sr.'s immediate question: "What is the status quo?"[41]

Fountain and Dillett were not the only ones leery of the idea of Colored conferences. Another leading minister put it this way:

There are some of our group who look forward to conferences because of exalted places and authority. There may be some of the other group who don't want to be bothered with us. Perhaps this is the reason they would like to have colored conference[s] to get rid of us.

J. L. MCELHANY (1880–1959), General Conference president and advocate for Colored (Regional) conferences. Courtesy of the General Conference Archives.

We should come together like the disciples. They realized their trouble. There was strife among them. They put it away and all their difficulties and the HOLY SPIRIT came upon them. (Joel 2:15–17.)

The colored conferences is not in my mind what we need. We need to get closer together and have a more cooperative spirit. We have now a form of organization to last until the Lord comes.[42]

One must assume, based upon his earlier remark, that the unexpected direction the discussion had taken now surprised and disappointed McElhany, who was chair of the meeting. It is also logical to conclude, given his opening remarks, that he felt relieved that the motion to maintain the "status quo" received less than enthusiastic support from most of the attendees. The record reveals that those who expressed themselves against "status quo" included ministers M. A. Burgess, A. Wellington Clarke, T. M. Rowe, J. G. Thomas, J. H. Williams, J. Gershom Dasent, and J. H. Wagner, as well as New York City layman Samuel Hooper. The remarks of Dasent and Wagner were particularly forceful.

Dasent (1879–1955), began his comments by referencing the progress made during the twenty-six years that Blacks had led the Negro Department:

The first five Regional conference presidents: H. R. MURPHY, South Central Conference (1946–1954); J. H. WAGNER, SR., Allegheny Conference (1945–1953); L. H. BLAND, Northeastern Conference (1945–1954); H. D. SINGLETON, South Atlantic Conference (1946–1954); J. G. DASENT, Lake Region Conference (1945–1949).

> We have had three colored leaders and God has blessed the work under their leadership. Oakwood is managed by a colored president. We have more students there than we ever had before. We look at the "Message Magazine." God has set His stamp of approval upon it.
>
> We are living in a time when the Negro is seeking for something more and better.... We shouldn't continue the Status Quo.... In 1930 I stood against this very thing of a colored conference. I believe the time has come when we need something more than what we have. The greater work is in front of us.[43]

However, J. H. Wagner (1903–1962), still in his early forties and destined to be a major voice in Black Adventism during the next eighteen years, put matters in the starkest of terms. His statement, expressing a view not offered before, urged:

> I believe we should adopt a plan that will be an advanced move for our people. In my recent effort held in Washington, D. C., a lady who was a member of one of the chain stores, cornered me and said, "We believe the Sabbath and that it is the right day. We can't get around that, but you are a minister in your denomination and how far can you go beyond that? What else is offered the colored people?" It was hard for me to answer that. I offered some kind of weak excuse. We must realize that there are certain things that we can do that will make it easier to reach our better classof [sic] people. By organizing conferences it will give us a great advantage in reaching this type of people.[44]

Then, using an analogy that no one else had ventured to make, he concluded:

> When the Emancipation Proclamation was received through President Lincoln, it was through God's leadership. When the slave owners told the slaves that they were free, the slaves still wanted to stay with their masters. They didn't realize what the emancipation meant. I don't mean that we are in slavery; this illustrates that because we have a difference of opinion, it doesn't mean that we are not on the right course. We preach of the United States in prophecy and we can see that he came up just at the right time.... It was for people who were looking for freedom.[45]

S. O. Cherry, beloved physician at Oakwood Junior College who would die a few years later in 1947, then spoke for the "status quo" in the following terms: "I believe that we should give more power to the present plan that we have now. The Southern Union Plan is the best plan we have, but it is void of power. If our leaders had more executive power they would be happy."[46]

J. H. WAGNER (1902–1962), key spokesperson for Colored (Regional) conferences. Courtesy of the General Conference Archives.

But it was clear that after Wagner's comments the tide had turned permanently. Following a number of other speeches against the "status quo" motion, H. D. Dobbins stated, "There is a motion before the house.... Since we do not seem to want to remain under the status quo, I wonder if Elder Fountain will withdraw his motion." Fountain's reply was, in part, "Whatever organization is selected, I assure you, that I will cooperate with it one hundred per cent.... We should get something started. If it will help any, I will withdraw that motion."[47] E. S. Dillett then withdrew his second.

At that point, H. D. Dobbins, who must be credited with focusing the pro-conference opinion for an appropriate vote, moved that a committee be appointed to "study the conference plan and bring back recommendations."[48] J. G. Dasent seconded his motion. During the question phase of the motion, several of the White General Conference leaders who had accompanied McElhany to the meeting, but who had not commented as yet, expressed themselves in favor of Colored conferences. Notable among them was W. A. Spicer, a past-president of the General Conference (1922–1930), who said, "I hope that this body will set its approval on the Conference plan."[49] Another was J. J. Nethery (1879–1971), at that time president of the Lake Union Conference, who commented:

> I believe in Local Conferences for our colored people.... I don't think that we should thing [sic] of 17,000 colored members and making 30 conferences. You can take your 17,000 members, or at least the membership in a few conferences, you could build a good conference with these members....
>
> It may be that we cannot organize a colored conference in every Union. Why not start with one or two and with the help and counsel of the brethren we can see how it works and later on we can start in another Union.
>
> I hope you will think kind of us for we believe in this proposition.[50]

H. M. Blunden (1885–1974), then secretary of the General Conference Publishing Department, also spoke, observing, "I don't see why this new conference set up couldn't work.... Of course, at first problems will be created but we can work it out."[51] The motion then carried and the delegates nominated the committee to take the recommendation to the "large body" of delegates.

The committee met April 10 and formulated the recommendation. It read in part:

> *Conference Organization:*
> 5. WHEREAS, The present development of our work among the colored people in North America has resulted, under the signal blessing of God, in the establishing of some 233 churches with some 17,000 members; and,
> WHEREAS, it appears that a different plan of organization of our colored membership would bring further great advance in soul-winning endeavor; therefore,
> We recommend,
> 1. That in unions where the colored constituency is considered by the Union Conference Committee to be sufficiently large, and where the financial income and territory warrant, colored conferences be organized.
> 2. That these colored conferences be administered by colored officers and committees.
> 3.That in the organization of these conferences the present conference boundaries within each union need not be recognized.[52]

At the first session of the Spring Meeting on Monday, April 10, 1944, the General Conference Committee adopted the recommendation.[53] Black Adventist protest had been successful: Colored conferences would be a reality.

The next day, April 11, at a specially-called meeting, a report of the committee's recommendations that the Spring Meeting had adopted went to the full complement of Colored delegates. Peters, serving as chairperson, began discussions with a brief statement about the progress of the Colored work and then launched into the matter at hand:

> There is one thing that I am grateful for, and that is, we didn't come here as a group of workers to make demands. We were the invited guests of the General Conference to listen to what they had proposed.
> This is not the same spirit that was in the 1930 meeting. I now feel confident that the time had not come in 1930 for this enlargement. There is a spirit of unity among the colored workers, now, that did not exist, then....

We should remember, all the way through, this thing is to propel a greater evangelism. We ought to go back to our field and assume a more careful and humble attitude than ever. All eyes will be turned upon us. We ought to go to work, and work harder for souls and missions than we have ever done before.[54]

J. L. McElhany followed with a statement further revealing his hopes that Black conferences would stymie racial dissention among lay people:

I am hoping that as these new organizations take affect that we have the fullest cooperation and confidence of our laity. This is of inestimable value. I believe this new organization among the lay members ought to be put out of existence as soon as they go back. . . . I thank you for the privilege of talking to you and telling you a few of the things that were on my heart.[55]

G. E. Peters then replied:

We thank you very much for your remarks. . . . Bringing about this organization, we feel that we need experience. . . . This new organization is not to push someone to a great station. The object in view is to bring more souls in the truth. We thank you for your words again. We want to assure you that we want to give you the assurance of our loyalty.[56]

Just before a number of tributes to Chairperson Peters for his wisdom and persistence, F. L. Peterson summarized matters:

I think this is one of the most outstanding moves that have ever been made for us. . . .

Whenever we used to say colored conferences many people thought we meant separation. I feel that it will be a very fine thing to give an explanation in the Review of this organization, so that our people will know that this is something that has been handed down by the General Conference to us. If this is done it will help us. They will understand that this is a General Conference idea. . . .

I think this is a very fine thing that we have come to. I believe that this means we are going to finish the work. I was told *never to mention conferences. Don't ever mention them!* I am glad I didn't mention them. I am more than glad that it is now here.[57]

In his fall 1945 report to the church in the *Adventist Review,* Peters provided the following details regarding the organization of the three initial Colored conferences:

Following the Spring Meeting, several Union Conferences invited a commission from the officers of the General Conference to give study to the plan of going forward with the proposed organization. The Lake Union was first to lead out in this direction.

September 26, 1944, the colored churches of the Lake Union, comprising 2,260 believers were organized into a conference taking the name Lake Region Conference of Seventh-day Adventists. This new conference embraces the states of Wisconsin, Michigan, Indiana, and Illinois. . . . This new conference which began its functions January 1, has a colored population of over 800,000 souls, which must be warned with the message of a soon-coming Saviour.

October 3 another colored conference was organized. This conference comprises the Atlantic Union territory (except Bermuda) and has taken the name "North Eastern Conference of Seventh-day Adventists." In the new conference is the Ephesus Church of New York City with more than 1,000 members. There is a total of 15 churches with a membership of 2,200. . . . The colored population of this conference numbers 1,106,000.

December 17 the Columbia Union Conference went forward with its new organization. This conference has 40 churches with some 3,800 believers and a colored population of 2,340,832. The conference includes the states of Delaware, Maryland, New Jersey, Ohio, Pennsylvania, Virginia, West Virginia, and the District of Columbia. The name adopted was the "Allegheny Conference of Seventh-day Adventists."[58]

The formal vote to organize the Allegheny Conference, typical of all the others, occurred after delegates of the constituent churches had met for three days and reads:

> After a full and free discussion of Agenda item No. 5, 'To Organize or not to organize a Colored Conference which would comprise the entire territory of the Columbia Union conference,' it was voted to organize a Colored Conference for the believers in the Columbia Union, the vote being 265 affirmative; 18 opposed."[59]

In his report, Peters, who on other occasions highlighted the operation of Oakwood Junior College and Riverside Sanitarium (Nashville, Tennessee) as evidence of Black leadership's ability, emphasized the development of another of its institutions, *Message* magazine, noting observations after nine years of existence:

> This magazine is a monthly, full-message journal, the only periodical of its kind in the world. Its psychology is especially adapted to meet the spiritual needs of the 13,000,000 colored people of the United States. At present it is going to all colored Universities, Colleges, Academies, and newspapers

editors. It is the ideal medium for making the primal contact with the wealthy families of our cities. . . . Since its origin nearly all the articles have been prepared by our colored ministers and workers.[60]

Peters concluded his report with a mixture of optimism and justifiable caution regarding his main focus—Colored conferences:

> These three conferences have been organized to meet present day conditions and to help in the speedy finishing of God's work on earth. Our colored workers and believers in North America are loyal and true to this Message.
>
> We realize that the organizing of these conferences will not be without trials and difficulties. But with God at the helm, as the Omnipotent Captain these newly launched ships will sail on to victory.[61]

## DEFECTIONS ALONG THE WAY

The epochal struggles of Black leaders during the first four decades of the twentieth century were not without significant loss. A number of prominent Black ministers and laity found the church's racial practices untenable, and their protests resulted in their leaving the church and sometimes taking significant numbers of other members with them.

## J. K. Humphrey (1877–1952)

The departure of the well-known Harlem pastor/evangelist J. K. Humphrey in 1929 is the most storied defection in Black Adventist history. After being rebuffed in several requests for funding for a community welfare project in Harlem as well as for administrative accommodations (Colored conferences), Humphrey led approximately 600 of his 1,000-member congregation (then known as Harlem #2 and now Ephesus) to independence in what he called the United Sabbath-day Adventist Conference.[62]

Because of his extreme popularity, Humphrey's leaving the denomination and beginning his own independent movement had a traumatic effect upon the North American church. He had arrived in the United States from Jamaica, British West Indies, in 1903; by the late 1920s he was, by virtue of his eloquence and dynamic leadership, a truly charismatic figure. He had started no less than seven Seventh-day Adventist congregations in the New York City region. By the time of his withdrawal he had followers not only in Manhattan (Harlem) but also in Brooklyn; Jamaica, Queens, Long Island; New Rochelle; and White Plains, New York. Eventually his independent support included congregations in several nations abroad, including Central America and the Caribbean.

In 1944 the *New York Amsterdam News*, a popular Black community newspaper begun in 1909, reported Humphrey's reaction to the formation of Black conferences. "According to Bishop Humphrey, his counsels, appeals and arguments to the general conference [sic] for a separate conference to manage and strengthen the work among colored people were ignored and he felt himself in conscience bound to withdraw from the white group."[63]

The article quotes him as stating: "This was in 1928 and 1929 that I urged the general conference [sic] to do the only logical and proper thing, but our leaders then could not see what I was driving at. Today, that is in April, 1944, a conference was called in Chicago to do the same thing that I advocated in 1928. If they are right now, I must have been right then."[64]

One of Humphrey's fellow clerics and ardent supporters, Maitland G. Nunez, in an article titled "Why Should It Be Thought a Thing Unchristian?" written in August 1931, delivered an eloquent apologia for Humphrey's cause:

> In the departments of a nation forming its economic, political, educational, inventive and religious background, when that which is called "new" is launched,—something which differs from the old method,—men everywhere rise up against it. But like the locomotive, the Bell Telephone, the Republican form of Government, the airship, the teaching that the world is round, the acceptance of the automobile, the Seventh-day Sabbath, and other ideas, it forces these same men to see light, reason, logic, and good sense in the "new idea," as they call it, and after a few severe tests are given according to their ability to test, they soon fall in line and loudly proclaim that the new thing which has come (to benefit humanity) is all right. So after the big fight against, there comes acceptance of, the new idea.
>
> ... The brothers and sisters north and south, homeland and foreign should cease the unwise cry. "The time is not ripe, we are not ready for such a master move." Let me ask, "When is the time going to be ripe?" If 1913 to 1931 does not bring a ripened time; if the briny tears of men and women among the Advent Negro believers who have had to groan in public and private, does not show ripened time; if the loss of hundreds of boys and girls of our Negro preachers and members in the Advent ranks, if the premature death of Negro Adventist preachers suffering under the oppression does not bespeak that the time has come; and if justifiable concern for the future as well as interest in our present condition does not spell the arrival of the time, when will it ever come?[65]

## John W. Manns (1881–1929)

Humphrey's was the most celebrated case of a Black leader leaving the denomination in response to the church's racial policies, and Lewis Sheafe's is one of the best documented (see discussion below). But perhaps the most hostile of all defectors was J. W. Manns, a popular minister of the early twentieth century, who, along with his brother Charles, a gifted musician, in 1915 left the Seventh-day Adventist church to establish a body that he named The Free Seventh-day Adventists. That the name was the same as that adopted by Sheafe was no accident. Sheafe had six years earlier held evangelistic meetings for Manns in Savannah, Georgia. Records indicate that while their formal affiliation was brief, Manns, nevertheless, retained the name that Sheafe had proposed.

On the occasion of the second biennial session of the general assembly of Manns's group from January 15 to 23, 1922, conducted at the Bethel Church of Free Seventh-day Adventists in Savannah, Manns excoriated his former Seventh-day Adventist brethren:

> Because bigoted white leaders among Seventh-day Adventists have failed to consider the necessity of such vital changes, but have fixed a permanent bar against the Negro leadership in the organization, many of the most intelligent Negro ministers are separated from the denomination, some of whom have become entirely disgusted and have sought other positions, such as doctors of medicine and chiropractic. Others have resorted to real estate speculations, and still others to the farm, etc. It is also true, that many have given up the Christian hope, and are looking to the cold world, from which there can be no lasting peace of mind.[66]

At the conclusion of his paper, Mann gave twelve reasons why he found it necessary to begin his independent movement. The final ones read as follows:

> Ninth. We are free because the white leaders of the Seventh-day Adventists denomination discriminate against colored people. They do this abominable, most detestable, discriminating in the organization, the Church, the office, the school and sanitarium, notwithstanding the Negro membership must make great sacrifices to aid in building up these wonderful institutions now owned by the S. D. A. denomination.
>
> Tenth. We are free because Negro Seventh-day Adventists, as a rule, are barred from Seventh-day Adventists Northern and Western schools, where schools of the world make no distinction among races.
>
> Eleventh. We are free because the white leaders of the Seventh-day Adventists denomination bar even Negro Seventh-day Adventists [sic] patients

from their sanitariums, when the worldly institutions of the same kind, accept colored people of every walk of life.

Twelfth. We are free, because Negro Seventh-day Adventists are barred from holding any clerical position in the Seventh-day Adventists Publishing houses, tract societies and conference offices.[67]

## Lewis C. Sheafe (1859–1938)

As discussed in Chapter 1, one of those who had striven mightily for full integration of Black and White church attendance as well as administrative functions was Lewis C. Sheafe. He was untiring in his attempts to tackle what he had referred to as the "color line" wherever he was assigned, North or South, both in and out of the church.

In 1907, after several years of unsuccessfully seeking full participation for Blacks, including his 1901 recommendation of a Negro Department (defeated then but established in 1909), Sheafe declared his independence from the policies of the Seventh-day Adventist church in a letter to A. G. Daniells. It conveyed the sentiments of his congregation in Washington, D.C.:

> The People's SDA. Church, assembled Wednesday evening, Jan. 9, 1907, to study conditions pertaining to its welfare, and to transact business. . . .
>
> We learn from scriptures that it is the right and privilege of the individual church to take part directly in all lines of missionary work, at home and abroad; to ordain persons for special work, at home or abroad; to exercise self-government, under the guidance of its exalted head, the Lord Jesus Christ; to collect and expend its means, such as tithes and offerings, furnished by its members; being subject to no foreign tribunal or court or review, the only recognized head of this church, above the pastor, is the Lord Jesus Christ.
>
> This church by [unanimous] vote decided to at once enjoy these and other scriptural rights and privileges,
>
> We therefore respectfully notify you of our action,
> Done by order of the church.
> (signed) Lewis C. Sheafe, Pastor.
> (signed) Elmira B. Greene, Clerk[68]

Efforts at reconciliation by several leaders failed, including those of Ellen White, who sent him a lengthy communication dated February 1, 1907, pleading with him to reconsider. After weeks of discussion, Sheafe, whose assignments had come directly from the General Conference, surrendered his credentials to church officials.

Among those who did not regret his departure was J. S. Washburn, the evangelist who had worked with Sheafe to establish churches in Washington, D.C. In a letter to Daniells, Washburn stated what most Black leaders assumed to be White leadership's opinion regarding racial parity: "The weaker you are, the more you realize what a terrible thing it would be to be under black government, under colored domination.... The more one knows of the colored people, the less he feels to blame the Southern white people, who feel that it will not do to let the colored man get on top, and it would be a terribly dangerous thing."[69]

Six years later Sheafe reconsidered his decision, and the Southern California Conference hired him. However, his reconnection with the church was brief. After holding evangelistic meetings that led to the formation of the Berean Church in Los Angeles, California, he left again. In September 1916, unhappy with various church racial policies and practices, he relinquished his ties to the denomination for good, taking with him most of the members of the Berean congregation. He named the movement that resulted the "Free Seventh Day Adventists."

In his biography of Sheafe, Douglas Morgan explains that "it was not so much a theory or model of church organization that Sheafe protested as the perception of heavy-handed authoritarianism on the part of church leaders—in particular an all-White hierarchy...."[70] However, by 1916, he further observes, Sheafe and his wife had added to that concern the authority of the writings of Ellen White, most pointedly the use of her 1915 counsels in volume 9 of her Testimonies regarding the separation of the races. With that conviction they publicly protested and departed, never to return.

## Arna Bontemps (1902-1973)

A racially influenced departure from the ranks of Adventism that cost the church more academic/intellectual loss than any other was that of Arna Bontemps. Born on October 13, 1902, in Alexandria, Louisiana, he had French, Cherokee Indian, Jewish, and African heritage, all of which, some thought, at times expressed themselves in his speech and personality.

His father, who became a Seventh-day Adventist and lay preacher when Arna was very young, moved the family to Los Angeles when he was three. Arna attended San Fernando Academy from 1917 to 1920, and in 1923 graduated with a bachelor's degree in English from Pacific Union College. While there, under the tutelage of well-known Adventist educator Charles E.

Weniger (1896–1964), Arna honed literary skills that would later bring him acclaim as one of America's most honored authors.

From 1924 to 1931 Bontemps taught at Harlem Academy in New York City, one of very few Black Adventist day schools at that time. It was during those years in the "Black Mecca," as many called Harlem, that his literary genius flowered and he gained prominence as a participant in the most recognized and revered of all African American literary movements—the Harlem Renaissance, the name given to the cultural, social, and artistic explosion that took place there between the end of World War I and the mid-1930s. While in New York City, despite Bontemps's growing acclaim as a poet and short-story writer, as well as his close association with various luminaries of the Harlem Renaissance, including Langston Hughes (1902–1967), he remained faithful to the church (Appendix 12).

Bontemps accepted an invitation to teach at Oakwood Junior College in 1931, where a confluence of events caused him to resign in 1934. After spending a short time in California, he moved to Chicago where he taught at Shiloh Academy and where in 1943 he earned a master's degree in library science at the University of Chicago. That same year he was appointed head librarian at Fisk University where he remained until 1964. Later Bontemps taught at the University of Illinois and in 1969 was made curator of the James Weldon Johnson Memorial Collection at Yale University. He was a frequent guest instructor and lecturer at various institutions of higher learning and recipient of numerous prestigious academic and literary awards.

The last three decades of Bontemps's life were spent apart from the Seventh-day Adventist church. One of the reasons he relinquished membership was the church's reaction to his authorship of fiction, an activity for which he received high acclaim but which countered the church's emphasis of contemplation of truth.[71] He also distanced himself from the denomination due to dissatisfaction with its racial attitudes. While his response to racism in the church and society was not highly vocal, it was effective. Bontemps's creativity and eloquence often led to a stirring emotional response, something a fiercer and bolder approach might not have accomplished.

It was during his service at Oakwood that tensions with White leadership became overwhelming for Bontemps.[72] What brought matters to such an uncomfortable level was the suspicion that he was involved in the well-organized student protest at Oakwood Junior College in 1931 in response to the denomination's continued appointment of White leaders at the institution. On the morning of October 8, 1931, the very day of the fall meeting of the school's board of trustees, the students refused to go to chapel, class, or the dining facility and demanded that the General Conference (Oakwood's parent body) place Blacks on the board and replace their White school head with a Black director.

In addition to their complaint to the board, the students shared their protest in a tersely-worded letter with thirty "representative persons":

> We are tired of lying. In view of the fact that conditions at Oakwood Jr. College are not favorable to mental, physical and spiritual advancement, we, the student body are appealing to our interested brethren in the field for help. It is our desire that they cooperate with us in a definite way for this worthy cause which will mean so much to the advancement of the work among our people.[73]

Response from the General Conference was immediate. One letter to then President J. A. Tucker read:

> Your students have addressed a letter to the General Conference. . . . We are surprised to discover that the students as a body have taken any step that ignores the college faculty or the board. We desire it to be clearly understood that the General Conference is always willing to do its utmost to adjust difficulties that arise in the work. But it cannot countenance action of employees or students that set aside faculty. . . . We have noticed especially the demand of your students that the president of your college shall be a Colored man. We find it hard to believe that in this important matter they want to dictate to the General Conference. . . . We desire to make it very clear that the General Conference will permit no such dictation by a student body in such a matter, but will hold itself absolutely free to choose whomsoever it will [to] serve as president of Oakwood Jr. College.[74]

On November 2, 1931, F. L. Peterson, then secretary of the Negro Department, wrote the students as follows: "No doubt, you have overlooked the fact that the General Conference has a world field to plan for, and it takes time. I will say that in making your request you put the General Conference in a very hard place when you cease all activities and then undertake to take over the school until the General Conference acts."[75]

W. W. Fordham (1911–1998), later to become the director of the Negro Department (1975–1979), was then a student and an active participant in the strike, and he described subsequent events:

> At length General Conference leaders became convinced that it was time to change presidents at Oakwood, but first they tried to get another White administrator. They called Professor Leon Cobb from Pacific Union College to

head the school, but Cobb refused the call. Next they invited Elder D.A. Ochs to take the responsibility. Ochs candidly told them he was fearful of the proposition. "I have never lived in the South," he said, "and I know nothing about Colored people and their ways. Up to the present moment I can't fully conceive how a German would deal with Colored psychology."

Finally, it was clear that the time had come for Black leadership at Oakwood. J.L. Moran, principle of Harlem Academy, was called to take the leadership of the school. He became the first Black president of Oakwood College on May 12, 1932.[76]

Bontemps, who in his own words had been hired by the institution with "some admitted reluctance," was accused by administration of subverting the students with racial ideas that contributed to "the rebellion," was ordered to discard all his writings—many of which referenced society's racial inequities.[77]

Bontemps lasted a little longer on the faculty but remained under suspicion as one who was, by his pen if not by spoken provocation, stimulating student and faculty opposition to the church's racial policies and practices. That, along with the fact that he felt "anathema" (the way he described it) because of his association with Langston Hughes, left him, he thought, with no alternative but to resign.[78]

That he understood that his Oakwood experience would be short-lived Bontemps expressed in the following portion of his letter to his good friend Hughes written in the wake of the protest of 1931:

> The boys here in school were successful in getting Tucker out. The board voted it last week, but they also voted to send the leaders in the strike home. So Herman Murphy, Allan Anderson, Earnest Mosely and Rashford and Fordham are gone (you may remember some) and the place is dreary as a result. I was also pointed out as being favorable to the revolution and, as a result, may not be rehired. I am not really bumped, but the faculty is to be cut in half (due to depression) and I may not be on the new slate.[79]

A racial event of the same year that drastically affected relationships, not only in Alabama but also the entire nation, was the celebrated case of the "Scottsboro Boys," nine Black teenagers accused of raping two White girls (one of whom lived in Huntsville) at a lonely railroad site near the town of Scottsboro some forty miles east of Huntsville. Even though repeated appeals over a seven-year period clearly eroded the girls' story, and one girl actually admitted to lying, several of the Boys still faced execution. The national outcry against Alabama's actions and the decisions of superior courts saved their lives, but only after years of heart-wrenching tension and litigation. In 1936 to 1937 the state dropped the cases against four, and the other five received long prison sentences.

Bontemps's good friend Langston Hughes visited Oakwood during a Christmas season in the early 1930s, and while in Huntsville attempted to speak with the rape accuser who lived there. "I wanted to interview Ruby Bates in Huntsville," he wrote, "but the Negro teachers at Oakwood thought I must be crazy. They would take no part in helping me to locate her, and none of them would accompany me to see her. Finally, they dissuaded me from the attempt on the grounds that I would be taking my life in my hands, as well as endangering the college."[80]

When he left Oakwood, Bontemps, in his own words, "fled from the jungle of Alabama's Scottsboro era to the jungle of Chicago's crime-ridden South Side. . . ."[81] In his more extended explanation he stated:

> As my year ended, I was given an ultimatum [by Oakwood]. I would have to make a clean break with the unrest in the world as represented by Gandhi's efforts abroad and the Scottsboro protests here at home. Since I had no connection or involvement with either, other than the fact that I had known some of the people who were shouting their outrage, I was not sure how a break could be made. The head of the school had a plan, however. I could do it, he demanded publicly, by burning most of the books in my small library, a number of which were trash in his estimation anyway, the rest, race conscious and provocative. *Harlem Shadows, The Blacker the Berry, My Bondage and Freedom, Black Majesty, The Souls of Black Folk,* and *The Autobiography of An Ex-Colored Man* were a few of those indicated.
>
> I was too horrified to speak, but I swallowed my indignation. My wife was expecting another child, and the options before us had been reduced to none. At the end of the following term we drove to California, sold our car, and settled in the small room in Watts in the hope that what we had received for the car would buy food till I could write my book. By the next Spring [1935] *Black Thunder* was finished, and the advances against royalties was enough to pay our way to Chicago.[82]

Several years later in a letter dated November 15, 1950, to his friend Herb Nipson, a reporter for *Ebony* magazine who had inquired about his view of the Seventh-day Adventist church, Bontemps gave a glowing portrayal of his former church in matters of education, health, and mission endeavor, and he had particular praise for his experience at Pacific Union College.

He concluded the letter, however, with the following terse comments regarding the church's racial attitudes:

> In race relations Adventists are retarded. Perhaps one should bracket with this the observation that as a whole they appeal to a better Negro than white element. . . . In their early years Adventists were solid on the race question. They began to compromise to appease the South. They are still doing it, and they suffer as a result. Their younger Negro leaders are fighting at every turn for an abolition of segregation and dual standards. They are not satisfied with their progress, I gather. And I don't blame them.[83]

Bontemps died at the age of seventy while reading a rosary of sorrow at the wake of Clara Perry, the wife of the Meharry Medical College president, in the Perry's home on June 4, 1973. Bontemps was never caustic or bitter, as some who left the church. He retained good relations with his sister, who was the wife of Owen A. Troy, Sr., and was proud of his nephew Owen Troy, Jr. (1927–2014), who served the church admirably in a number of capacities, including a lengthy tenure in the Communications Department of the North American Division.

By the time of Bontemps's death, the Seventh-day Adventist church had made significant strides in the matter of race relations. Its schools of higher education had dropped their quota systems, its hospitals admitted Blacks in all parts of the country, and the hiring of Blacks in the upper echelons of church administration was becoming more commonplace. The struggle for admission of Black students into local day schools and congregations in some sections of the country was still in process, but much had changed since Bontemps left the church.

## AVOIDING SCHISMS

It is remarkable, given the level of racial insensitivity that existed and the obvious charisma of the several Black leaders who did defect, that so few schisms occurred prior to the creation of Colored conferences in 1944. It is further noteworthy that those fractures that did develop did not eventuate in the kind that has split so many denominations into wholly separate structures. That the majority of Black leaders never seriously advocated a separate church can be attributed to several discernable factors; among which are:

- An apocalyptic emphasis that minimizes expectations for justice in the present world even among the oppressed.
- A system of "belief transmission" or socialization through church schools and youth societies that transmits theological and social values to succeeding generations.
- A fear of heavenly disapproval for harming the church by exposing its weaknesses.
- The stellar efforts of a long line of eminent Black preachers and teachers who with uncommon gifts of pen and voice spanned the century with the gospel proclamation of hope in Christ and sacrificial loyalty to the church they served.

A rich example is the tone of G. E. Peters's February 20, 1949, letter to Francis R. Scott, a pastor in faraway Burma. Scott had been approached by a national believer explaining what he thought were Ellen White's less than adequate responses to racial inequities in the United States. Scott wrote Peters for an explanation. Peters replied:

> Dear Brother Scott:
> Your letter of January 24 has been received. I can readily see the problem you are facing in helping this Karen brother to understand certain statements made by Mrs. E. G. White in the Testimonies concerning the colored question. It is quite difficult, I admit, for our brother, so far removed from the United States and conditions in the South, to grasp the meaning of Sister White's instructions. May I state that her position is understood and accepted by Negro Seventh-day Adventists....
> 
> The plan of separate churches in the South works quite well. It is understood and accepted by both groups and has resulted in thousands of both races won for the kingdom. The truly converted white man and the truly converted Negro love all races and with them there is no color line, although they must live up to the law of expediency. The Apostle Paul wrote in his epistle to the Corinthians, "All things are lawful unto me, but all things are not expedient..." 1 Cor. 6:12. The white S. D. A. and the colored S. D. A. in the South understand the situation. Should we attempt to ignore conditions between the races in the South, the work for both whites and Negroes would be seriously jeopardized.[84]

Peters's allegiance to the "law of expediency," which sounded very much like Spalding's "principle of policy," indicates that even as the walls of segregation began to crumble in the mid-twentieth century, most Black Adventist leaders determined, while working for change, to protect the church's image with both their members and the public.

That protectionist attitude of Black leadership was never more clearly demonstrated than by the reply of F. L. Peterson (then Associate Secretary of the General Conference) to F. W. Hale, Jr. (then a professor at Central State University) regarding the younger, more militant Hale's plans to expose the church's racial weaknesses to the press. Peterson reprimanded his former student in a letter (April 27, 1961) that, in part, read:

> To organize against the church because of any wrongs that may be seen in the church is neither a Godly or Godlike act. To seek to nullify the work of the Seventh-day Adventist church because of racial reasons will produce only chaos, and we have nothing to gain from chaos. The race to suffer the most damage will be the race that made the disorderly attack. We have a better way and a better plan. God would have us use it.
>
> Please, Dr. Hale, do not let it be chalked up against you that you would confederate against God's church because of racial prejudices. Make your appeal in a different way. . . .
>
> Remember that it does not make any difference who bores the hole in the ship, when the boat goes down everyone on board will get wet. Those who bless you now will curse you later. Do not do it.
>
> There are some things that Baptist, Methodist, Congregationalist, etc. can do, but Seventh-day Adventists cannot.[85]

Hale's courteous reply lauding Peterson for his sacrificial ministry to the Adventist Church, but nevertheless reaffirming his intention to press vigorously for correction of racial ills within the denomination, is a classic example of a thoughtful but firm resolution to move ahead with his plans. Early on in his May 6, 1961, letter, he stated:

> Elder Peterson, I will always have the highest regard for your qualities as a man, for the source of inspiration which you have personally been to me, and for your counsel through the years . . . and I accept your caution in the right spirit. . . . I am aware that this action (1) will cause some to consider me as a "heretic, rebel and flaunt"; (2) will cause others in key positions "to pull the shade" on my career as far as my future service to the denomination is concerned; and (3) will cause still others to even challenge my motives and sincerity of purpose.
>
> So I have no doubt about what personal damage could result; however, I can no longer "hide my light under a bushel" in these matters. . . . *I maintain that there is no circle in the church that could sustain segregation and discrimination for one moment, if it were not sustained in the circle of leadership.* (Appendix 13)

While the methodology of Hale and the layman group he led (discussed further in the next chapter) pierced the veil of existing Black Adventist caution with regard to public protest, the majority of the Black pastorate and laity still hesitated to expose the church's racial sins. The rules of social engagement structured by ethics gained from traditional theological understandings would simply not allow most Black Adventists, lay or clergy, to engage in public protest.

Since many of those who had protested vigorously within the church (i.e., Sheafe, Humphrey, Mann, Nunez, Bontemps) had all finally left the denomination and in the minds of church leaders and members were eternally "lost," vigorous protest of any kind now had a distinctly foreboding aura. That posture changed dramatically during the first three decades of the second half of the century, causing considerable tension in many cities. It included an attempt by one pastor of the Black-administered South Central Conference, Randolph Stafford, to bring legal action against the White-administered Alabama-Mississippi Conference (Appendix 14). That the spirit of protest endured until then is remarkable.

My most unforgettable demonstration of Black leaders' willingness and ability to shield their members from discouragement was provided in the late 1960s when I visited with Pastor J. G. Thomas, one of the more colorful and celebrated Black Adventist evangelists of his era. We had enjoyed pleasantries for some time in his home when quite abruptly this aging warrior pulled from under his bed, near where he was seated, two large boxes filled with newspaper clippings of Blacks being beaten, hanged, and stoned. I was amazed that he had quietly collected these materials over several decades. I had heard of him for many years and seen him a number of times, but never suspected that intrepid soul-winner was so privately gripped and aggrieved by the nation's, and it must be assumed his church's, racial weaknesses. That he had refused to let these injustices sour his public proclamation or persona struck me as remarkable, and that refusal was critical to shielding his audiences from racial animosities. I view his mindset as typical of the many heroes and heroines whose demonstrations of church loyalty prevented major church fissures both before and since the organization of Regional conferences.

## THE WEST COAST DIFFERENCE

No discussion of the creation of Regional conferences would be complete without attention to developments on the West Coast of the United States where matters evolved quite differently.

The minutes of the General Conference Committee for April 29, 1929, show that the Pacific Union Conference was one of the several unions included in Black leadership's original appeal for Colored conferences.[86] The others were the Atlantic, Columbia, Lake, and Central Unions, in each of which a Colored conference was eventually formed. However, neither the Pacific Union, comprising the states of Hawaii, California, Arizona, Nevada and Utah, nor its fellow western neighbor, the North Pacific Union, incorporating Alaska, Idaho, Montana, Oregon, and Washington, were included in the 1944 actions that gave birth to Negro conferences.

F. L. Peterson, O. A. Troy, Sr., and Norman McLeod, all at that time respected ministers in the West, were present at the 1943–1944 sessions and indicated approval of the proposition. However, their support did not translate into obvious, and certainly not successful, efforts for conferences in the Far West.

The Black work "Out West," as believers east of the Rockies often refer to the church structure in those two union areas, began with congregations organized in Berkley and Los Angeles, California, in 1906. Progress for many years was slow. As late as 1910, fewer than fifty Colored believers lived in the West. With the addition of one other church (Blythe, California) and one branch Sabbath School (Allensworth, California), membership approximated two hundred in 1920.[87]

Membership also grew slowly during the 1920s. Congregations were added in San Diego, Oakland, San Francisco, Los Angeles, and Pasadena, California, and Salt Lake City, Utah. Nevertheless, by 1930 the Black West Coast membership, still growing slowly, numbered only approximately 350.[88]

In the thirteen years between 1930 and 1943, Los Angeles gained other churches along with those established in San Bernardino and Fresno, California, and Phoenix, Arizona. Augmented by these additional congregations and, very importantly, the surge of members migrating from the East and South (particularly from Texas and Mississippi), by 1943 the Black West Coast membership approximated 1,500, a modest but not unprecedented number with which to begin a local conference. That Black leaders and laity did not request inclusion in the 1943–1944 decision reflected factors both organizational and environmental.[89]

A significant organizational factor was F. L. Peterson's appointment as secretary of the Colored Department for the territory of the Pacific Union made just one year prior to the beginning of the Regional conferences. The fact that the position was a significant first for Blacks on the West Coast, that many saw it as dealing with the primary reasons behind the need for Colored conference organization, and that the position might be taken away were a Negro conference organized, all tended to dampen any enthusiasm for having a Colored conference in the Pacific Union.

A second such factor was that the Black Adventist community on the West Coast, still less than four decades from its beginnings, had not undergone the intensity of racial discontent as had its counterparts in the South and East.[90] It must be remembered that by the time of the 1944 Regional conference organization, Black Adventists in those areas had already witnessed the protests of Sheafe, the Manns brothers, Humphrey, and Nunez; the untimely death of Green; the Colored conference rejection of 1929–1930; the student revolt at Oakwood in 1931; and numerous other racially-driven events. Black West Coast believers native to the area had not experienced such trauma, and many of those migrants from other areas may have wished simply to forget them and move on.

The primary environmental factor that shaped events is what may be described as "West Coast Exceptionalism." This included the belief that social conditions on the West Coast were, in almost every way, better than elsewhere in the country. It also involved the advantages of semi-tropical scenery, clean air, the variety and abundance of fruits and vegetables, the lure of newly constructed communities, the increased prospects of employment, and the proximity and variety, for Californians in particular, of snowy mountains, sunny weather, and the usually placid Pacific Ocean, all earning for this part of the country the appealing appellation "Golden West."

But it was not only these environmental features that gave Westerners, both in the general society as well as in the church, the feeling of difference and advantage. It was also pride in a greater mixture of races. Whereas in the East and the South in particular, racial interaction usually involved just Blacks and Whites, and that often negative, the West, the land of new beginnings and fresh opportunities, displayed a rainbow of humanity, including significant percentages of Asians, Pacific Islanders, and Hispanics.

The obvious needs addressed by the Peterson appointment to Colored Department secretary notwithstanding, this wide range of cultural contact in much of their territory gave most West Coast Black believers hope and expectation of full integration at the level of local conference functioning—a pursuit long before abandoned by most Adventist Blacks elsewhere.

That hope has, despite the presence of problems echoing those in the rest of America, remained for most Black West Coast leaders and laity the driving principle of racial association. In April 1990, Earl A. Canson, Sr. (1927–2003), then secretary of the Pacific Union Regional Affairs department, gave clear expression of this position in his article "An Argument against the Regional Conference Proposal" printed in the *Pacific Union Conference Regional News*. He reasoned:

> Acts 2:1 says "They were all with one accord in one place." There must have been some significance in being in one place while they were with one accord. It's easy to get along with someone when you are separated from them, but to be with one accord in one place is quite an accomplishment. The Bible teaches that TOGETHER IS BETTER.... Ellen G. White believed that TOGETHER IS BETTER. She said, "God wants the different nationalities to mingle together, to be one in judgment, one in purpose. Then the union that there is in Christ will be exemplified."—9T, 180. She also said on the same page, "... not to build up a wall of partition between different nationalities."
>
> Ellen White said that the world "needs to see the Lord's people sitting together in heavenly places in Christ"–9T, 188. That means Black people and White people should be sitting together in our churches, our conference meetings, our campmeetings, our evangelistic meetings and our workers meetings. These are heavenly places.[91]

As is usually the case, as Black numbers grew so did relational issues in churches, incidents with racial overtones at schools, and mounting frustration regarding lack of administrative hiring and appointments in hospitals, education institutions, and conference offices. As a result, by the mid-1950s there began the first of a long series of moves to establish a Regional conference in the Pacific Union.

Major C. White (1927–2003; Black), the highly respected secretary of the Pacific Union, reported on these attempts in the February 1990 *Regional News*:

> The idea of organizing a Black or Regional Conference in the Pacific Union is not new. This idea has been thoroughly discussed and officially voted on in the Pacific Union three times by Black ministers in the union 1955, 1965 and 1975 and unofficially once by the laity in the Southern

California Conference in 1965. On each occasion the concept was voted down. The great majority of ministers and laity voted to continue working toward integration and togetherness in all ethnic groups.[92]

However, W. D. Felder, at that time Black Ministries Coordinator for the Northern California Conference, refuted the idea that the West Coast Black ministers had categorically rejected the idea of Regional conferences. In his article, "An Argument Supporting the Regional Conference Concept," printed in the February 1990 edition of the *Regional News*, Felder wrote:

> On or about March 5–8, 1989, the Black workers of the Pacific Union met at Soquel [California] to discuss, among other things, the feasibility of a regional or Black conference in the Pacific Union. After much debate, pro and con, the larger number of votes were cast for the desirability of a regional conference in the Pacific Union. Other votes were cast for an improvement in the current system, or not ready at this time. Significantly, not one vote was cast for maintaining the present system as it relates to Blacks.[93]

In the same article Felder sought to counteract the arguments made by those opposing the Regional conference concept:

> Here in the Pacific Union we have elected to have Black coordinators to speak out on, and represent Black issues and problems. The Black coordinator, however, has no executive authority. He only advises on Black issues and problems, and many times that advice is ignored or given low priority.[94]

A number of widely published articles in the *Regional News* supported Felder's position. They included Helvius Thompson's "The Biblical Theology That Supports Regional (Black) Conferences," John E. Collins's (Associate Director of Community and Health in the Northern California Conference) "An Argument Supporting the Regional Conference Concept," and Timothy P. Nixon's "An Idea Whose Time Has Come."[95]

One should note that generally those who advocated Regional conferences had transferred from the East or South and had attended Oakwood College, an almost entirely Black school, while those who spoke against them (e.g., Canson and White) had spent their college years at Pacific Union College, then an almost exclusively White institution, and thus had never been employed outside of the Pacific Union. That was not without notice or influence in what by the early 1990s had become an increasingly heated debate in the Black Adventist West Coast community.

Furthermore, it was also observed that many of those who most fiercely opposed the establishment of Regional conferences on the West

Coast had come from existing Black conferences, bringing with them horror stories of personal indignities and sufferings. Typically they were pastors and church school teachers who told of late paychecks, sparse budgets, and inferior facilities as being common throughout Regional conferences and therefore "good reason not to have one out here." They also complained about the lack of Christian education (local church schools) and leaders who were highly autocratic and politically motivated.

Objective observers recognized that the latter charges were no greater a phenomenon in Black conferences than in those administered by Whites. However, they also acknowledged validity to some of the concerns. Black conferences, struggling to get on their feet, were functioning with a pay structure the same as that of "White conferences"; but with a roughly 35 percent lower income base (tithe and offerings), they could not match their counterparts in such matters of hiring ratios, land acquisition, and school facilities.

The North American Division has had since the 1960s financial policies (appropriations) particularly helpful to conferences handicapped by limited income. Notwithstanding, because of the disparity between White and Black income in the United States (approximately 30 percent even today), finances still remain a major challenge for Black conference leaders. The fact that they do not equal White-administered conferences in matters of evangelism budgets, education scholarships, and appropriations for building projects is a chief reason that even today many West Coast Blacks would rather retain their status quo.

Until the early 1990s it was the Southern California Conference where protest had its most strident voice. Aided by spokespersons from the other California conferences as well as the Nevada-Utah Conference, also a part of the Pacific Union, their most visible effort was the creation of *The Layman's Voice,* published from 1989 through the early 1990s. Copies of the short-lived publication, edited by lay persons, went far and wide, expressing a fervent desire for a Regional conference "Out West." In the early 1990s another lay-led protest body, the "Westerners United for a Regional Conference" (WURC), whose motto was "The Time is Now," superseded *The Layman's Voice.*

WURC consisted mainly of Southeastern California Conference (SECC) lay members chaired by Gaines Partridge (1923–2009), former Oakwood College professor and later Director of Student Affairs at Loma Linda University. It promoted its cause, with the guidance of sympathetic pastors, with what some regarded as "do or die" energy throughout the SECC until the end of the decade.

WURC's methodologies paralleled in many ways those of another Southeastern California Conference protest, that of the Conference's Black Caucus (SECBC) chaired during the 1990s by Anthony Paschal, director of that conference's Regional Department. The SECBC possessed a decidedly larger membership since it was a regularized entity comprised of pastors and church delegates conference-wide. WURC, however, taking advantage of the fact that it was not directed by conference employees or confined by policy restrictions, often presented its arguments in language more strident than its clergy-led counterpart organization felt free to use.

As during the early 1990s the stronger push for a Regional conference came from a lay-led group (WURC), so did opposition to the idea. It did so via a group named "Blacks for Correction and Improvement without Separation." The latter organization's leading voice was Eva Bradford-Rock (1912–2009), sister of Charles E. Bradford, president of the North American Division (1979–1990) and mother of the author of this study.

Bradford-Rock, listed in *The Laymen's Voice,* January 1990, along with Vera Panton, as co-chairperson of "Blacks for Correction and Improvement without Separation," served over the years on a number of committees and commissions tasked to study the matter of a Black conference in the West. Blessed with excellent speaking, writing, and organizational abilities, she was not only the leading lay force against the idea, but, other than Canson and White, its most influential opponent.

GAINES R. PARTRIDGE (1923–2009), West Coast protest leader. Courtesy of the General Conference Archives.

While it is true that "Blacks for Correction and Improvement Without Separation" (also referred to as "Blacks for Modification Without Separation") became more visible in the debate beginning in the early 1990s, it had been involved in what one could best describe as behind-the-scenes contacts with church members and conference officials for many years.

An example of its dealing with the latter group appears in various statements produced in response to Bradford-Rock's early 1990 request of White church administrators for assurance of their unbiased regard toward Black Americans. Following are replies to her request for written affirmation:

- Herman Bauman (president, Arizona Conference): "I firmly believe and am committed to the Bible truth expressed in Acts 17:26. 'And have made of one blood all nations of men for to dwell on all the face of the earth.' I believe wholeheartedly that God has made us all equal, that there is absolutely no difference in capabilities, and that there should be no difference in opportunities either. . . . There is no race of people in this world that is superior to any other, and I believe the true Christian will be absolutely color blind."[96]
- L. Stephen Gifford (president, Southeastern California Conference): "It is the position of the president of the Southeastern California Conference, that BROTHERHOOD of BELIEVERS must be the norm and not the exception for this conference. This implies that all shall be afforded fair treatment, without regard to their race or national origin. That is how Jesus worked, and acted, and lived. And this is how we, the followers of Jesus Christ, must work and act and live today."[97]
- Thomas Mostert, Jr. (president, Pacific Union Conference): "When God looks on His human creation, He relates to all of us on the same basis. Language spoken, color of skin, rich or poor, educated or not, God does not play favorites or discriminate. His children should relate in the same way. But to truly be brothers and sisters in Christ means actively seeking to break down the barriers that separate. Status quo in most cases is unacceptable, though for some more comfortable. We need more church members who will make personal plans to improve communication and understanding between ethnic groups. Only when brotherhood is a priority can we truly make progress in working together."[98]
- Herbert H. Broeckel (president, Central California Conference): "I wish I could say that I have always practiced Brotherhood as carefully, and strived to achieve it, as urgently as I do now. Because we are all human, I am sure that I still fall far short of the mark of what God would have me to become in regard as to how I treat every man, woman, or child of whatever race, ethnic group

they are from. Because truly, we are all one in Christ.... I pray that none of us will ever forget our ethnicity and that we can all make our contributions to society and to the church without being discriminated against."[99]
- G. Charles Dart (president, Southern California Conference): "It is my belief that the brotherhood of man is at the core of the gospel. The 'good news' Jesus wants us to share is that every human being is as important as another. My belief is based not only upon direct scripture, such as Paul saying we are all one blood and that God is the Father of all mankind, but also in the actions of Jesus while He lived on this earth.... Whether they are young or old, rich or poor, black or white, brown or yellow, we all are children of our Heavenly Father and He considers us all of equal importance and wants us to have that same attitude and concept of one another. To me that is very good news! It should be the responsibility of the church to demonstrate this good news to the world."[100]
- Don C. Schneider (president, Northern California Conference): "All people stand before our God with the same needs. We are all equal at the foot of the cross. All are sinners in need of grace. But thanks be to God, the saving power of our Lord is available to all people. Because Jesus looks upon all people as the same, we must too, and therefore we must do all we can to bring the gospel to all people."[101]
- Darold J. Retzer (president, Nevada-Utah Conference): "The very heart of the gospel and the love demonstrated by our Lord indicates to me that we are brothers and sisters in Christ. Though we all are different, yet we all stand equal before Him.... It appears that our Creator enjoyed variety. He made us with different features, with different talents, with different abilities, with different personalities but He loves us all. I appreciate the diversity in the Adventist church and feel that each race benefits by coming in contact with others. We all need each other."[102]

"Blacks for Correction and Improvement Without Separation" promoted such statements as evidence of the spirit of fairness by White leadership in the Pacific Union. However, neither they nor their opposites in WURC found their principles satisfactorily demonstrated in the political and social life of the union's conference offices, churches, and various other institutions. The hiring of Blacks in administrative positions was still at a minimum, Black students experienced discrimination in schools, and all-White or partially mixed congregations soon turned all-Black when appreciable numbers of the latter group began to attend. Throughout the first half of the 1990s, "Blacks for Correction and Improvement Without Separation," while steadfastly defending its anti-Regional conference position, also continued to identify glaring racial inequities and to press for change.

Meanwhile, WURC, in tandem with SECBC, pointed to these same racial incidents and disparities and vigorously pursued the Regional conference option. They did so in spite of the results of an extensive (sixty-two-page) feasibility survey conducted by Canson's office during April through July 1990 that, with the assistance of the Pacific Union's office of Church Ministries, showed most Black believers in support of changes within the system rather than the development of a separate conference.

The study, involving all fifty-four Black congregations in the states of California, Arizona, Nevada, and Utah, elicited responses from 3,052 believers in majority-Black churches (a return rate of 36 percent of surveys issued to members). To the question, "I favor a Regional Conference because it will meet the special needs of the Black work," 42.2 percent of respondents said yes and 57.8 percent said no. And to the question, "I favor the present system but with sufficient modifications to meet the special needs of the Black work," the response was 76.8 percent yes and 23.2 percent no.[103]

The brief period between late 1990 (when the feasibility study released its results) and early 1994 (when a chain of events particularly affecting the fate of the Regional conference initiative took place) saw deepening division between the supporters and the opponents of the Regional conferences option. The survey brought relief and assurance to the advocates of modification. On the other hand, Black conference advocates found reason to question the validity of key elements of the survey questions and analysis and responded in a "no confidence" posture toward its results and the objectivity of its framers.

Two young Black pastors pointedly expressed the determination of WURC and SECBC during this period to promote their vision. The first response appeared in a letter printed in WURCs "Proposal to Establish a New Conference," January 1994. The author, Cleveland Hobdy III, wrote an article titled "The History of Regional Conferences," containing this excerpt:

> Over the last few years, throughout the Pacific Union, there has been a cry for equality of African American descent.... After many lengthy discussions, a

survey that many believed was incorrectly developed and administered, and a lack of implementation of recently proposed modifications, the issue of Regional Conference is again being discussed. However, the discussions have taken the more direct route of deciding whether to move to a Regional Conference of governance instead of comparing it with the recent set of proposed modifications. The present Anglo majority has not implemented the modifications. It is currently believed that these modifications might never take place.[104]

The second, even more strident commentary, "Why We Need a Regional Conference" by Timothy Nixon, concludes:

> There are some who feel that our journey toward a sister/brother conference is "unwise and untimely." In 1963, a similar criticism was leveled against the Southern Christian Leadership Conference during its desegregation campaign in Birmingham, Alabama. From a Birmingham jail, Dr. Martin Luther King, Jr. wrote:
> 
> *"I have never yet engaged in a direct action movement that was 'well-timed.'... For years now I have heard the words 'Wait!' It rings in the ear of every Negro with a piercing familiarity. This 'Wait' has almost always meant 'Never.' It has been a tranquilizing thalidomide, relieving the emotional stress for a moment, only to give birth to an ill-formed infant of frustration."*
> 
> We Adventist African-Americans have also heard that word, "Wait." I, for one, can wait no longer. A sister/brother conference, administered by the constituent African-American churches, is an idea whose time has come.[105]

A number of significant encounters that would shape the outcome of the debate began in early January 1994 with the visit of Thomas Mostert, president of the Pacific Union Conference, with members of WURC and SECBC, to the Kansas Avenue Adventist Church in Riverside, California. During the meeting Mostert advised the group that their local conference (SECC) must consider any request for a sister conference before the union conference could hear it.

The next significant event was the presentation by WURC to the Southeastern California Executive Committee on January 27, 1994. In a fifty-seven-page report by the WURC—presented by Darrell White, WURC representative and SECC Executive Committee member—it was pointed out that eight of the ten Black SECBC congregations had voted in business sessions in favor of organizing a Regional conference and thus desired to move forward. The conference committee responded to the report in this way:

> VOTED, since local conferences form churches, and union and divisions form conferences, Southeastern California Conference Executive Committee is referring the issue of a Regional Conference to the Pacific Union Executive Committee for study and action. (Vote: 20 Yes and 2 No).[106]

Two weeks later, the *Pacific Union Recorder*, the union's official news communiqué, reported on the January 27 action of the SECC as follows:

> In response to church business meeting votes in eight of Southeastern's ten African-American churches expressing their desire to form a sister, regional conference, the Executive Committee voted to refer the matter to the Pacific Union Conference Committee for further consideration and implementation....
>
> Under formal discussions since the 1988 PUC Black Workers' meeting at Soquel, California, the move toward a regional conference has continued to gain momentum over the years, finally culminating with the votes by our black churches and the Executive Committee.... it seems likely that the votes by the churches here will encourage African-American churches in other conferences in our union to consider the opportunity, with several likely to join.[107]

Upon receiving the SECC request, the Pacific Union leadership informed the SECC that it could not become involved in the matter unless the conference presented the union with a clear recommendation of its own, not merely a request that the union study a matter on which it had, itself, not made a clear decision and recommendation.

Told of the Union's position, WURC's directors, feeling manipulated, asked the Pacific Union's leadership for an audience to discuss matters and were denied. Disappointed by the flow of events and convinced that the union was deliberately arranging events to thwart them, the WURC and SECBC decided to lead their followers in mass protest at the very next union committee meeting on March 2, 1994, in Thousand Oaks, California, ninety-eight miles away.

C. Elwyn Platner, Pacific Union communications director, had learned that the demonstration was scheduled for 10:00 a.m. at the Westlake Village office of the Pacific Union Conference. He issued a press release the day before (March 1) stating that a group of members desired to create an independent entity and had presented the request to the Pacific Union Conference Executive Committee, but that the conference would not consider it until after the suggested protocol was followed.[108]

The next day, the *Riverside Press Enterprise* carried the headline "Black Adventist Churches Want Own Conference." The second and fifth paragraphs of the seven-paragraph article that followed read:

> The Rev. Anthony Paschal, vice president for the denomination's Southeastern California Black Ministries in Riverside, said 200 black Adventist leaders will hold a protest demonstration in Thousand Oaks at the church's Pacific Union Conference headquarters, which administers 613 churches with 190,000 members in five western states....
>
> Paschal said the church's Southeastern California leadership has endorsed the formation of a small black Conference—similar to ones in other parts of the country.[109]

The protesters, traveling in cars, vans, and buses, arrived as planned on the morning of March 2, 1994. For several hours they were denied an audience with the fifty-member Pacific Union Conference Executive Committee or even entrance into the building. Meanwhile, they marched in front of the Union office with such picket signs as "We Must Be Heard," "No More Stalling," "Self Determination," and "We Shall Overcome!"

The following day, March 3, *The Thousand Oaks News Chronicle* headlined the event as "Group Protests Adventist Control" and sought to place matters into perspective:

> About 150 demonstrators gathered outside the Seventh-day Adventist regional headquarters Wednesday to demand that the church's Pacific Union Conference allow its black churches to take steps toward independence.... At stake is more than $2 million the 10 churches send to the Pacific Union and its local conference and property that would be transferred to the new conference.... The 22 black churches throughout the union would have the option of joining a new conference, increasing their revenue potential to around $10 million, said Jessie Wilson, pastor of the Kansas Avenue Church in Riverside.... The staff at the Adventist's media center were warned the group planned to demonstrate and had security personnel on hand.[110]

The same day the *Ventura County News* headline read, "Blacks Protest Adventist Operations." The report stated:

> About 250 African American churchgoers who want to govern their own religious affairs protested White control of the Seventh-day Adventist Church outside the church's Thousand Oaks headquarters Wednesday.... Waving banners that read, "Let My People Go," the crowd was locked out of a meeting of the 50-member Pacific Union Executive Committee, which

governs church operations in five states. Eventually five representatives were allowed to address the panel. . . . "They have not gone about this the right way," said church spokesman Elwyn Platner. "That's why the executive committee didn't want to discuss the issue today."[111]

Erylene Piper-Mandy, a sociologist with a PhD and a protest member of the Ephesus Adventist Church in Los Angeles, when asked by one news reporter of her assessment of events, replied:

> They have just locked the door to a building I helped to build. . . . We have different problems from the European-American urban neighborhoods and they must have funds to address those issues . . . it is not just an issue of independence, but parity . . . the church facilities in the Southeastern Conference are decrepit while facilities in the White-dominated areas are 'top of the line'. If color doesn't matter then how do you explain the difference in this beautiful building and the shambles we have?[112]

Helen Horton, SECC Bible instructor and member of WURC, wrote a letter a week later to Pacific Union president, Thomas Mostert, voicing the prevailing sentiments of those who had made the protest at the union headquarters:

> I trust that by now you are convinced of the determination of African Americans in Pacific Union to organize a Regional conference similar to those in the other parts of the United States. The happenings of March 2, 1994, could have been avoided if you had put this initiative on the Union executive committee.

Her letter concluded:

> I am sorry that because of your culture you cannot empathize with us. I know that this can only come to pass as there is a willingness on your part to be educated, to listen, to face reality, and to learn from the experience of others who have had to face similar problems that confront the African American.[113]

The Pacific Union Executive Committee minutes of the March 2 proceedings include this statement:

> After consultation with the North American and General Conference leaders, the following procedure is suggested:
> 
> 1. The Pacific Union Conference Executive Committee is asking the Southeastern California Conference to evaluate the validity of the request from the eight churches to form a conference.
> 
> 2. The Southeastern California Committee is asked to deny or recommend formation of a new conference before the Union Committee by August 31, 1994.

3. If the Southeastern California Committee action is to recommend ... the Pacific Union will consider the recommendation, and if it favors the proposal, shall forward it to the Division for consideration. If the Southeastern California Committee action is to deny ... and the decision is appealed ... the Union Executive Committee will review the Southeastern California's findings of facts to determine what, if any, further evaluation is appropriate.

4. The division committee will make the final decision based on information from the Pacific Union, or from a survey committee they appoint to evaluate the proposal.[114]

Eight days later, on March 10, Lynn Mallery, president of SECC, reported to the executive committee that the union conference committee had refused to hear the matter and had referred it back to the SECC requesting a more definitive position. The decision was made to structure a committee to study the matter and make further recommendation concerning the formation of a Regional conference to the Pacific Union Executive Committee.

SECC's response to the union's request for a clearer position was expressed by the following action of June 16, 1994:

VOTED, that we recommend the formation of a Regional Conference within the Pacific Union beginning with the eight churches of the SECC that have already voted to do so, provided an agreement is reached on a philosophical and financial plan of operation and asset distribution, to be determined at a called Executive Committee August 11, 1994 at 9:00 a.m. The Regional Conference Recommendations will be the main agenda item at its meeting.[115]

At the August 11 meeting the SECC Executive Committee voted the following:

1. That we are unconvinced by the philosophy for the formation of a Regional Conference.

2. That we do not believe that the 8 churches have sufficient finances to form a Regional Conference.

3. That we support the formation of a Regional Conference in spite of the reservations.

4. That we accept the Treasurer's recommendations for the operating budget and asset distribution.

5. That we request the 8 African-American Churches to vote on the detailed financial proposal without modifying it.

6. If these recommendations are accepted by the 8 African-American Churches, then these recommendations will go to the SECC constituents for further action.

7. If approved by the constituents, the recommendation will be sent to the Pacific Union.[116]

Meanwhile, understanding better the requirements of the Pacific Union and wishing this latest vote of the SECC to avoid the fate of prior SECC submissions to the union (January 27 and July 16, 1994), WURC and SECBC leaders asked for clarification of the latest SECC statement. The SECC Executive Committee's reply to their request, recorded September 22, 1994, was:

> **VOTED,** that Conference Administration will meet with select members of WURC who want clarification of the Regional Conference Resolutions voted on August 11, 1994. If there are clarifications needed, Administration will bring these concerns to the Executive Committee.[117]

The SECC's next formal action on the matter of a Regional conference occurred almost ten months later on June 22, 1995, after its officials had visited all eight of the committed churches and closely investigated such issues as budget and assets distribution. Their decision that day reads:

> **VOTED** that based on the input, supporting data, prior SECC Conference actions, and agreement on the operating budget from the churches in the SECC, it is recommended by the Southeastern California Conference Executive Committee that the Pacific Union Executive Committee pursue further the forming of a Regional Conference.[118]

It is not exactly clear what impact conversations with the two protesting groups (WURC and SECBE) had in framing the language of SECC's June 22, 1995 endorsement. What is certain is that shortly after that decision, the union conference leadership decided that the local conference's language met the threshold for its participation and scheduled a hearing on the matter with its executive committee.

The union committee considered the SECC request on November 29, 1995, granting thirty minutes to Regional conference proponent spokespersons Anthony Paschal and Darrell White to make the case for a Regional conference and thirty minutes to Major White (union conference executive secretary and uncle of Darrell White) to respond to their presentation. Following a period of discussion, the committee, by secret ballot and in executive session, adopted the following position by a vote of forty yes and nine no:

While recognizing:

1. The legitimate concerns of the African-American churches of the Southeastern California Conference that have led to their request to form a Regional Conference; and

2. The frustration in the conduct of business that has led to a desire for greater self-determination; and

3. The racism of the society around us that seeps into the church and the need to resist its pernicious influence; and

4. The need to nurture and develop multi-cultural leadership for the whole church; and

5. The just aspirations for full participation in the administration of the church; and

6. The special circumstances and the special challenges churches face in the inner city;

It is felt that:

1. We are stronger as we address these issues together. We are convinced that a multi-cultural expression of God's gift to the church is the best way to achieve our mission to bring the Gospel to every nation, kindred, tongue and people; and

2. The work of the church would suffer loss if deprived of the best each group brings to the organization as a whole; and

3. Characteristically, Regional conferences were formed where there were primarily two cultural groups, whereas the Pacific Union is multi-culturally diverse.

Therefore:

1. We consider it not in the best interest of the work of the church to approve the request of the Southeastern California Conference at this time; and

2. We are committed to continue, with the churches of Southeastern California Conference the search for more effective ways to work together toward the accomplishment of our God-given mission.

3. Working together, we will develop an agenda to guide our on-going discussions by the February 22, 1996, Union Executive Committee meeting.[119]

The resolution's receipt by the SECC committee members at its meeting on December 14, 1995, closed the loop of protocol requirements connected with the appeal. However, it did little to ameliorate the concerns of the WURC and SECBC.

The WURC and SECBC were encouraged that the union vote recognized that their concerns were legitimate; their frustrations were understandable; that racism in the church, as elsewhere, is pernicious and must be resisted; and that Black churches faced special challenges in the inner city. But they were disturbed by what they felt was the way they had been unnecessarily shuttled back and forth between the local and the union conference; by the fact that the executive committee of the SECC, which had been told by the union that it was their approval alone that it (the union) would consider, had been assigned no responsibility for making the case on December 29; by the union committee's granting them just thirty minutes to make their case; by the union assigning an individual whose proper place it was to hear evidence with the rest of the committee and assist in making the decision (its second ranking officer, the committee's executive secretary) with equal time to discourage approval; and by the body having prepared ahead of time a nearly 300-word response negative to their position. It was a litany of actions that confirmed in their minds that while SECC officials were at least willing to allow the process to move forward, union conference leadership was prepared to do whatever necessary, even if blatantly arbitrary, to prevent Regional conferences.

Letters of appeal from the WURC and SECBC for help in getting what they regarded as a fair hearing went to both division and General Conference leadership. But as is standard procedure in matters of disagreements between individuals or even churches and their local or union conferences, neither of the higher levels of authority agreed to intervene.

Additional attempts to sustain the Regional conference appeal did surface during the latter half of the 1990s. One was by Western Lay-Persons for a Regional conference (WLPRC), a small group of former, more militant (some regarded as "die hard") members of WURC led by David L. James. WLPRC's newsletter headlines clearly reflected the mindset of its outspoken leaders. Among the more suggestive were: "Unity: a Proffer or a Deception?" (July, 1998); "The Western Plantation?" (October, 1998); "The Disease to Please" (July, 1999); "If Withholding Is the Choice?" (December, 1999); "How Long, Oh Lord?" (March, 2000), "Justice Delayed Is Justice Denied!" (November, 2000); "Regional Conferences and the Seven Last Plagues" (November, 2000); "The Illusion of Inclusion" (October, 2000); and "It's Broken! Fix It!" (April, 2000).

WLPRC's editors targeted not only White church leaders, whom they regarded as insensitive in racial matters, but also Black leaders, whom they charged as betraying the cause by either remaining silent once in office, or, even worse, assisting in implementing policies restrictive to racial freedom. Many Black pastors and members quietly cheered WLPRC's boldness, but most steered clear of identifying with an organization whose tactics and opinions were so confrontational as to be regarded as extreme.

So it was that as the century ended, WURC, apparently lacking legitimate channels for a fair hearing, discontinued its activities. WLPRC, its more militant derivative, lasted into the early days of the twenty-first century but lacking substantial support, also gradually dissolved. Meanwhile, the conference-authorized SECBC, while having numerous caucuses and discussions regarding a Regional conference, never developed the support to proceed.

The "Regional Fellowship," a small group of lay and clergy led by WURC supporter Anthony Paschal, succeeded in sustaining the conversation for the first few years of the present century. However, as West Coast protestors before them, they found that not only was Pacific Union leadership unhappy about the idea of one or more Regional conferences in its territory, but that the majority of Pacific Union Black believers and their pastors were less than convinced that they were necessary.

While no records exist of group protest for Regional conferences in other States in the West, several individual African-American members had felt compelled to speak out during this era. One was Samuel L. Bond, an activist public school teacher, local church officer, and member of the Arizona Conference who lived in the Phoenix area. He was particularly concerned by the implications of a letter written in October 1978 by a concerned White pastor of a large Adventist Church to all of the other pastors of the Arizona jurisdiction. It read in part:

PASTORS OF THE ARIZONA CONFERENCE—URGENT—URGENT—URGENT—URGENT

Gentlemen,

We have an *emergency*! It is absolutely *imperative* we act *NOW*! If we delay—if our people delay—it could mean the closing of some of our schools.

The IRS has drawn up a regulation to remove tax exemption privileges from private schools which do not meet the racial integration quota of 20%. . . . Even though our schools are open to all races to attend, a racial imbalance will subject us to the ruling. It is a violation of the judicial procedure "Innocent until proven guilty."

Please copy the second attached information to make a bulletin insert. Have the members write AND mail Saturday night. If we wait until the weekend passes the mail may not reach Washington in time to have any affect [*sic*].[120]

Bond responded in a letter dated October 16, 1978, with thoughts typical of the Arizona Black church membership at that time. He wrote:

> Dear Pastor,
>
> Your letter of October 11, '78 to all the pastors of the Arizona Conference of Seventh-day Adventists regarding the racial imbalance of our schools, and the loss of tax exemption privileges was a great shock to my spiritual well-being.
>
> It shocked me that not one clause of your letter suggested that our conference has a job to do to right a situation that has long gone wanting for Christian equality, and social justice and progress. You in effect have only pleaded that we hasten appeals to our government not to let the hammer fall on us despite the fact that we cannot stand, what may be called, "the acid test" of judgment.
>
> We are guilty of the sin of omission, if not also guilty of the sin of commission. While the sixteen elementary schools, and the one senior academy of our conference are open to minority students, it is glaringly true that *not one* of them *has even one Black professional on its* teaching or administrative *staff*. Neither is there an affirmative action program on foot to correct this situation. We are not innocent; and we have no need to be proven *guilty*....[121]

Another individual protest expressive of the concerns of Black members in the Northwest in that same time frame came from lay leader Leroy B. Washington, of Seattle, Washington. His five-page communication sent to the president of the Washington Conference, headquartered in Bothell, Washington, on December 4, 1979, was particularly descriptive. Washington, a government probation officer, decrying conditions that he regarded as the discriminatory practices of the Washington Conference, penned the following blunt assessment, with copies to the members of the conference executive committee and other up-line people:

> This letter contains some observations of the conditions of the Black work in the Pacific Northwest....
>
> Over the years I have become increasingly aware of the double standards which exists between what is preached and verbalized about race relations and civil rights within the Church, and the reality of what really exists and happens on many levels....
>
> What I have observed here in Seattle is not unique from what is going on in North American Adventism at large. The very ingredients which served as a basis for Black leaders throughout this Country to push strongly for Black Unions exists on the local conference level here; i.e.,

proportionate economic support and the lack of a power base to meet the needs of the minority membership. . . .

In order to get a clearer picture of the needs which I address, perhaps some of the Conference Officials should move their membership to Spruce Street Church [a Black Adventist church in Seattle, Washington]. This will provide a weekly reminder of the Conference's obligations within the Inner City, and the need for adequate worship facilities. Perhaps your families should come and sit on the hard wooden benches, your wives tear holes in their nylons from kneeling to pray to our Lord on hard wooden floors that are splintering because of age. Perhaps they should go to lavatories, to take care of nature's needs, which are less than hygienic with poor worn-out sluggish plumbing. Perhaps they should walk through the facilities moving from one area to another when the precipitation is high and dodge puddles, dripping roofs, and buckets on the floor to catch the water. Perhaps your families should shiver through services in poorly heated and poorly ventilated rooms. Perhaps then you may get a sense of the needs and problems which I address. . . .

Washington signed his letter, "Your 'Brother' in Christ."[122]

The president's reply of December 21 reveals that he took umbrage to Washington, sending his letter of protest to the entire conference committee without having spoken to him first, highlighting Washington's position as an officer at the U.S. courthouse, and, as he interpreted Washington's comments, trying to convict the Washington Conference without a fair trial (i.e., adequate and accurate information). In a four-page reply, he did take the time to address some of Washington's concerns, although perhaps not to Washington's satisfaction. He concluded his response to Washington with this observation:

> I would request that if there are situations which appear to be unfair, that you come to us first to resolve the situation to everybody's satisfaction. If you are ever denied such an opportunity, then I believe you would be justified in taking your case to higher church levels. To circulate information widely before visiting with us personally is both unChristian and inappropriate.

Then softening somewhat:

> While these words may appear to be very blunt on paper, they are said with a Christian warmth and a real desire to achieve the kind of relationship with you, Leroy, that you would voluntarily remove the quotes from around the word, brother, in your salutation.[123]

Seattle resident Bert B. Reid, son of the much-loved African (Caribbean) American pastor D. B. Reid, also protested conditions in the Black sector of the conference. While in his eight-page letter he criticized what he described as the president's unnecessarily harsh reply to Washington, his language was decidedly more gentle and less threatening. His closing comment was more of an appeal than a protest:

> I beg of you and the committee to pray seriously and take an active role in addressing the needs of Spruce St., Maranatha, and Mt. Tahoma. We have special problems and needs and require all the assistance and expertise you can send our way. I can guarantee that if you are sincere in your efforts the people will rally behind you so that together with God's help we can finish the work and go home to glory. . . . I have some ideas in mind that I hope will help us to resolve some of these long outstanding problems.[124]

This brief survey demonstrates that no area of the country was exempt from racial tensions. However, whereas in the rest of the country the push for structural accommodations formerly articulated in 1929–1930 ended in 1943–1944 with the organization of Regional conferences, in the West it began in earnest in the middle 1950s, peaked there in Southeastern California in the mid-1990s, and for reasons held by the majority of its faithful Black clergy and laity, largely waned to a whimper as the century concluded.

### Notes

1. Robert A. Gibson, *The Negro Holocaust: Lynching and Race Riots in the United States, 1880–1950* (New Haven, CT: New Haven Teachers Institute, Yale University, Feb. 4, 1979). http://www.yale.edu/ynhti/curriculum/units/1979/2/79.02.04.x.html.

2. Ibid.

3. Jacob Justiss, *Angels in Ebony* (Toledo, OH: Jet Press, 1975), 146. (http://www.blacksdahistory.org/files/101257366.pdf)

4. "Minutes of the Three Hundred Fifth Meeting of the General Conference Committee," Takoma Park, Maryland, March 3, 1929, 802. (http://documents.adventistarchives.org/Minutes/GCC/GCC1929-03.pdf)

5. See "Minutes of the Three Hundred Twenty-Fifth Meeting General Conference Committee," Takoma Park, Maryland, April 29, 1929, 838–839. (http://documents.adventistarchives.org/Minutes/GCC/GCC1929-04.pdf)

6. "Minutes of the Three Hundred Twenty-Fifth Meeting of the General Conference Committee," Takoma Park, Maryland, April 29, 1929, 838–839. (http://documents.adventistarchives.org/Minutes/GCC/GCC1929-04.pdf)

7. "Minutes of the Three Hundred Eighty-Third Meeting of the General Conference Committee," Columbus, Ohio, September 26, 1929, 947–950. (http://documents.adventistarchives.org/Minutes/GCC/GCC1929-09b.pdf)

8. Minutes of Special Pre-Spring Council Session, Washington, D.C., April 11, 1944, 1. (http://documents.adventistarchives.org/Resources/RegionalConf/RCO-02.pdf)

9. G. E. Peters, General Conference Autumn Council, Battle Creek, Michigan, 1941, General Conference Archives.

10. See the Claude A. Barnett Papers catalogue here: http://explore.chicagocollections.org/marcxml/chicagohistory/31/vm4333p.

11. Claude A. Barnett to H. J. Klooster, December 31, 1938. Oakwood University Archives, Eva B. Dykes Library, Huntsville, Alabama.

12. The ill-fated compromise signed in Munich, Germany, on September 30, 1938, between England, France, and Italy with Hitler that relinquished all of the Sudetenland to Nazi Germany.

13. "7th Day Adventist Jim Crow Called 'Uncle Tom' Sellout." *The New York Amsterdam News*, January 7, 1939.

14. Barnett, Claude, "Chicago Adventists Deplore Jim Crow at SDA College: White Head of School Refuses to Comment on Situation, as Does Chicago Clergyman, Pressed for Interview," *Chicago Defender*, January 25, 1939. The *Claude Barnett Papers*, Chicago Historical Society Library, Chicago, Illinois.

15. Ibid.

16. In C. B. Rock private collection.

17. Claude A. Barnett to F. L. Peterson, February 21, 1939, Oakwood University Archives, Eva B. Dykes Library, Huntsville, Alabama.

18. See "Haynes, Carlyle Boynton," *Seventh-day Encyclopedia*, 2nd rev. ed., A-L (Hagerstown, MD: Review and Herald Publishing Association, 1996).

19. *Claude Barnett to J. L. McElhany*, Oakwood University Archives, Eva B. Dykes Library, Huntsville, Alabama.

20. See F. W. Hale, Jr., *Angels Watching Over Me* (Nashville: James C. Winston Publishing Co., 1996), 184–186.

21. I am indebted to Benjamin Baker, formerly of the General Conference Office of Archives, Statistics, and Research, for uncovering additional and corrective elements of the oft-transmitted stock narrative. This draws from his "The Real Lucy Byard Story," unpublished, November 9, 2016.

22. James H. Byard to G. E. Peters, September 28, 1943, cited in Baker, "The Real Lucy Byard Story," 3.

23. Robert A. Hare to J. L. McElhany, W. E. Nelson, et al., November 15, 1943, cited in Baker, 4.

24. Baker, 5.

25. First Jamaica Seventh-day Adventist Church to J. L. McElhany, October 25, 1943, cited in Baker, 5.

26. Sharon Seventh-day Adventist Church to J. L. McElhany, December 23, 1943, cited in Baker 6.

27. Justiss, *Angels in Ebony*, 43, 44. (http://www.blacksdahistory.org/files/101257366.pdf)

28. Ibid., 44.

29. Ibid., 44.

30. For years DeWitt Williams's *She Fulfilled the Impossible Dream: The Story of Eva B. Dykes* (Hagerstown, MD: Review and Herald, 1985) has been the authoritative work on Dykes's life. However, fresh research is being done on her remarkable life.

31. See "Morgan v. Virginia (1946)," *Encyclopedia of Virginia* (https://www.encyclopediavirginia.org/Morgan_v_Virginia).

32. Minutes of the Three Hundred Forty-Sixth Meeting of the General Conference Committee, November 3, 1943, 1123 (http://docs.adventistarchives.org/docs/GCC/GCC1943-10-AC.pdf#search=%22colored%22&view=fit).

33. Minutes of the Three Hundred Seventy-First Meeting of the General Conference Committee, January 13, 1944, 1219 (http://docs.adventistarchives.org/docs/GCC/GCC1944-01.pdf#search=%22colored%22&view=fit).

34. Minutes of the Three Hundred Eighty-Seventh Meeting of the General Conference Committee, March 9, 1944, 1280 (http://docs.adventistarchives.org/docs/GCC/GCC1944-03.pdf#search=%22colored%22&view=fit).

35. Minutes of the Three Hundred Ninety-Fifth Meeting of the General Conference Committee, April 7, 1944, 1311. (http://docs.adventistarchives.org/docs/GCC/GCC1944-04-SM.pdf#search=%22colored%22&view=fit)

36. Minutes of the Pre-Spring Council, Washington, D.C., April 8, 1944. (http://documents.adventistarchives.org/Resources/RegionalConf/RCO-02.pdf)

37. Ibid., 2.

38. Ibid.

39. Ibid., 4.

40. Minutes of the Pre-Spring Council, Washington, D.C., April 9, 1944. (http://documents.adventistarchives.org/Resources/RegionalConf/RCO-02.pdf)

41. Ibid., 5.

42. Ibid., 6.

43. Ibid., 8.

44. Ibid., 10.

45. Ibid.

46. Ibid.

47. Ibid., 11.

48. Ibid.

49. Ibid.

50. Ibid., 11, 12.

51. Ibid., 12.

52. Ibid., 14, 15.

53. Minutes of the Three Hundred Ninety-Sixth Meeting of the General Conference Committee, April 10, 1944, 1315. (http://documents.adventistarchives.org/Minutes/GCC/GCC1944-04-SM.pdf)

54. Minutes of Special Pre-Spring Council Session, Washington, D.C., April 11, 1944, 1. (http://documents.adventistarchives.org/Resources/RegionalConf/RCO-02.pdf)

55. Ibid., 3.

56. Ibid., 3, 4.

57. Ibid., 4.

58. G. E. Peters, "Development of the North American Colored Department," Official Report, 1945, 2. (http://documents.adventistarchives.org/Resources/Regional-Conf/RCO-02.pdf)

59. Ibid., 9.

60. Ibid., 3.

61. Ibid.

62. The best source on Humphrey's life and apostasy is R. Clifford Jones's *James K. Humphrey and the Sabbath-Day Adventists* (Jackson: University of Mississippi Press, 2006).

63. "Adventism among Negroes: Its Origin and Development," *The New York Amsterdam News*, May 13, 1944.

64. Ibid.

65. M. G. Nunez, "Why Should It Be Thought a Thing Unchristian?" August 1931, Oakwood University Archives, Eva B. Dykes Library, Huntsville, Alabama.

66. John W. Manns, *Why Free Seventh-day Adventists?* (The Banner Publishing Association, undated), Heritage Room, James White Library, Andrews University, Berrien Springs, Michigan, 2–3.

67. Ibid., 13.

68. Lewis C. Sheafe to A. G. Daniells, January 15, 1907; quoted in Morgan, *Lewis C. Sheafe*, 309.

69. J. W. Washburn to A. G. Daniells, February 20, 1907, quoted in Morgan, *Lewis C. Sheafe*, 321.

70. Morgan, *Lewis C. Sheafe*, 381.

71. See Philippians 4:8.

72. For an extended treatment of the protest, see W. W. Fordham, *Righteous Rebel* (Hagerstown, MD: Review and Herald Publishing Association, 1990), 25–34; Holly Fisher, "Oakwood College Students' Quest for Social Justice before and during the Civil Rights Era," *The Journal of African American History* 88, no. 2 (Spring 2003): 110–125; and Mervyn A. Warren, *Oakwood! A Vision Splendid Continues* (Collegedale, TN: College Press, 2010), 108–159.

73. Justiss, *Angels in Ebony*, 76.

74. Ibid., 77.

75. Ibid., 76, 77.

76. W. W. Fordham, *Righteous Rebel* (Hagerstown, MD: Review and Herald, 1990), 34.

77. Arna Bontemps, *Black Thunder: Gabriel's Revolt: Virginia, 1800* (Boston: Beacon Press, 1968), xiv.

78. *Arna Bontemps-Langston Hughes Letters 1925–1967*, selected and edited by Charles H. Nichols (New York: Dodd, Mead & Co., 1980), 5.

79. Ibid., 18, 19.

80. Langston Hughes, *I Wonder as I Wander: An Autobiographical Journey* (New York: Rinehart & Co., 1956), 62.

81. Arna Bontemps, *Black Thunder: Gabriel's Revolt: Virginia, 1800* (Boston: Beacon Press, 1968), xiv.

82. Ibid., xxviii–xxix.

83. Arna Bontemps to Herb Nipson, November 27, 1950, Syracuse University Libraries.

84. G. E. Peters, Letter to Brother Scott, February 20, 1949.

85. Frank L. Peterson to F. W. Hale, April 27, 1961, Oakwood University Archives, Eva B. Dykes Library, Oakwood University, Huntsville, Alabama.

86. Minutes of the Three Hundred Twenty-Fifth Meeting of the General Conference Committee, April 29, 1929, 838. (http://documents.adventistarchives.org/Minutes/GCC/GCC1929-04.pdf)

87. See 1921 *Annual Statistical Report*, General Conference of Seventh-day Adventists. (http://documents.adventistarchives.org/Statistics/ASR/ASR1921.pdf)

88. See 1931 *Annual Statistical Report*, General Conference of Seventh-day Adventists. (http://documents.adventistarchives.org/Statistics/ASR/ASR1931.pdf)

89. Earl Canson, "The Light Rises in the West—The Story of Black Men and Women Who Pioneered in the West," *Regional Voice*, June, 1987, 5; July, 1987, 7. (http://documents.adventistarchives.org/Periodicals/RV/RV19870601-V09-04.pdf; http://documents.adventistarchives.org/Periodicals/RV/RV19870701-V09-05.pdf)

90. "South and East"/"East and South" is shorthand for the area where the original Regional conferences were formed in the eastern or right half of the United States.

91. Earl Canson, Sr. "An Argument against the Regional Conference Proposal," *Pacific Union Conference Regional News*, March 1990, 1.

92. Major C. White, "An Argument against the Regional Conference Proposal" in *Pacific Union Conference Regional News*, February 1990, 1.

93. W. D. Felder, "An Argument Supporting the Regional Conference Concept" in *Pacific Union Conference Regional News*, February 1990, 1.

94. Ibid., 2.

95. John E. Collins, "An Argument Supporting the Regional Conference Concept," *Pacific Union Conference Regional News* (April 1990): 1; Timothy P. Nixon, "An Idea Whose Time Has Come," *The Trumpet* (February 1994): 5–8.

96. Herman Bauman to Eva Bradford-Rock, February 20, 1990. Arizona Conference of Seventh-day Adventists, 1. C. B. Rock Private Collection. This response and those that follow appear in letters from a box of records that my mother gave to me several months prior to her death, at the age of ninety-six, on January 20, 2009—the same day as Barak Obama's first inauguration. Her rather casual statement was: "Here are some things that you might want to look at someday." Thinking that they were family records—letters and other memorabilia (she was devoted to such materials)—I put the box in the corner of my study closet intending, as she suggested, to investigate "someday." That day came five years later when I opened the box to discover a treasure-trove of materials illumining the opposition that she and her group organized against Black conferences on the West Coast. Among these valuable records were the replies of distinguished leaders of the Pacific Union Conference to her request for written affirmation of their position on matters of racial parity.

97. L. Stephen Gifford to Eva Bradford-Rock, February 21, 1990. Southeastern California Conference of Seventh-day Adventists, 1. C. B. Rock Private Collection.

98. Thomas Mostert, Jr., to Eva Bradford-Rock, February 23, 1990. Pacific Union

Conference of Seventh-day Adventists. C. B. Rock Private Collection.

99. Herbert H. Broeckel, "Statement Regarding Brotherhood," March 1, 1990. Central California Conference of Seventh-day Adventists, 1–2. C. B. Rock Private Collection.

100. G. Charles Dart to Eva Bradford-Rock, March 13, 1990. Southern California Conference of Seventh-day Adventists. C. B. Rock Private Collection.

101. Don C. Schneider to Eva Bradford-Rock, May 2, 1990. Northern California Conference of Seventh-day Adventists. C. B. Rock Private Collection.

102. Darold J. Retzer to Eva Bradford-Rock, May 3, 1990. Nevada-Utah Conference of Seventh-day Adventists. C. B. Rock Private Collection.

103. Feasibility Study Report—Regional Conference Opinion Survey, Pacific Union Conference of Seventh-day Adventists (March, 1990).

104. Cleveland Hobdy III, "Regional Conference in Harmony with Church Guidelines," *The Trumpet* (February 1994): 3.

105. Timothy Nixon, "Why We Need a Regional Conference," *Adventist Today*, May/June 1994.

106. Response to the Southeastern California Conference Executive Committee Action 12–94, January 27, 1994.

107. "Regional Conference Proposed," *Pacific Union Recorder*, February 21, 1994.

108. C. Elwyn Platner, "Pacific Union Conference Press Release," March 1, 1994.

109. Marlowe Churchill, "Black Adventist Churches Want Own Conference," *Riverside Press Enterprise* (March 2, 1994).

110. Margaret Daly, "Group Protests Adventist Control," *The Thousand Oaks News Chronicle*, March 3, 1994, A1, 8.

111. "Black Protest Adventist Operations," *Ventura County News,* March 3, 1994.

112. *Los Angeles Times* Religious Section, March 23, 1994.

113. Helen I. W. Horton to Thomas Mostert, March 9, 1994, 1–3.

114. Pacific Union Conference's Executive Committee, "Response to SECC's Request to Form a Regional Conference," March 3, 1994.

115. Southeastern California Conference Executive Committee Minutes, June 16, 1994.

116. Southeastern California Conference Executive Committee Minutes, August 11, 1994.

117. Southeastern California Conference Executive Committee Minutes, September 22, 1994.

118. Southeastern California Conference Executive Committee Minutes, June 22, 1995.

119. Pacific Union Conference Executive Committee Meeting, November 29, 1995.

120. Letter to pastors of the Arizona Conference, October 11, 1978.

121. Samuel L. Bond Letter, October 16, 1978.

122. "Leroy B. Washington Letter to [the president] and Members of Conference Committee," December 4, 1979, 1–5.

123. Letter to Leroy B. Washington, December 21, 1979, 3–4.

124. Bert B. Reid Letter, February 4, 1980.

# 3
# THE PUSH FOR BLACK UNIONS, 1969–1980

The Black Adventist clergy's third major protest movement was the push for modified autonomy (i.e., Black unions). Like the first movement (the push for full integration in membership and administrative participation within the church structure) and like the second one (the push for Colored conferences), the third movement was fueled primarily by a desire for increased leverage in gospel witness. It began as a request but developed into the most public and fiercely fought deliberation of them all.

## BACKGROUND AND IMPETUS

As was the case with the first two protests, events in society as well as the church lent strong impetus to the call for Black unions. The twenty-five-year period between the establishment of Colored conferences in 1944 and Black leadership's formal request for Black unions in October 1969 was one of explosive protest and seismic change in the socio/political arrangements of the nation. In 1946, President Truman signed Executive Order 9808, addressing anti-lynching laws, abolition of the poll tax, desegregation of the military, fair housing, education, health care, and employment. The country was alive with racial confrontation and altercation. For example, in 1947, Jackie Robinson (1919–1972) became the first Negro to enter baseball's major leagues. On July 26, 1948, President Truman signed Executive Order 9980, instituting fair employment practices in civilian agencies of the federal government, and Order 9981, which directed the armed forces to provide "equality of treatment and opportunity for all personnel without regard to race, color, religion, or national origin (the latter a qualification added for the first time in civil rights legislation). And in 1950 the NAACP led sixty advocacy organizations comprising over 4,000 delegates in a mass Washington D.C. lobby, resulting in the establishment of the Fair Employment Practices Committee and further organization of what was named The Leadership Conference on Civil Rights.

It was in the wake of such events that the truly historic Civil Rights Movement (1954–1968) blossomed. In 1954, the Supreme Court struck down "Separate but Equal," and in 1964 the Civil Rights Act was signed by President Lyndon Johnson. Major credit for these advances in the nation's racial profile must be attributed to the movement. However, as sampled above, actions during the prior ten-year period (1944–1954) were rife with events that significantly altered the social determinations and expectations of Black Americans, including, of course, those of Black Seventh-day Adventists.

By 1969, when the Black Union proposal emerged, the Black Adventist North American Division membership had increased from 17,891 (when Regional conferences were organized) to approximately 75,000. Meanwhile, the church, as most Protestant bodies, was lagging behind the secular government in the implementation of human rights. Memberships and admission were still not being granted in White churches, schools, and hospitals in the South and much of the Midwest. And there was yet a perceptible insensitivity on the part of White leadership in general.

That insensitivity was painfully obvious to Black Adventists on April 15, 1969. The Southern Union's official news organ, the *Southern Tidings*, announced that conservative radio commentator Paul Harvey was producing thirteen one-half-hour Bible Story television programs at the cost of $75,000 for the union's publishing department.

During the 1960s, Paul Harvey had staunchly opposed socially progressive programs and principles deemed helpful by Black Americans. He had done so, first, by regularly upholding the social conservative agenda on his popular daily radio broadcast, and, second, and very noticeably, by his vigorous support for conservative Senator Barry Goldwater (1908–1998) in his failed bid for the United States presidency in 1964. Struggling minorities did not consider Goldwater as a friend. He had called for the end of liberal domestic policies supported by the New Deal coalition, among other actions. It seemed highly insensitive to Black Adventists that

Harvey, one of his most energetic supporters, would be presented to the public as an ally in the church's mission.

Whereas Black Adventists viewed the Harvey involvement as harmful, a similar endorsement the following year provoked even greater consternation. That event unfolded on Friday, December 25, 1970, when the *Birmingham Post Herald* announced that Alabama's governor, George Wallace, would begin the New Year reading the Bible in the headquarters for the Voice of Prophecy international radio broadcast at midnight on December 31.

There could not have been a more racially tainted personality imaginable for this role than this man who had not many years prior (June 11, 1963) earned international press by defying the government's school desegregation orders. The negative consequences of this arrangement throughout Black Adventism were predictable. I expressed my personal concerns by telegrammed appeals to General Conference president Robert Pierson and Voice of Prophecy director H. M. S. Richards, Jr., (Appendix 15), knowing them both to be regretful of such errors.

The trigger event for major changes in race relations in the nation in the mid-century was the vigorous protest of the Civil Rights Movement (c. 1954–1968). The parallel influence within the church was the frontal challenge to its racial practices conducted by the Laymen's Leadership Conference (LLC).[1]

The LLC had its birth on February 26, 1961, at the Neighborhood House in Columbus, Ohio. It was a response to what Frank W. Hale, Jr. (1927–2011), its founder, described as a "state of race relations within the Seventh-day Adventist Church [that] would reveal gross injustices and demonstrate a monolithic unreadiness by the church fathers to make any monumental efforts to erase those excessive practices."[2]

The formal statement of its goal, written in Article 2 of its constitution and by-laws, declares, "The purposes of the LLC are to weld Seventh-Day Adventist laymen into an effective, powerful adjunct of the clergy: to assist in the achieving of Christian goals; to challenge each other to deeper, richer, fuller and more useful living; to preach the brotherhood of man."[3] By June 1961 the organization had jelled with surprising speed. During that month, led by Hale and Martin, the LLC sent out a mass mailing to Regional conference constituents with copies to General Conference officers, Regional conference officers, and Regional conference pastors. The communication read:

Dear Fellow Believer:

Now is the time for us to declare the WHOLE TRUTH.

On February 26, 1961, an organization was formed to unite all Seventh-Day Adventist laymen into common bond to combat racial segregation and bias among Seventh-Day Adventists.

We hate to admit that the evidence supports the fact that Negro Seventh-Day Adventists serve a subordinate role in the life and program of the denomination. Too long we have equivocated—too long we have excused.

For decades we as Negroes have adjusted. We have adjusted to segregated churches. We have adjusted to regional conferences. We have adjusted to quota systems in our colleges and professional schools. We have adjusted to the philosophy of "White Teachers Only" in our institutions of higher learning. We have adjusted to the philosophy and practice of "menial tasks only" for the few Negroes who have served in such units as the Review and Herald Publishing Association and the Voice of Prophecy....

We have adjusted and adjusted. Now is the time to readjust!... Communication is a two-way street. Too long has the information been funneling down; now is the time for some information to start bubbling up.

We are appealing to groups all over the country. Our success will depend upon two things: God's blessings and our personal preparation.

We anticipate that every effort will be made to block to scuttle [sic] this program. Yet we must not fall nor be discouraged. "Let us march on 'til victory is won!"[4]

Hale later described the response to this statement as producing, within a short time, files "pregnant with letters from faithful Black Adventists who have been confronted with racially embarrassing circumstances and who wanted to share their experiences with the LLC... hoping that we could help to remedy an excruciatingly painful experience that has plagued our denomination for years on end."[5]

LLC's focused determination and its willingness to utilize the help of public media—a tactic prior groups, both clergy and lay, had been reluctant to employ—was seen in its landmark protest at the church's 1962 worldwide General Conference session in San Francisco, California. This confrontation was occasioned by the refusal of church leadership to meet with LLC's officers prior to the session for discussions regarding the church's racial conduct. The protest catapulted the group into national attention and remains its most celebrated effort.

The leaders of LLC had decided to go public at the session with their complaints if church officers refused to meet with them or if such a meeting was not productive. Church leaders did refuse, and on July 28, at 3:00 p.m. in the ballroom of San Francisco's Jack Tar Hotel, LLC officers laid out the case of the church's racial inequities through the years before a standing-room-only crowd of hundreds of General Conference attendees and a large contingent of the San Francisco area's news media.

The impact of the meeting was immediate and extensive. Articles reporting the protest of racial injustice in the Seventh-day Adventist Church appeared in papers throughout the country. Among the headlines were: "Adventists Challenged to End Racial Segregation" (*San Francisco Chronicle*, July 28, 1962), "Open Letter on Adventist Racial Bars" (*San Francisco Chronicle*, July 30, 1962), "Adventist Head Asks Patience of the Church's Racial Critics" (*New York Times*, August 1, 1962), "Adventist Head Denies Race Bias" (*Oakland Tribune*, July 28, 1962), and "Lower the Church Bars" (*San Francisco Call-Bulletin*, July 30, 1962).

*The Oakland Tribune* ran the following report on July 30, 1962:

"Total integration of the Seventh-day Adventist Church must happen now," Dr. Frank W. Hale, Jr., leader of a Negro Adventist integration drive declared . . . because "there aren't two Gods—a white God for the whites and a black God for the blacks." Hale, founder and head of the Layman's Leadership Conference said, "The day of reckoning has come. The world is too small, too crowded, too perilous, and too rapidly changing to permit further temporizing with bigotry and discrimination.[6]

F. L. PETERSON (1893–1969), first Black to be elected as a General Conference vice president. Courtesy of the General Conference Archives.

The most visible result of LLC's protest actions at this General Conference Session was the election of F. L. Peterson, then sixty-nine, as one of the General Conference's four general vice presidents—the first Black to be so honored. Ironically, Peterson, who had a year and a half earlier chastised Hale regarding his intention to go public about the church's negative racial practices, became the first and arguably the most significant beneficiary of Hale's tactics.

While no statement by church leadership confirms that it was LLC's protest that influenced Peterson's election to the vice presidency of the General Conference, it did not escape the attention of Black church members that his appointment occurred on the same day as the hotel rally and that it had been rumored for days that his age (sixty-nine) was being used to disqualify him for that position.

LLC's protest presence was eventually eclipsed during the 1970s by the activities of those pushing for Black union conferences. However, it is indisputable that during the 1960s it was the LLC, more than any other factor, that raised the hopes of Black Adventists for fuller social freedom within the church.

It is also indisputable that a significant consequence of the bold approaches of the LLC was its impact upon a number of younger Black pastors. The fact that Hale, LLC's militant leader, was just four years later in 1966 elected as president of their beloved Oakwood College, a General Conference institution, emboldened them as the earliest spokespersons for the most fiercely fought of all Black Adventist leadership protest endeavors: Black union conferences.

## THE PROCESS, THE POLITICS, AND THE VOTES

Black leadership formalized its desire for Black union conferences[7] at its annual Regional Advisory Committee meeting, April 7–9, 1969, at the Biscayne Terrace Hotel in Miami, Florida.[8] The vote was the first of twenty-five actions taken at the meeting addressing the needs of the Black work and read as follows:

> Whereas, the present structure of Regional conference organizations has been blessed of God in soul winning endeavor, and
> Whereas, it now seems in order to suggest that the organizational idea move up one step,
> Voted, that we recommend to the General Conference that a representative committee be appointed to study the advisability of the organization of a Regional union or Regional unions in the United States.[9]

Eight months later a letter signed by eleven local church pastors appealed to GC president Robert H. Pierson (1911–1989) for action. The letter, with an abbreviated copy to then secretary of the Regional Department H. D. Singleton (1908–2010), who had chaired the April 7–9 meeting, read:

On December 3, 1969, a group of concerned Black Seventh-day Adventist clergymen from all the Regional Conferences assembled to discuss some of the urgent problems confronting them in their continuing effort to serve particularly the Black community.... It was the unqualified consensus of the participating pastors that in view of the mood of the Black population both within and without the church, the effectiveness of our ministry mandates the administrative accommodation termed "Black Unions." (Appendix 16)

Those who signed the letter were: Luther Palmer, Jr., H. L. Cleveland, S. A. Hutchins, J. L. Butler, Jessie R. Wagner, R. L. Willis, W. L. DeShay, M. M. Young, Donald Crowder, and Hector Mouzon. The letter lists Jessie Wagner (1930–1978), then pastor of the prestigious City Temple Church in Detroit, Michigan, and later president of the Lake Region Conference headquartered in Chicago, Illinois, as the contact person.

Wagner, son of J. H. Wagner, Sr. (remembered for his rather strident response to church president McElhany's urging at the historic April 1943 meeting that Colored conferences be created), was blessed with a bold but charming personality and enjoyed unique insights into church structure resulting from his upbringing in the home of his influential pastor/administrator father. His combination of talent and savvy insight positioned him as leader of the group of young pastors that pressed the matter forward when the April 7–9, 1969, Biscayne Bay appeal seemed to have been ignored.

Seven of the eleven signatures were former schoolmates at Oakwood College (six during Frank Hale's tenure there as a teacher, 1951–1959), eight were still in their thirties, and four later became conference presidents. All eleven individuals were my friends. R. L. Willis was a childhood companion from back in New York; M. M. Young, was a schoolmate from Los Angeles Academy; and Jessie Wagner was a colleague at Pine Forge Academy in Pottstown, Pennsylvania. In addition, six of them—Hutchins, Muzon, Palmer, Wagner, Willis, and Young—were my schoolmates at Oakwood College. On a very personal note, Luther Palmer and I married sisters, daughters of F. L. Peterson. These relationships, plus the fact that I was at that time pastor of the Ephesus Church in Harlem, New York, one of the more prestigious Black Adventist pulpits in the country, made it logical that they would seek my signature as well.

When I noticed, however, that none of the current Black local conference presidents had signed, I refused to do so. They explained that they had not asked the officials to sign because it would not be politically prudent for them to do so. I found that reasoning unsatisfactory, and in an approach that I tried to follow throughout my ministry, including my sixteen years as a General Conference vice president, I refused to take the lead on an issue that my immediate supervisor seemed unwilling to discuss publicly or that might embarrass him.

That was the case, years later, in the matter of women's ordination, a process that I have always heartily endorsed but was guarded about publicly promoting during my GC years, because the three leaders with whom I served (Neal C. Wilson, Robert S. Folkenberg, and Jan Paulsen), for reasons they felt prudent, did not do so.

The Black union proponents held that Black unions would have the following benefits, unavailable in the existing system:

- vertical mobility or opportunity for promotion within the church administrative system;
- horizontal mobility or the need and privilege of transfer and fellowship with those in other Regional conferences;
- better direction for Regional conference administration;
- joint programming and planning among Regional conference and union;
- accurate representation of Regional conferences at higher administrative levels (the division and General Conference);
- a natural presence on the Union Presidents' Council—the most prestigious administrative committee in the North American Division; and
- increased employment opportunity for Black Adventist laypersons.

Officers of the North American Division (NAD) responded to the appeal for study of the request by forming a commission. NAD president[10] Neal C. Wilson explained:

> The commission was appointed in close counsel with black church leaders in North America and consisted of 71 black and 21 white members representing all phases and areas of denominational interest. Of this number, 16 were laymen and 17 were pastors (16 black and one white). The commission met first on January 13, 1970, and spent approximately 14 hours discussing the question.[11]

At the conclusion of the discussion, the commission voted to table the motion that the NAD give study to establishing two Black unions in its territory, and instead consider the issues involved and make alternate recommendations for the good of the Black work. That was done with the understanding that the commission which met on January 13 would be later reconvened to hear the recommendations. Meanwhile, the General Conference appointed a number of committees to structure the recommendations and settled upon their ideas at the meeting of the North American Spring Meeting, April 1–3, 1970. The commission of "representative" pastors and laity whose work was tabled on January 13 was reassembled on April 16, 1970, and provided, in lieu of a recommendation for Black Unions, a sixteen-point document (known as "The Sixteen Points") for the betterment of the Black work.

Church leadership asked the commission to accept this document formally titled "Regional Conferences and Human Relations" (reminiscent of the 1929 Resolution) rather than proceed with further discussion regarding Black unions. Their recommendation was carried by a vote of forty-one to twenty-eight (Appendix 17).

While the Black Union appeal failed, one positive consequence of the studies and discussions was a new level of consciousness on the part of NAD leadership regarding the needs of its Black constituents, and what appeared to be a strong determination to address those needs. But there was also a negative result of the April 16, 1970, decision and the studies that preceded it: the deepening polarization among Blacks themselves. Those who spoke and voted against the Black union proposition were, in the main, individuals in union, division, and General Conference positions—those inside the church's system. Those who voted for it were almost entirely ministers and leaders in local conference and pastoral service—in other words, those outside of the system's hierarchy.

This was carefully but pointedly addressed in an open letter to the church leadership by Charles E. Bradford, at that time president of the Lake Region Conference:

> If my analysis is correct, and I believe it is, the [Black] representatives from the field voted decisively in favor of the unions. The General Conference, Union and institutional delegates voted overwhelmingly against Black Unions. I am led to conclude that the men who serve the people, who are closer to the rank and file, were outvoted by men who are twice removed from the field. It is regrettable that a voice of the delegates from the field was drowned out by the non-field segment. (Appendix 18)

Thus, the battle lines formed not only between Blacks and Whites in the system's upper leadership levels, but also with Blacks against one another.

One reason the visionary propositions of "The Sixteen Points" did not satisfy the proponents of Black unions was their skepticism regarding White leadership's ability to deliver on the majority of the sixteen propositions. Their skepticism was justified. Consequently, in 1975, after five years of disenchantment with "The Sixteen Points" document, Black leadership, in a response akin to that of their predecessors' reaction to the 1929 Resolution, abandoned hope for its success and again appealed for Black unions.

This time the formal appeal was directed by the Regional conference presidents themselves, several of whom (Harold Cleveland, Donald Crowder, Paul Monk, Luther Palmer, Jr., and Jessie R. Wagner) had signed the original request as local church pastors. Church leadership granted the second request for consideration, and a blue-ribbon commission convened at Andrews University in Berrien Springs, Michigan, on August 26, 1976, to decide the reasonableness of granting another full-fledged appeal.

The August 1976 meeting resulted in the decision to ask the President's Executive Group on Administration (PREXAD) to hear the renewed proposal. On January 25, 1977, W. S. Banfield, a staunch opponent of the Regional presidents' proposition and chairperson of a fact-finding commission established by PREXAD, sent out letters outlining an elaborate plan for the second full review. Between that month (January 1977) and that year's Annual Council (October 1977), several committees met and researched the issue with a depth not seen in the original discussions of 1969 and 1970. This time leadership asked a number of eminent scholars, both White and Black, to participate.

But the outcome was the same as before. At the Annual Council, on October 13, 1977, Neal Wilson, then president of NAD and speaking for PREXAD, read to the church leadership in attendance a historic position paper regarding the advisability of Black unions:

> After the most careful deliberation, it is the confirmed belief of PREXAD that it would not be judicious nor wise to organize regional "black" unions. The following are some of the reasons that have led to the decision:
>
> 1) a major consideration in the thinking of PREXAD is the concern to keep our people as close together as possible spiritually and organizationally. . . .
>
> 3) PREXAD feels that we must reject any philosophy which says that only black people can make decisions for black people, or white people for whites, or for that matter any ethnic or language group only for itself. . . .
>
> 4) The goal of unity of the body of Christ with the parts operating in

sympathetic relationship does not seem to suggest going in the direction of black unions. . . .

6) Any further organizational separation than now exists would be misrepresented both inside and outside the Seventh-day Adventist Church. . . .

7) If North America consciously moved in the direction of further fragmentation, thus reducing interchange between all ethnic and cultural groups, it could set the wrong example and have an adverse influence on our sister divisions around the world.[12]

The Regional conference presidents rejected the position of PREXAD (its second negative decision) and indicated to Robert Pierson, the General Conference president, that they intended to pursue the matter further (Appendix 19). Pierson replied to them in language typically fatherly and kind, expressing hope and confidence that they would accept the decision and move forward (Appendix 20).

Meanwhile, the eight presidents (Harold L. Cleveland, Allegheny West; Robert Woodfork, South Atlantic; Charles E. Dudley, South Central; George R. Earle, Northeastern; William C. Jones, Southwestern Region; Charles D. Joseph, Lake Region; Samuel D. Meyers, Central States; Luther R. Palmer, Allegheny East) asked E. E. Cleveland, at that time director of Missions at Oakwood College, and me, Oakwood's president, to join them, labeling the group "The Committee of Ten." This Committee decided to publish a booklet supporting their cause to be sent to all Regional conference churches. R. C. Brown, then secretary of the Lake Region Conference and later its eighth president (1990–1994), edited and published the sixteen-page booklet titled *Together for a Finished Work* in January 1978. The widespread distribution of the booklet, along with information sessions conducted by members of The Committee of Ten, stirred church leadership to further consideration of Black unions, and the matter unexpectedly appeared for a decision on the agenda of the General Conference at its Spring Meeting, April 11–14, 1978. This body of approximately 400 church leaders from around the world, most of whom had little or no exposure to the issues involved, listened to PREXAD's October 13, 1977, unfavorable reasoning. Surprisingly, after two-and-one-half days of discussion, they decided to delay action until the fall meeting in October 1978.

In an attempt to define the options for what was now a puzzled North American and international membership, the *Adventist Review*, in its September 7, 1978, edition, presented contrasting opinions by two Black leaders titled "Black Unions: Yes and No." Industrial psychologist and lay preacher

Allan Anderson wrote the "no" position, and this author, then president of Oakwood College, authored the "yes" article.[13]

The Annual Council took up the question of Black unions on October 12, 1978. The Black union proponents approached the meeting with higher hopes than ever. Many White leaders around the country, perhaps as a result of sheer weariness of debate, had privately expressed their intention to vote in favor this time around. The proponents were genuinely optimistic.

As the deliberations proceeded, the possibility of approval was palpable. It seemed to the excited advocates that in spite of what they regarded as the "stacking of the deck" against them in the past with the study committee chairmanships and membership, success was now at hand. The positive comments that had been made by the time the question was called on the motion indicated to the proponents almost certain approval. The direction was so obvious that the chair, General Conference president Neal C. Wilson, apparently felt something had to be done. He had politely entertained debate from both sides during the discussion of the question. But immediately prior to the vote, he abandoned all appearance of neutrality, and, while still holding the chair, appealed to the delegates to defeat the motion.

Neal C. Wilson (1920–2010), president of the North American Division and later of the General Conference. Courtesy of the General Conference Archives.

Wilson's comments had a chilling effect, and the supporters of Black unions believed ever after that those strong comments had dramatically shifted the outcome of the secret ballot that immediately followed. The recommendation to establish Black unions was voted down.[14]

That Wilson's bias while chairing the crucial Black union vote was obvious to the delegates and observers was confirmed in the *Washington Post*, October 20, 1978, account of the proceedings by staff writer Marjorie Hyer. Headlined "Adventists Reject Blacks' Proposal," her report reads in part:

> Black leaders of the half million-member Seventh-day Adventist Church in North America suffered a resounding defeat last week in their 11-year battle for a separate administrative structure within the church.
>
> The largely white annual council of the church, at its annual meeting in Takoma Park, rejected by a vote of 190 to 53 the black leaders' appeal for a realignment that would give blacks greater control of their religious life. . . .
>
> In the flow of rhetoric that continued into a late-night session at the denomination's spacious Takoma Park Church last week, the central reason for rejecting appeals for black unions appeared to be a public relations problem—the fear that the creation of all-black structures would be viewed as segregationist. . . . The image of the church as a racially inclusive body is particularly prized because a large amount of the church's mission efforts are focused on urban black areas. . . .
>
> *The case against separate black judicatories was presented largely by Neal Wilson, 58, president of the North American Division of the church, who also chaired the day's discussion.*[15] (emphasis supplied)

That Wilson himself considered his remarks pivotal to the defeat of Black unions was confirmed in private conversations with this author on several occasions during later years. The essence of his comments was: "I believe you fellows might have had it" (referring to a positive vote). "I had to do what I did!" I kept my responses very general and brief. Firstly, I knew that his motives were good. Secondly, in spite of his repeated invitation to do so, I felt uncomfortable rehearsing the events with him. As the years went by, I had become reconciled with the fact that we had done our best and needed to move on.

Since then I have regretted not telling him that, but I believe that my willingness to assume difficult responsibilities and subsequent loyalty as one of his vice presidents must have reassured him of my deep respect. He was, in my opinion, a truly exceptional leader. That his strong courage sometimes expressed itself as arbitrariness was a characteristic that I tried not to model, but which I later came to appreciate and, to a degree, emulate when convinced that an issue would have lasting negative consequences for the world church.

Wilson's action was not unusual. It was common, in fact expected in Adventist deliberations, that on sensitive issues the ranking officer had the "privilege" of a final statement or opinion before the vote. At this point in the church's history, administrators paid scant attention to Roberts' rules or any other rules of parliamentary order. Sessions were conducted in the hopeful assumption that all parties were persons of good will, and that the majority vote—after prayer, sufficient vetting by the group, and, many times, comments by the chair (often solicited by the voters when weightier matters were being decided)—should be accepted as the will of God.

When the chairperson of the meeting was also the ranking officer of the unit involved, the possibility of voting results that differed from his or her wish changed from rare to almost never.

The Committee of Ten, knowing that Wilson had always been a friend to Black causes, but feeling that they had been denied by what they regarded as his very arbitrary intervention while chairing the vote, four days later fired off to him a letter:

> Dear Elder Wilson:
>
> Black leadership deems it necessary to state that the recent Autumn Council proceedings demonstrate, once again, the impossibility of fair and candid treatment of their request for Black Unions or any other request, for that matter, which is opposed by Church leadership. The reasons as we see it are as follows:
>
> Problem #1. *Lack of a Tangible Parliamentary Code.*
>
> When asked at the inception of our October 12, 1978 discussion to pin point the parliamentary code that guides at our councils, the Chair replied that there are no adopted guidelines; rather, that we are a Church and, as such, choose to be led by a general spirit of cooperation not specific procedures. We view this as a huge disadvantage to any minority, especially one opposed by the Chair. For it is quite evident that when the chairman is aggressively involved in defeating a proposition, the petitioners can be overruled, outflanked and silenced at any point at which the Chair exerts its authority. It is also self-evident that appeals to the floor for help are futile when the majority is fully aligned with the Chair and depending upon him to be chairman and parliamentarian, as well.[16] (Appendix 21)

Their protest letter further stated:

> We can understand how some Blacks, who have spent considerable time overseas, are still hopeful of full integration in America and willing to suffer and wait. We know that there is a general time-lag that they must overcome.... We also understand how some Blacks, who reside in areas where there is no self-determination, might be happy with their status of limited or quasi assimilation.
>
> We can understand how some liberal Whites, who honestly wish that our Church would function as one culturally and functionally, would still hold onto their dreams. We can understand that some paternalistic Whites,

who think they know what's best for Blacks, cannot trust our leadership and would be reluctant to see it happen. But we do not understand, nor do we believe, that top administrative leadership in our division or of our Church fail to get the point . . . the real issue with them is not the danger of a separate Church, or world opinion, but *money* and *power*! . . .

Several of our White friends in leadership in local and Union and General Conference positions have come by night to tell us so.

And this brings us back to where we began. Even though the ballot is secret, as long as our discussions and votes must be conducted in an arena where the judge is also the prosecuting attorney, parliamentarian and Chairman of the jury, justice cannot be had—impartiality is [an] impossibility . . . we suspect that the issue will never be voted until the judge, himself, decides to recommend it. . . .

It is distressing to know that (even in 1978) not only has Black leadership no power or the option to chart its destiny along the legitimate, philosophical and structural lines of Church administration, but also it is denied a proper arena within which to debate its needs.[17]

Given the reaction of knowledgeable Black Adventists to Wilson's role in the defeat of the Black union proposal, one might understandably ask how he nevertheless retained their confidence as a champion of racial justice. The answer is that, for many years since his presidency at the Columbia Union, he had boldly modeled the hiring of Blacks at both the union and the North American Division levels, and consistently encouraged others to do so.

Wilson's most bold and meaningful act, however, was his chairing the November 2, 1978, meeting of the nominating committee that chose C. E. Bradford as the General Conference vice-president for North America (a job description later changed in September 1986 to president of the North American Division of Seventh-day Adventists). Just days after the October 12 negative vote on Black unions, General Conference president Robert H. Pierson announced his retirement. Wilson had been immediately elected as his successor, and thus chaired the meeting, held in the Takoma Park, Maryland, church to select his own replacement in North America.

Wilson found himself and the sixty-eight-member nominating committee (twelve of them Black) facing an unexpected dilemma. Four of the five nominees the delegates had settled on were White: Cree Sandefur, president of the Pacific Union; Max Torkelson, president of the North Pacific Union; and Lowell Bock and Francis Wernick, both vice presidents of the General Conference. C. E. Bradford, then associate secretary of the NAD, was the only minority in the group.

All four of the White nominees came short of final nomination. That unexpected outcome began with Sandefur's withdrawal, in spite of the obvious favorability of the General Conference leadership to him. In the voting for the four names that remained, support for Wernick waned. That was mainly, it seemed, because Wilson warned that Wernick's responsibilities as chair of the Loma Linda boards was too critical to leave at that time, and asked the committee not to nominate him for the position. Bock, another capable administrator, thought to be Wilson's choice for the position, faced strong opposition from the Pacific Union delegates for reasons that most of us did not understand, and thus failed to receive substantial support. All of this dictated that the final ballot had only two names: Bradford and Torkelson. The result of that ballot was Bradford 18 and Torkelson 50. Later conversations confirm that all twelve Black delegates voted for Bradford, meaning that six others joined in support for him. The Torkelson vote came just as the morning session ended. Wilson advised committee members that we would have Torkelson's response when the session resumed at 1:00 p.m., thus allowing him time to make his decision. And, he added, Torklelson had asked to speak with him about what was at stake.

The twelve Black members of the nominating committee were very unhappy. We felt that Bradford's slim support reeked of racial preference by the White committee members, especially in light of the fact that several times during the process the General Conference treasurer and other church leaders had asked that we not vote for "Brad" because they had something bigger and better in mind "down the line" for him. After one such comment by a GC official, I was recognized by the chairman and asked, "Since the office of world presidency is already filled, exactly what in the Adventist structure is bigger and better than the leadership of the NAD?" Whatever he had in mind, he did not say.

We assembled after lunch fully expecting to have Torkelson introduced as the nominee for vice president for North America. We were, it seemed, hopelessly outnumbered, once more being "steam-rolled" by superior forces. Looking back, it was the same helpless feeling I had during the assault in the park on the edge of Harlem when I was ten: we were whipped and there was nothing we could do about it. That's why I couldn't understand what Bradford meant when he happened to pass me sitting alone in a church hallway during the lunch break, with what I am sure was forlorn body language, and, not stopping, said what I remember as: "It's not over. Just pray; you never know." I didn't understand then what he could have possibly meant, but I was soon to find out.

His hint became clear when Wilson began the afternoon session by announcing that Torkelson had declined to be considered for the NAD presidency. He had done so, later conversations revealed, because his view of NAD's proper function was considerably more expansive than what new GC President Wilson thought wise or immediately doable. It was a philosophical disagreement of which Bradford and others who worked at headquarters were aware; we were not. Stunned by this surprising development and obviously unhappy, several delegates pressed to begin the nominating process all over again, an act requiring a brand new slate of names. The Black delegates protested. Bradford's was the only name left of the five from which we had agreed to choose, and we insisted that a vote on his name should be taken.

Wilson listened and refused, as several were urging, to accept a motion to restart the process, solemnly lecturing the delegates regarding the appearance of racial bias resulting from not voting Yes or No on Bradford's name, the only one surviving. He mentioned the tensions of the emotional Black union debate and the optics of assembling new names before exhausting the present slate. Then, after assuring the group that "Brad could do it," he called for a Yes or No vote that approved Bradford by a wide margin. A specially called General Conference Committee meeting then confirmed his name on January 11, 1979.[18]

Upon returning to Huntsville, one of my first stops was the office of E. E. Cleveland to whom I gave an enthusiastic eyewitness account of how, as a delegate and participant in history, I had seen matters work out in our behalf. He listened impassively, and when I finished responded, "You don't know what you have done."

"What do you mean," I asked, genuinely puzzled.

"You have just killed Black unions," he replied. "It will be very difficult if not impossible for a Black president to support them. And further," he continued, "the members, Black and White, are going to reason, 'You have a Black division president, isn't that enough?'"

While Bradford's election opened to Black Adventists a world of good otherwise unachievable, Cleveland's assumption had validity—if not entirely for the reasons he gave—because it took from the Black union proposal's active support one of its most respected voices and potent pens.

As for the fairness in parliamentary procedure and voter freedom about which the Committee of Ten protested to Wilson, it should be noted that there now exists more voter independence in church deliberations, thanks to a formalized "General Conference Rules of Order" adopted in 1989. Members of the Committee of Ten have privately credited their protest letter to Wilson about the Black union vote with sparking the implementation of this more equitable protocol.

The tradition that allows the ranking officer to offer a final comment still frequently surfaces, but with less effectiveness than in prior decades. In the past, voter independence was often muted by the allocation of inordinate authority and status to the office of "president" at any level of organization (especially that of the General Conference). Voter independence is now much more prevalent than before. One example is the willingness of major elements of the North American Division to vote contrary to the widely-published appeal of the present General Conference president, Ted Wilson, son of N. C. Wilson, that women not be ordained.

Even almost forty years later, a few Black leaders still privately bemoan the defeat of Black unions. However, given Black lay and clergy joy over the subsequent placement of Blacks in meaningful positions in the church's division and world conference structures and the acceptance and success they have achieved, further appeal is very unlikely.

While we have no way of really knowing, it is also unlikely that the considerable number of Blacks who have, since the debates, occupied the officer and departmental posts in the union conferences in the United States would have been so honored had not the Black union debates taken place. It is notable that since that time, Blacks have been elected to the presidencies of the Atlantic Union, Lake Union, Columbia Union, Pacific Union, Mid-America Union, and Southern Union—six out of the nine unions in the NAD—as well as to the other officer positions and most departmental posts.

Whether these and many other leadership opportunities for Black Adventists now exceed those that might have come had the church established Black unions, for some, remains debatable. What is not in doubt is that the goal of interracial functioning at the local church level, a major tenant of "The Sixteen Points" that was to substitute for Black unions, has not materialized. As with similar proclamations in previous documents issued by church committees in the wake of Black protest, calls for collaborative fellowship of distinctly differing cultural congregations have proven impractical. In retrospect, the most obvious benefits of the eleven-year discussion regarding Black unions have been an impetus for opening doors of service for Blacks at national and international (world church) administrative levels; an impetus for in-depth focus on the sociological and theological principles of church structure and relationships; and an impetus and example for protest efforts by the later Black twentieth-century leadership.

## BLACK LEADERS FOR AND AGAINST BLACK UNIONS

From the very beginning of their struggles for justice, the social ideology of Black Adventist leaders has varied. Some wished for greater freedom within existing systems, while others called for new structural forms as the means to progress. The eleven-year debate regarding Black unions forced Black leaders to more critically evaluate and articulate their varied social and theological convictions than had been done in the past.

The result was a number of thoroughly researched and passionate appeals produced by Black leaders in articles and speeches both for and against the Black union initiative. While the majority of Blacks wrote and spoke with considerable skill for Black unions, those against them made their case just as adroitly and with equal passion. It was thus that the two camps came to oppose each other both theoretically and, as we shall see, emotionally as well.

I have chosen to examine in some detail the thought and methodologies of six individuals, whose written expressions I judge to have given particular clarity to the nature and consequences of the debate. The first three (the "Integrationists") opposed the Black union initiative from a desire to fulfill Martin Luther King, Jr.'s dream of integration, the key element of the Civil Rights Movement he led, and they fought to pursue this. The last three (the "self-determinationists") regarded true integration of the races, both public and private, as illusory and opted instead for a system (Black unions) that involved modified self-determination in light of what they regarded as the unshakable realties of social pluralism in society as well as the church.

### The Integrationists

Like many African Americans in the latter three decades of the twentieth century, the individuals profiled below regarded tendencies toward self-determination as "giving up the struggle"—not just for inclusion but for long-sought equality.

## Warren S. Banfield (1925-2006)

One of the individuals whose voice and pen spoke eloquently against the Black union idea and for the continued effort to integrate the existing structures was Warren S. Banfield. His impressive service portfolio included pastorates in North Carolina, Georgia, and Florida; president of the South Atlantic Conference of Seventh-day Adventists (1962-1971); associate secretary of the Southern Union Conference (1971-1975); associate secretary in the Regional Department of the General Conference (1975-1978); and director of the Human Relations Department of the General Conference (1978-1989).

Banfield first became active in racial affairs during his pastorate in Tampa, Florida, from 1956 to 1962. In 1956 he shocked his conservative members and surprised his ministerial colleagues around the country by accepting the presidency of the Tampa Branch NAACP, a position he held for a two-year period. This occurred at a time when many Black Adventists were skeptical about joining protest groups such as the NAACP, not to mention taking leadership roles in them. Banfield was consistently vocal regarding racial issues both within and without the church, and Blacks and Whites alike saw him as a forthright spokesperson for justice.[19]

What distinguished Banfield's protest effort in the church was his regular involvement in both official (church-appointed) and unofficial (lay-voluntary) human relations forums and study groups. While most other leaders sought redress through rigorous debate and various pressure tactics, Banfield's chief effort was participation in dialogue and fellowship with integrated boards and committees.

Typical of such groups was the Human Relations Committee of the Southern Union Conference on which Banfield and I served together in the late 1960s. Its organizational preamble reflects its philosophy:

WARREN S. BANFIELD (1922-2006), staunch advocate for integration. Courtesy of the General Conference Archives.

> WHEREAS, There are many forces in the world seeking to disrupt the unity of the Seventh-day Adventist Church, and
>
> WHEREAS, There should be present in these last days in the church the spirit enunciated by Christ in His prayer for His disciples that we be one as He and the Father are one, and in harmony with His teaching that we should love our neighbor as ourselves and do unto others as we would have others do unto us,
>
> WE RECOMMEND, That stronger efforts toward unity and brotherhood be made in the conferences of the Southern Union and in the churches. (Appendix 22)

An even earlier committee connection that demonstrated Banfield's orientation, and one on which I also served while living in Atlanta (1967–1969), was the Concerned Christian Council, comprised of White and Black laity and clergy who organized in the Atlanta area during the late 1960s. Banfield was listed as both charter member and co-chair of its education committee, which stated its purpose in even stronger language than did the Southern Union Human Relations Committee. Its preamble reads in part:

> The purpose of the Concerned Christian Council is to promote understanding and foster Christian fellowship among all segments of the Seventh-day Adventist Church, and to implement the Human Relations Guidelines as spelled out in the Bible and Spirit of Prophecy and formally adopted by the Seventh-day Adventist General Conference, Union Conference, and Local Conference Human Relations Committees. It is the Council's desire to implement these purposes by those legitimate and Christ-like means afforded us through the denominational organization. (Appendix 23)

The minutes of Banfield's education committee for May 19, 1969, typify his focus. Among other things, committee actions called for workshops for teachers of newly integrated schools in the Atlanta area, awards for speaking or writing on integration issues, live-ins, in-service training for teachers in Black history, booths on racial integration issues at teachers' conventions, traveling forum groups to visit various churches and answer questions, and letters of invitation and copies of CCC guidelines to post in each church in the Atlanta area.[20]

Banfield was single-minded in the possibilities envisioned by his group. It was largely his energies in cross-cultural group activities that earned for him the leadership of the General Conference Office of Ethnic

Relations, later renamed Office of Human Relations. His sincere faith in these processes as the proper path to social justice is revealed in his thoughtful statement on cultural interaction written about the time of that appointment:

> One of our church's greatest assets resides in the diversity of the cultural and ethnic origin of its membership. People who historically and traditionally represent strong antipathies and hatreds, should be getting a taste of "this new thing", a new race, a new hope, a new nation, and thus participating in God's developmental process in the universe, *His unfinished task of creation....*
>
> Social distance has a direct bearing on human relationships. Proximity, intimacy and communication are interrelated and have social consequences. In a given area, wide social distances and the absence of proximity and intimacy tend to make communication between races difficult, to perpetuate stereotype thinking and contribute to human misunderstanding. We gain a knowledge of people by entering into a relationship with them.[21]

It is not too much to say that as a proponent and participant of interracial fellowship activities designed to foster racial understanding with the hope of eliminating discrimination, Banfield stood out among Black Adventist leaders.[22]

### Earl A. Canson, Sr. (1927–2003)

EARL A. CANSON, SR. (1927–2003), Director of Regional Affairs for the Pacific Union Conference. Courtesy of the General Conference Archives.

Earl Canson, who began his ministerial service in 1948, held several pastorates in the state of California, and distinguished himself in other administrative capacities. In 1978 he was appointed director of Regional Affairs for the Pacific Union Conference. In this position, Canson actively dissuaded Blacks in the union from supporting the later push for the organization of Black Conferences. As a man whose disposition was more amelioratory than revolutionary, Canson quietly managed to diffuse most Black political unrest on the Pacific Coast, while at the same time championing the cause of integration. His long-time friend and fellow clergyman, Major White (1926–2004), whose more aggressive personality effectively complemented that of the mild-mannered Canson, partnered with Canson in his efforts.²³

Like Banfield, Canson saw the need for drastic changes in the church's racial policies and practices. However, both placed more hope to affect this end in amiable negotiations than in the long-range benefits of education by association. Canson's skills as a witty, low-key diplomat and non-confrontational negotiator appealed to White leadership and provided him with a high degree of acceptance among the Blacks on the Pacific Coast.

MAJOR WHITE (1926–2004), West Coast "unity" proponent. Courtesy of the General Conference Archives.

Canson's article, "The Pacific Union Conference Regional Department: Facts and Figures," is typical of the diplomatic language by which he was able to combine spiritual appeal with political thrust. In concluding his paper in which he explained why Blacks in the Pacific Coast area need not apologize for refusing to organize Black Conferences, Canson states, in language typically inoffensive:

> I would be the first to admit that opportunities to develope [sic] leadership are greater in the Black conference for us Blacks than it is here. But we are rising. My plea is to prepare for greater service and the God of earth and heaven feed us and we will be satisfied. I maintain that if we decide to go Black Conference we will do it not because we have to but because we want to. Our wants are not always best for us, God certainly knows what we need. I'm willing to submit my opinion to His will——Are you?²⁴

Some contested Canson's philosophy of organization and his understanding of full justice, but never his skills as a mediator and negotiator. His soft-toned approach was unquestionably effective.²⁵

### Frank W. Hale, Jr. (1927–2011)

As one of the better-known Black educators in the United States, Frank Hale's lengthy career included professorships and chairs at several universities, the presidency of Oakwood College (1966–1971), and vice provost for minority affairs and professor emeritus at his alma mater, Ohio State University (1971–1988 and 1999–2005, respectively).

Mainline Black clergy, unlike the educator Hale, generally functioned with the assumption that they should shield laypersons as much as possible from the racial foibles of the church, lest their loyalty suffer. Not so with Hale—he led with the belief that the threat of public disclosure was, in fact, a legitimate tool. It was, as discussed earlier, a successful strategy in his work with the Layman's Leadership Conference. However, while he was quite willing to go to the press in order to bring pressure to bear in the struggle for internal change, Hale was just as concerned that the church make public its principles and programs that were characterized by fairness.

An example of both of these elements is on display in Hale's October 1963 response to then *Adventist Review* associate editor, Raymond F. Cottrell (1911–2003). Cottrell had, in a *Review* editorial of October 17, 1963, agreed with David Lawrence, editor of the *U.S. News and World Report*, in criticizing church groups who had participated in the now historic March on Washington on August 23, 1963. With Lawrence, Cottrell reasoned that such participation violated the principle of separation of church and state.

Hale expressed his vigorous disagreement in a letter to Cottrell:

> My brother, I cannot abandon my conscience by not recording my protest against what appears to be a subtle, yet cynical, disregard for the principle of human freedom as it affects the Negro in particular. . . .
>
> How shall we ever convince the world of our sincere concern for human equality, while we openly join hands and ally ourselves with those who make their livelihood by generating and fertilizing the prejudices of men?
>
> You indicate that the church should not "enforce its opinion" in legislative matters. But do not Adventists seek legislative support and influence public opinion for their positions in the areas of temperance, Sunday laws, and health reform? (Appendix 24)

Hale's attention to organizational church responsibilities during his six-year presidency of Oakwood College (1966–1971) somewhat muted his reputation as a crusader. However, LLC's involvement in the Black union debate thrust him to the forefront of protest again. He was a firm proponent of the integrationist point of view: as many other Black Adventists, Hale saw the Black union proposal as dishonoring the hard-fought victories of the yet unfinished Civil Rights Movement.

The fact that Hale later served as personal confidant to Jesse Jackson of Operation PUSH and a member of its board heightened his profile as a maverick among Black Adventist protest personalities, and as one whose activities and influence went far beyond the conventional boundaries of usual Adventist social protest. He did nothing to reduce the apprehension of many, White and Black, when in January 13, 1970, he wrote:

> Where do we go from here? If our hearts are right, we must plan an effective strategy for racial desegregation in the Seventh-day Adventist Church. On each church level considered, effective strategy will require a variety of actions that are interactive and mutually supportive. Included should be such strategies (1) emphasizing the changing of attitudes and (2) emphasizing direct changes of social patterns and institutions through active intervention.
>
> There is no valid ethical ground for categorical insistence on restricting strategy to techniques of "persuasion" and "education" in the removal of racial barriers in the church, notwithstanding the common assertions to the contrary. The very existence of such barriers is not ethical, and the racial composition of the membership and basis for participation in the church is not properly a matter requiring the consent of persons in the church.[26]

FRANK W. HALE, JR. (1927–2011), renowned civil rights activist, educator, and president of Oakwood College. Courtesy of the Oakwood University Archives.

While we should note that we have no written evidence of Hale ever abandoning his integrationist views for the self-determinationist position, his post-Black union debate shift of membership from the mostly White congregation in Worthington, Ohio (a part of the White-administered Ohio Conference) to the almost completely Black Ephesus Church in Columbus, Ohio (a part of the Black-administered Allegheny West

Conference), could suggest a softening, if not entire reversal, of position. In sum, Frank Hale was, without a doubt, the face of Black lay leadership protest during a most critical period of debate in Adventist social history.[27]

## The Self-Determinationists

Unlike their counterparts, the spokespersons discussed below preferred to pursue modified structural autonomy rather than pin their hopes on what they and others viewed as the impossibility of wide-spread cultural assimilation.

### Charles E. Bradford

Charles Bradford, as did all the other protest leaders we are considering with the exception of Hale, also began his career as a church pastor. After sixteen years of pastoring in the states of Louisiana, Texas, and New York, he entered administrative service. Transitioning among pastoral, evangelistic, and conference departmental work for many years in three conferences (Southwest Region, Central States, and Northeastern), he became president of the Lake Region Conference in 1961, a post he held until 1970. In 1971, Bradford became associate secretary of the General Conference, where he served until 1979. As discussed above, in 1979 the church elected him president of the North American Division. He was the first, and to this date only, Black so honored.

What distinguished Bradford's protest career from other leaders was his emphasis on specific policy remediation. His concern was not so much that of integration or even desegregation, but that of strengthening Black institutions and enhancing Black economic status through policies and projects best described as restitutional. That is, while he promoted programs that emphasized education, better relationships, and negotiations, he primarily spent his

CHARLES E. BRADFORD, first Black president of the North American Division. Courtesy of the General Conference Archives.

energy in seeking material remediation in the form of funding or set-asides for Black causes.

Bradford did not, as others, function with the hope of White acquiescence to the demands for full freedom. He respected but did not fantasize about King's dream of an America where someday justice will "ring from the prodigious hilltops of New Hampshire" to "every hill and molehill of Mississippi," so that all will be "free at last!"[28] For him there would be no happy, fully-integrated American society. He did not think that group discussions and cross-cultural programing would drastically change America's long history of discrimination.

In Bradford's view, the superiority of numbers and materials possessed by the larger group (Whites) could best be accessed through political statesmanship rather than protest of another kind. Superior White authority was not so much to be boycotted, protested, or even neutralized, as it was to be manipulated. His approach was typical of that class of minority leaders who advance to meaningful positions in the administrative structure by combining skills of negotiation with the working dictum, "Don't get mad, get smart."

In an undated document titled "An Appeal to the Leadership of the Seventh-day Adventist Church to Give Special Study to the Position of the Negro Seventh-day Adventist in American Society and in the Church," probably written in early 1966, Bradford reiterates his strong preference for the restitutional motif as an instrument of justice with the following reminder:

> Mrs. White called for a positive program to help the recently freed slaves to become good Christians and useful citizens. . . . During the 1890s and early 1900s she used the columns of the *Review* to make direct appeals to the church, both leadership and laity. The servant of the Lord did not equivocate. "Upon the white people of the United States the Lord has laid the burden of uplifting this race. But, as yet, Seventh-day Adventists' have done comparatively little to help them. . . . The American Nation owes a debt of love to the colored race, and God has ordained that they should make restitution for the wrong they have done them in the past. Those who have taken no active part in enforcing slavery . . . are not relieved from the responsibility of making special efforts to remove, as far as possible, the sure result of their enslavement."[29]

Having quoted Ellen White's position on the matter, Bradford then spoke for himself:

The leadership of this denomination must recognize the gravity of the situation and not allow precedent or established policies to hamper positive remedial action.... To state it in a different way—compensatory and massive remedial measures are necessary to bring existing Negro institutions and facilities up to date and to prepare more Negro youth to serve the church.[30]

Bradford's practical approach reaped a number of financial benefits for his race during his years in the North American Division as associate secretary and president. The projects he influenced, such as the financial initiatives cited below, had the distinct character of set-asides or affirmative action. They included: the Large City Evangelism Fund providing special help for the inner cities (1966); the annual Regional conference tithe appropriation (initially 2.5 percent) for Oakwood College (1967); the Small Conference Assistance Plan providing tithe reversion monies for conferences with tithing capita of $100 per member per year or less (1968); and the Regional Scholarship Fund providing special scholarships for Black students in graduate schools (1971).

Before he joined the General Conference, Bradford had used his pen often to protest inequities and appeal for justice.[31] That he became president of the North American Division and thereby a vice president of the General Conference, despite such outspokenness, is noteworthy. Critical to any study of his career is the observation that throughout his ministry he succeeded in the difficult posture of an "organization man"—as he has often referred to himself—while at the same time remaining active in programs that benefited the Black constituency.

## E. Earl Cleveland (1921–2009)

E. Earl Cleveland's career after finishing his studies at Oakwood Junior College in 1942 was nothing short of mercurial. He left the pastorate after five years of service in the states of North Carolina and Kentucky to become a full-time evangelist in the Southeastern United States. After thirteen years of highly productive ministry, he was in 1954 appointed General Conference associate ministerial secretary, a position with worldwide evangelistic responsibilities. During his term of duty, he held campaigns in more than sixty countries and preached on every continent. In 1976 he accepted the position as director of Church Missions and teacher at Oakwood College.

During his earlier years of service (the 1940s to 1960s), Cleveland had the reputation among many as a fierce apologist for the status quo. However, by the time of the vote on the Black union issue in 1978, Cleveland's reputation as a social conservative and defender of the establishment had turned 180 degrees. By then many looked upon him as the most strident of the more militant wing of Black Seventh-day Adventist leadership.

No one can be certain, but many regard the action of the General Conference in 1966, which placed a younger, less experienced White man as head of the General Conference Ministerial Department, as the critical factor in Cleveland's emergence as a racial activist. What solidified his image as a militant spokesperson are both the volume and the often strident tone of his statements. The eleven books he authored, many of which deal directly with scriptural principles of brotherhood, clearly portray his views. Those views are sharply focused in his articles regarding racial challenges in general and Black unions in particular. His many editorials in the *North American Regional Voice* (a monthly news magazine begun by Black leaders in the wake of the 1978 Black union defeat) were classic examples of both his style and social thought.[32]

The level of Cleveland's protest intensified with time, but his basic method of seeking to change social attitudes through the use of his pen did not. Both as a defender of the faith prior to 1966 and as a social activist afterward, his form of protest was journalistic rather than administrative. Unlike the other protest leaders observed in this study, Cleveland never served as head or representative of a voting constituency of the church. However, the lack of an administrative platform in no way limited his effectiveness. While the others profiled here primarily focused on specific challenges within the church's structure or with particular incidents of injustice suffered by laity or clergy, Cleveland sought to clarify what he called the church's "misunderstanding and abuse" of the social principles of the Bible and the writings of Ellen White.

E. EARL CLEVELAND (1921–2009), General Conference Ministerial Secretary and vocal activist for Black unions. Courtesy of the General Conference Archives.

Cleveland's attitude toward those statements in the writings of Ellen White, that some might view as supporting negative racial policies, we find poignantly revealed in a letter to Ron Graybill, then a research assistant of the Ellen G. White Estate (the organization that maintains White's writings). In colorful and passionate language, Cleveland wrote:

> I don't want to be surprised by the enemies of the faith with quotations that I have not seen nor heard, that could prove damaging to the reputation of the prophet, or embarrassing to me as a Believer. Also, so many of our White believers have misunderstood the intent and content of so many of her published racial observations, that such a book [*Ellen White on Race Relations*] would prove enlightening and helpful to them. It is therefore a work long overdue. I hope that when you have completed this work it will carry the official stamp of approval of the E. G. White publications committee. This would give it some denominational responsibility and backing. The church owes us this. Black people, in our communion, have suffered too long at the hands of Administrators and members who have *misread*, *misunderstood*, and *misapplied* the writings of our prophet, feeling that she has sanctioned their prejudice.[33]

Ellen White statements that Cleveland found especially subject to misapplication include the following:

> Every species of animals which God had created was preserved in the ark. The confused species which God did not create, which were the result of amalgamation, were destroyed by the flood. Since the flood, there has been amalgamation of man and beast, as may be seen in the almost endless varieties of species of animals, and in certain races of men.[34]

> The colored people should not urge that they be placed on an equality with white people.[35]

> Common association with the blacks is not a wise course to pursue.[36]

Cleveland's demand that the church carefully explain or print such statements only in their context as well as in relation to Ellen White's other statements on the subject had much to do with the reprint of *The Southern Work*, the ninety-six-page collection of Ellen White's articles and letters on the subject of race relations written in the years 1891 through 1899. Cleveland thought that, placed in context, White's writings would decry rather than support the prevailing notions of racial superiority. He was correct.

Although Cleveland asked the White Estate to responsibly address these quotations, he himself was an able exegete of such controversial statements. His interpretations lend a sometimes provocative quality to his literary corpus and earned him the reputation as the most outspoken of all Black Adventist twentieth-century freedom exponents.

A typical example of the way in which he handled White's statements that seemed to some as prejudicial is his following reply to a friend, who wrote to him questioning the meaning of her observation that "in heaven there will be no color line; for all will be as white as Christ Himself."[37] Cleveland's response was:

> I received the statement from the pen of Mrs. White concerning the color of Jesus. If you will study it closely you will notice it does not say how white Jesus is. Let me quote the phrase: "In Heaven there will be no color line, for all will be as white as Christ Himself."
>
> But I raise the question, How white is Christ Himself? Neither the scriptures nor Mrs. White have dared to say. Now the nearest thing that is descriptive on the subject is from Revelation 1:14, 15. It speaks of ". . . His feet like unto fine brass as if they burned in a furnace. . . ." Now . . . feet that look like they have been burned cannot be white. But an objector may say, "John was a Prophet and this was simply metaphoric language." To this I would reply that Ellen White was a Prophet and therefore her language was also metaphoric. In the flesh, Christ was a Jew and there is no evidence that the Semite was White.[38]

Unsurprisingly, as the frequency of Cleveland's statements, letters, and inquiries on the subject of racial justice accelerated, and as their tone became more pointed, his activist positions became more and more uncomfortable for his White colleagues at the denomination's headquarters and many constituents across the North American Division. I was, at that time, president of Oakwood College, and I believe that it was this tension, more than anything else, that led Robert Pierson, president of the General Conference, to appeal in 1975 to me to find a job for Cleveland at the school. By this time, fully aware of the attitude toward him at denominational headquarters, Cleveland cooperated with the plan and accepted a position at Oakwood. Removed from the more restricted atmosphere at church headquarters, he found additional freedom at Oakwood to both teach and preach as well as continue in his journalistic endeavors to promote racial justice in the church. His protestations were frank, direct, insightful, and without fear of sanctions, political or otherwise.

In sum, Cleveland was by far the most prolific writer and social commentator in the history of Black Seventh-day Adventism. Specifically, his effort to improve the lot of his people by clarifying the social and racial principles of the Bible and the writings of Ellen White had a far-reaching effect during the Black union discussions.

### Charles E. Dudley, Sr. (1927–2010)

Charles Dudley's pastoral ministry included the states of Alabama, Kentucky, Louisiana, Tennessee, and Texas. He is best remembered for his thirty-one years (1962–1993) of highly productive service as the president of the South Central Conference. Headquartered in Nashville, Tennessee, this conference has oversight of the Black program in Alabama, Kentucky, Louisiana, Mississippi, Tennessee, and parts of Arkansas. From its inception it has had a strong influence on the growth and dynamism of Black Seventh-day Adventists.

It was into this area (Mississippi) that the historic vessel *Morning Star* sailed in the mid-1890s with a special ministry for families of the recently freed slaves. The region of South Central saw the first Black Adventist congregation organized in Edgefield Junction (now Nashville), Tennessee, in 1883. Here, from 1927 to 1983, Black Adventists from all over the country came to Riverside Hospital for medical treatment. Also vital is that in the South Central Conference, in Huntsville, Alabama, is Oakwood University, which has been Adventism's sole school ranked among the "Historically Black Colleges and Universities" (HBCU) since 1896. Such denominationally-significant institutions, set in the backdrop of the often tumultuous racial conditions of that region prior to and during Dudley's tenure, dictated for him a highly active and visible social agenda of Black self-determination.

CHARLES E. DUDLEY, SR. (1927–2010), longtime president of the South Central Conference. Courtesy of the General Conference Archives.

Dudley distilled his firm support for the principle of self-determination in his statement that "history testifies that people receive better understanding when the leadership comes from their own group."[39] He illustrated his conviction with the following observation:

> Missionaries, business magnets [*sic*], political leaders and armed forces from outside organizations have in the past entered a community to help its people develop a better way of life for themselves; but more recently, these outside groups have not been readily received by nationals as in times past. Nationals are urging that they be given the opportunity to serve their own countrymen.[40]

Surprisingly, at first blush, but perhaps more understandably on second thought, Dudley encountered far less opposition to his self-determination theories from White Southerners in his region than did Black leaders from Whites in more socially liberal areas of the country. The fact is that the latter wished not to believe that America was incapable of at least posturing like all of its cultural pieces had melded together, whereas White Southerners were more realistic and happy to structure ways that some regarded as an "us-and-them" relationship.

Dudley's lengthy presidency of the South Central Conference and marked skepticism about White leadership's intentions, earned for him the role of leader of the Black union protest group. Typical of his belief regarding the motivation of the majority leadership of the church is the following statement:

> Since the organization of Regional Conferences in the United States in 1945, the work has realized tremendous blessings in growth in membership and financial income. As Joseph said to his brethren when they moved to Egypt during the famine: "You meant it for evil, but the Lord has made it a blessing for the entire family."[41]

Reflecting more generally upon the birth of Colored conferences, he wrote:

> The leaders of the church had been charged by African-American laity to integrate all of the church's facilities immediately. They made no request to separate from the existing conferences; however, instead of agreeing to integrate church facilities and open the doors to all people regardless of race, color or ethnic origin, the leaders moved to organize separate Colored conferences to be manned by Black leaders. This plan turned out to be the best route for the growth and development of the work among Black people in the church.[42]

Dudley was also vocal at the various church counsels and committees that discussed issues in which Blacks had an interest. By virtue of his status as leader of Black Adventism in the most racially contested area of the country, his views received special attention both for the need and the urgency of their implementation. In each of these concerns, Dudley was unerringly bold and resolute.

Throughout his presidency, Dudley addressed the challenges of racial injustice with a soft, determined voice and a pointed, potent pen. While his primary written expressions came after the Black union debate had concluded, his involvement in its unfolding was direct and meaningful. Dudley authored two studies of historical significance for the sector of the church that he served: *Thou Who Hath Brought Us: The Development of the Seventh-day Adventist Denomination Among African-Americans* (1997) and *Thou Who Hath Brought Us Thus Far on Our Way–II* (2000).[43] His volume, *The Genealogy of Ellen Gould Harmon White* (1999), while disputed by the White Estate, strengthened Black Adventists' long-standing suspicion that Ellen White was Black.[44]

Dudley's devotion to the needs of both the Black sector of the church and wider community was unrelenting. He repeatedly refused to accept invitations to advance to higher levels of administrative responsibility, because he wished to serve his people at the point of personal and immediate contact. He will go down as one of the most important protest voices.

## Integrationist Overview

The three supporters of the integrationist position (Banfield, Canson, and Hale) showed general agreement on a number of conclusions undergirding that position. Among other things, they believed (1) that self-determinationism is tantamount to separatism or nationalism and should be understood as a form of reverse segregation; (2), that because the idea of Black unions is separatist, it is contrary to the principle of unity mandated in the Bible and the writings of Ellen G. White; and (3) that non-Adventist society (both religious and secular) would view Black unions as a sign of the inability of the races to live in harmony in the Seventh-day Adventist Church.

In advancing the first of the points above, Banfield commented:

> Black leaders in and out of the church, have had to consider paramount the search for the answer to the question "How does a black person gain social and economic parity in a racially prejudiced society?" Historically, they have addressed themselves to the question from two distinct positions. They advocated either nationalism or integration.[45]

Hale addressed the second assumption above in his article "Commitment vs. Capitulation" as follows:

> Consequently, the philosophy of separatism is gaining within our church as it has in secular circles. When we must admit to ourselves that we do not have the spiritual courage to come to grips with the problems that make mockery of our faith, then we may be admitting that our faith is a mockery.[46]

Banfield reinforced Hale's concern that the organization of Black unions would be a negative reflection on Adventist race relations:

> The decision in favor of true integration of our current unions will enable the church to provide a less ambiguous, a more articulate and meaningful Christian witness to the world.
>
> The church is struggling to be the headlight and set the pace in race relations for the communications media, the business, educational, sports, and entertainment world, not the tail-light bringing up the rear. Secular society considers this to be one of Christianity's most obvious failures. In this matter the "true" or "remnant" church is hoping not to be weighed in the balances and found wanting. This is our great opportunity! Let us boldly move ahead![47]

All three established allegiance to the second proposition above with repeated statements that depicted integration as the "ideal" relational pattern in light of the instructions of the Bible and the writings of Ellen G. White. None did it more plaintively than Canson when he observed: "I am of the opinion that the text that says, 'Gather yourselves together, yea, gather together, O nation not desired; before the decree goes forth . . .' (Zeph. 2:1-2) is referring to the Seventh-day Adventists."[48] Or later when he commented:

> Mrs. E. G. White makes the following statement: "We are to practice the principles of heaven here below. In heaven there is one grand meeting place." (9T 197) I am not saying that we should forget that there are different races and that we melt into one society, but I am saying . . . let us be careful lest we further complicate the situation which will make it difficult for us to work in unison with our White brethren.[49]

As noted, however, while the integrationist forces all made the same general case, they did so from a variety of theoretical perspectives.[50]

Canson's dominant emphasis was cultural blending as a consequence of association between the races. He attacked what he called the "narrow thinking of cultural pluralism" and explained his fears that self-determination would prevent desired acculturation (integration) between the races, observing:

> Didn't Sister White say that "... God calls for a harmonious blending of a variety of talents?" In those churches where Whites and Blacks meet together ... a great opportunity exists for the harmonious blending of a variety of talents and every member can participate in a blending process.
>
> In those areas where the Blacks and Whites are members of different conferences, much of the blending is lost; but [there is a] uniting influence of the Union Conference.... There is a blending of talents of the Union Committee and a harmonious working together of an integrated staff in the Union office....
>
> Should our Regional Conferences be organized into Black unions, the only official blending of talents of the Whites and the Blacks would be on the General Conference Committee, which meets twice a year; at the General Conference Session, every five years; and at various Advisory Meetings.... We would not only be living in a pluralistic society, we will be part of a pluralistic church.[51]

Banfield gave more attention to the spiritual aspect of racial relations. He was convinced that Blacks must love even if it is "one-sided love," and that all methods should embody that principle, both as a means of reflecting true Christian values and as a weapon for softening the consciences of those guilty of oppression. "It is the nature of love to be sacrificial, and one-sided if it is genuine," he said. "This is love's strength and the distinctly Christian dimension of love contained in the meaning of the word *Agape*."[52]

And again, in his comments to the Advisory Board of the Office of Human Relations on October 9, 1979, he stated:

> In order for this vision to become a reality, we must help to develop in and among God's people a spirit that will enable them to transcend their ethnic, cultural, and physiological differences, likes and dislikes and to willingly become obedient to unenforceable obligations which are beyond the reach of the policies of the church or the laws of society.... Such obligations are met by an inner higher law written in our hearts which produces love. Human problems cannot be solved without the spirit of love and brotherhood. Love is still our most potent weapon for personal and social transformation.[53]

As discussed earlier, Hale differed from his integrationist colleagues in the matter of how he expressed his protest as well as in tactics. He was not only willing to speak out in the public arena, but appeared convinced that it was both proper and necessary to do so. Complementing the social emphasis of Canson's argument and the spiritual approach of Banfield was the *ethical* stress of Hale. His articles and speeches show consistent concern for the morality of self-determinationism. For him, moving to modified autonomy (Black unions) was tantamount to giving up on or deserting the fight for parity in the church. He ardently hoped that Black Seventh-day Adventists would not be guilty of ethical weakness by giving up a course (integration) for which so many (particularly Martin Luther King, Jr.) had fought and died; settling for less than the gospel "ideal" (integration) by yielding to a "philosophy of separatism" (Black unions) would be self-serving and reactionary rather than mediatory and unifying. In Hale's view:

> It is better to make it not by letting things ride, but by having some idea of where things ought to go and doing whatever is possible to make them go in that direction . . . the critical gap that exists between the nature of our witness and the calibre of our actions. . . . The opportunity for leadership holds out the buoyant hope that solving the problem within the ranks of Adventism may point the way toward elimination of the nation's most corrosive social illness and toward a more healthy state of the national conscience.[54]

And though Hale's later pronouncements were among the more provocative in the debate with the pro-Black union forces, his view was that all sides should seek peace: "The caution that must be observed, however, is in the area of strategies and tactics, for our cause is not *secular*, but *spiritual*. There is a fine line in many instances, we would agree, but Christians have never endorsed the philosophy that the *end* justifies the *means*."[55]

The irony of Hale's adamant opposition to Black unionists was not lost on those whose courage to protest for them had in no small sense been inspired by the boldness of the Layman's Leadership Counsel that Hale founded. In fact, it contributed to the awareness that determined integrationists, though differing as to solutions, were no less earnest than self-determinationists, both passionately motivated to protest.

## The Self-Determinationist Overview

Bradford, Cleveland, and Dudley supported their self-determinationist position with a number of common beliefs, such as (1) that cultural pluralism is so strong a reality of race relations in the United States that it requires, for a major minority, specialized arrangements; and (2) that the contemporary situation of African Americans in the Seventh-day

Adventist Church speaks more to the need for indigenous, local community authority than it does for additional access to the White community, and that one can justify this position not just sociologically but theologically—that is, by the counsels of the Bible and the writings of Ellen White.

Speaking about the issue of cultural pluralism, Cleveland wrote:

> My visits to South America and many other parts of the world convinced me that control of union conference organizations by indigenous leaders does not lessen the fervor with which they love their white brothers nor their faithfulness in the prosecution of the work. Rather, it forms what Ellen White calls a "unity of diversity" which has strengthened the church work.[56]

In similar language, he later observed:

> I should point out that the Spanish-speaking people had already requested of the General Conference that they consider organizing conferences simply because white America has not and will not assimilate them. Now these Spanish-speaking people are European and Caucasoid in origin. If the white man doesn't assimilate or integrate them, and they are having a hard time, what future do you hold out for the black man who is even farther from their ethnic strain? This is why we know that the only solution to our present problem is a larger degree of self-government. . . . Oh, and this goes for the Chinese and Japanese and all others.[57]

Both Bradford and Cleveland made strong arguments against accepting uninformed usage of terms implying oneness or unity. Cleveland put it this way:

> Let us not be lulled to sleep by slogans and phrases that mean one thing to us but quite another to our white brethren. Whether the words "unity," "togetherness" or "oneness" come from the lips of black or white, we must press for a definition of terms and discover the bottom line. . . . There is no substitute for limited autonomy in the organizations led by men. In the new earth, where "the kingdom will not be left to other people," we will experience the utopia where "a man is a man" for all that. Men are capable of limited justice, for all men are limited. But when the administrator is all-powerful, all-wise and everywhere present, justice may indeed run down like water and righteousness like a mighty stream.[58]

For Bradford, the dominant reason for seeking self-determination was for its practical benefits—increased mobility, better planning, and the consolidation of talent and resources. His was the pragmatic approach of one who understands clearly the functional problems at stake. He explained:

> It was because the climate in the predominantly white church made it impossible for the black man to exercise his gifts in freedom that black churches were organized. It was because the black minister was restricted on the conference level that the black conferences were organized. The same holds true on the union level.... The ultimate in separation is not separation of structures but of persons. The segregated church is not a creation of the regional conference. All things on the local church level remain as they were before 1945 [organization of regional conferences], no more, no less segregated. The creation of one or more Black Unions simply brings together existing conferences so that each may learn from the other so that the work may be unified and the structures more responsive to patent needs.[59]

Cleveland, on the other hand, appealed primarily to the principles of racial pride (dignity) and group solidarity for the acceptance of self-determination. He never more clearly expressed his concerns than when he wrote:

> We will not live quietly any longer with a *system* that denies our equality and insults our intelligence. We will *henceforth* resist being administered as a colony. We *insist* that the system be adjusted to accommodate our natural growth.... We *insist* that when men *who represent us* are being considered for high office that the decision be made by us....
>
> We say to our Brethren in Washington: We await some long-delayed hearty action that will alleviate our distress. Our liberality does not deserve the conservative financial policies now practiced toward us. Our past cooperation does not indicate contentment with the *organizational bottle-neck* that locks us in. We would, with one voice, solemnly urge you to take some "*hearty action*" to alleviate our distress![60]

While Dudley would agree with both Bradford and Cleveland in the views above, his primary appeal was for fairness—the freedom of what he would call the oppressed but loyal minority to chart its own destiny within the broad tent of unity in diversity.

In summary, while the theorists of both groups share much in common, we should see each as having an individuality that gives distinct character to his contributions in the struggle for equality in the Adventist Church.

## Latter Twentieth-Century Black Seventh-day Adventist Leadership Protest Styles

| NAME | EMPHASIS | PRINCIPLE | MEANS | BENEFIT | RISK | OBSTACLE |
|---|---|---|---|---|---|---|
| E. Canson | Blending | Unity | Association | Togetherness | Tokenism | White Flight |
| E. Cleveland | Political Empowerment | Practicality | Accommodation | Self-Determination | Separatism | Seen as Divisive |
| W. Banfield | Fellowship | Cultural Sharing | Education | Cultural Enhancement | Political Emasculation | Cultural Density |
| C. Bradford | Justice | Reparations | Policy Revision | Material Enhancement | Restitution as an End | Seen as Reverse Discrimination |
| C. Dudley | Fairness | Equality | Protest Within | Parity | Gradualism | Minority Inferior Voting Power |
| F. Hale | Rights | Just Laws | Protest Within / Without | Rights De facto | Rights De jure | Majority Fear of Loss of Power |

## DISSONANCE AND CONFLICT

As is often the case when leaders maintain fundamental differences of opinion in regard to strategies, the Black union controversy resulted in fissures of personal and professional relationships within Black Adventist leadership. The self-determinationists listed several actions of the integrationists to which they took exception and viewed as contributing to the breach.

One of the actions the self-determinationists particularly resented was the vocal resistance to the union proposal by Blacks holding jobs on the union and General Conference levels. Since the union proposal embraced reorganization at the local conference level, its proponents viewed as "meddling" the opposition of those Blacks no longer directly involved in the administration of Black local conferences and churches. The Black local conference presidents, in particular, disliked the fact that Blacks on the union and General Conference levels publicly contradicted their professional opinions as to what was best at the local conference level.

Another action that produced tensions was the opposition of individuals on the West Coast, where Regional conferences did not exist, and where, in the opinion of Black unionists, the question of creating Black unions was irrelevant. Black union proponents viewed the statements of representatives from that area as interference in affairs in which they had no stake and, therefore unethical, and as much as anything else, a defense of their own political status.

Another way that the integrationists irritated the self-determinationists was their use of deprecating rhetoric in their analysis of both the motives and capabilities of Black union proponents. That was especially so with regard to language used by leaders of the Laymen's Leadership Conference, the group that had for decades fought so hard to combat prejudice within the church and who saw the Black union thrust as a retreat from the Civil Rights Movement's demand for justice. LLC leaders not only disagreed with the Black union thrust as demonstrated in their statements, they also viewed its leaders, Black clergy, as less than capable in terms of academic background and structural freedom to accomplish such a radical change.[61]

Self-determinationists saw themselves demeaned by the public issuance of comments such as these:

- Being *"so-called"* leaders[62]
- Being dubbed the *"Black Union Boys"*[63] and *"would be"* statesmen[64]

- Being characterized as captains "decidedly shaky on their chart, compass, and steering apparatus"[65]
- The charge that they were administratively and operationally inefficient, and for which racism was but a "smoke screen"[66]
- Allegations that they employed "un-Christian" and "un-democratic" tactics[67]
- The charge of being *"actors and hustlers playing revolution,"* who would discredit the contributions of everyone other than themselves[68]
- The charge that the Black community needed to be aware that there is a difference between the *"committed"* and the *"comedians"*[69]

C. E. Dudley's letter of August 20, 1979, addressed to the four signatories of the LLC "open letter" referenced above, reflects the ire that the self-determinationists felt. He expressed his displeasure in a sternly worded communication:

> ... please reread your open letter to see if there isn't something that you should retract. The General Conference has organized a Committee on Litigation that deals with matters such as this. . . . P.S. When you have your meeting of the laymen from the regional conferences at the Harambee House in Washington, D.C., on September 12, I hope that your documents are correct and will stand investigation.[70]

Other practices of the integrationists that disturbed Black union advocates included:

- Use of the *North American Informant* (the periodical of the Black work) by the integrationist directors of the Office for Regional Conference Ministry (Fordham and Banfield) as a forum to discourage Black lay sympathies with the Black union movement
- The refusal of Fordham and Banfield (chairpersons of the Regional Advisory) not only to "carry the ball" but also to at least remain silent or neutral when they could not conscientiously support the actions of leaders they were elected to represent
- Their collaboration with Whites on an issue in which the White power structure already held the distinct advantage

With respect to the latter point, Black unionists thought it highly unfair that in addition to all the other handicaps with which they had to deal, they were disadvantaged by church leadership's consistent appointment of individuals (White and Black) negative to the Black union proposal as chairpersons of the study commissions; chairpersons of the discussion often openly agreeing with their opposition; and church administration regularly preceding each critical vote with articles in the *Adventist Review* stressing unity, a not too subtle implication that they viewed the Black union plan as divisive. Proponents of Black unions regarded such actions as crass political exploitation. They felt disrespected and "stepped on" by White leadership, and sabotaged by their Black brothers who joined forces with the White administration.

On the other hand, integrationists, many of whom had once been officers in the Regional conference structure, also had reasons to feel mistreated by the self-determinationists. One of the causes of resentment on the part of the integrationist group was their exclusion from strategy sessions held during the early stages. Being left out of the Black caucuses, where for so many years they had participated and even held leadership, was painful. Later, as the battle lines sharpened, neither side expected inclusion in the other's planning sessions. That, of course, given the escalating debate, was understandable but hurtful nevertheless.

Another self-determinationist action that disturbed the integrationists was the tendency of the Black unionists to think and speak of the integrationists as "sellouts." Since opposition to the proposal was weighted with individuals serving in upper-level administrative roles having less contact with the local church, and its proponents being primarily persons involved in local church conference and community activities, the derogatory slavery analogy of "house Negroes" versus "field Negroes" was easy to suggest in the heat of battle.

This differentiation between those Blacks who once served in easier jobs in the homes of slave owners from the more likely to rebel field hands who worked the land outdoors was, of course, for the most part, undeserved. While some may have opposed Black unions because they feared loss of their positions or prospects for higher places in the existing structure of Adventist administration, most, as the three leaders examined above, did not. They were convinced, as Canson, put it, that "Together is Better" and that even if over time not achieved, a state of togetherness is something Scripture mandates believers to pursue.

Perhaps the most serious or lasting fissures resulted from integrationist resentment with what appeared to be a number of vindictive measures employed by the Black union advocates. Among such measures were:

- The discontinuation of support for the beloved *North American Informant* magazine, used by the Regional Department editors to discredit the Black union idea
- Aggressive insistence on a change of the editor of *Message* magazine who also took sides against them
- Refusal (after the October 12, 1978, vote) to attend any meetings chaired by Banfield or Fordham
- Declining to attend any of the traditional Human Relations Councils called at the union or General Conference levels
- Refusal to invite Blacks on the union and General Conference staffs who publicly opposed them to the local conference functions that they might normally attend, such as camp meetings or ministerial workshops
- The organizing of national and regional caucuses (called departmental councils) without the participation or authorization of either the unions or the General Conference

But perhaps the most drastic consequence of the Black union proponents' unhappiness was the discontinuation of the Regional Department. Feeling betrayed by Fordham and Banfield, its director and associate, respectively, several leading Black union advocates (most of whom were Regional conference presidents) approached Neal C. Wilson, then NAD president, and convinced him to terminate the department. Whether or not Wilson was surprised or disappointed, he cooperated, and in 1979 successfully influenced its demise.

Warren Banfield, in a speech presented at the Laymen's Dinner Meeting at the Harambee House in Chicago, Illinois, on September 12, 1979, titled "Events Precipitating the Demise of the Regional Department," stated the case of the department's termination, frankly and accurately:

> The Regional Department and its journal *The Informant* became victims of the heated black union controversy. The General Conference decision to do away with this department was at the unanimous request of the regional conference presidents in a signed statement to the Vice President of the General Conference in charge of North America. This was done during the period of the Annual Council of 1977. At a called meeting of the Regional Presidents by N. C. Wilson, during this same session, at which W. W. Fordham and I were invited, it was verbally stated by several of the presidents with the assent of all that the department no longer served their needs and would no longer receive their support.[71]

Banfield further observed:

> I suggested to the President of the General Conference and the Vice President in charge of North America that there was no way the Regional Department could fulfill its mission without these leaders' support, and that it would probably be prudent to comply with their request. One of the main reasons given for the request to do away with the Regional Department was the fact that its directors, Elders W. W. Fordham, and W. S. Banfield, would not give personal support to the . . . request for black unions.[72]

The Black unionist Committee of Ten had dealt with this last point almost a year earlier, December 4, 1978, in correspondence replying to Banfield's notification of his appointment to head the newly created Department of Human Relations:

> We wish you well and believe that the department of "Ethnic Relations" can be helpful in building inter-group understandings. What we do not like about your letter is the inference in the final paragraph that we allowed a mere difference of opinion to rupture relations and interfere with a healthy working climate. If, in fact, relationships have been affected in the current debate, it is not that you differ, but in our opinion, you were unethical and discourteous in the use of your office. . . . Please do not mistake our disenchantment of such conduct with the inability to be disagreed with; it is, rather, the unwillingness to allow those who supposedly represent us to undermine and combat our objectives. (Appendix 25)

## CRISIS AVERTED

As sobering and serious as were the fissures of personal and professional relationships occasioned by the Black union debates, a more threatening consequence had developed: the potential for structural schism within the body of believers. The Black unionists, in the bitter wake of their 1978 defeat, developed plans to organize what they termed "Regional Territories." In effect they were quasi Black unions staffed along existing union lines, but for strictly evangelistic programming (Appendix 26).

C. E. Dudley, now the unofficial but undisputed chairman of the self-appointed Committee of Ten, issued the official notice of the first meeting of the Regional Territories' Councils in Huntsville, Alabama, on December 3, 1979. It included all of the Regional conferences complete with conference delegates and rules and regulations mirroring standard union constituencies (Appendix 27).

Black union advocates let it be known that they considered the Regional Territories' Councils as a means "to do Black unions anyway." However, in retrospect, it is highly probable that had the meetings taken place and territorial councils established, they would have, in short order, absorbed more of Regional conference energies and loyalties than the existing unions. Further, it is not too much to say that given this potential, had Territorial Councils begun, it is very likely that it would have elicited disapproval and even sanctions, moral and otherwise, from higher levels of the church.

Given the positions and influence of the chief planners, sanctions of any kind against them and their followers would have created the possibility of structural fractures much more broad and pervasive than those that occurred during the push for Colored conferences. The planners were not unaware of this potential.

What emboldened the planners to contemplate such a radical step and to confront its consequences was what they interpreted as the extremely unfair way in which the various study committees had been structured and the meetings conducted. They could not forget that more often than not, chairpersons opposed to the proposal officiated over the study committees and usually found ways to weigh-in against the Black union concept. What they saw was consistent, organized opposition from Blacks in the upper echelons of church administration and, in their view, the outside interference of Blacks on the West Coast, where no functional issues were involved. This appearance of programmed unfairness gave most of the advocates a sense akin to that of martyrdom, thus creating a willingness to do whatever necessary for what they saw as right.

The stakes could not have been higher: The Huntsville meetings could have caused a major rift in the Seventh-day Adventist Church in North America—and this, not only in terms of structural fragmentation, but, considering the existing moods and tensions, the service careers of a number of the proposal's proponents. Realizing what was at issue, the planners, at the last minute, changed the date to January 14, 1980, and the location from Huntsville to Atlanta, Georgia, a less politically charged site.

While the shift of date and location gave the chief planners more time to shape the Regional Territorial Councils, it had other consequences. One was the request for participation by dedicated sympathizers around the country. Another was the excitement generated among those who felt that, given the racial indignities perpetuated through the decades, this was the moment when Black Adventists, like their counterparts in many other denominations, might break away and begin their own branch of the church. On the other hand, the delay gave time for reflection and second thoughts by certain Black union supporters, who were not willing to brave the likely consequences of any hardening of positions and probable denominational reprisals. The most significant consequence of the delay, however, was that it gave time for church leadership to act preventively—and it did so in the most unexpected but persuasive manner imaginable: the request from C. E. Bradford, former Black union advocate and now president of the church in North America for approximately one year, that the meeting not be held.

On January 9, 1980, less than a week before the rescheduled meetings, the Regional Conference presidents received from Bradford an urgent telegram: "Because of the intensity of the discussion occasioned by the decision to set up territorial councils, I feel that [the] January 14 meeting should be cancelled."[73] Bradford followed up his telegram with a letter to conference presidents, including Dudley, his dear friend and former ally in the movement, with further rationale for his position. The two-page letter has as its key sentence, "Elder Wilson and the union presidents are, of course, concerned. But I, above all the rest, sense a deep concern because all that I had hoped to be to you and your fields is on the line" (Appendix 28).

With that very direct counsel and appeal in hand, Dudley canceled the meeting. His communication to the delegates, both ministerial and lay, explained his decision:

> Some of the brethren have learned, so I am told, that the Regional Conference presidents have been credited with Elder R. H. Pierson's early retirement and failing health, with the early retirement of Elder W. W. Fordham from the G. C., with the closing of the office of Regional Affairs in the G. C., with planning the dismissal of Elder L. B. Reynolds from the editorship of the Message Magazine and now with the possibility of the vice president's [Bradford] dismissal from his job. These charges are not true; however, some of the leaders felt that if the Atlanta meeting was to place the vice president's position in jeopardy with his brethren on the union and general levels, it would best to honor his request that we cancel the meeting on January 14. (Appendix 29)

Bradford's appeal and Dudley's rather grudging concurrence notwithstanding, several Black leaders decided to meet in Atlanta anyway and were dissuaded only after it was determined that there were too few others willing to attend to accomplish anything significant, and their efforts were not worth risking blame for hampering the work of the first African-American president of the North American Division. Thus concluded the third, and most divisive, of the major twentieth-century freedom protests of Black Seventh-day Adventist leadership.

### Notes

1. For the most extensive treatment of the LLC and its protest at the 1962 General Conference, see Frank W. Hale's *Out of the Trash Came Truth* (Columbus, OH: Frank Hale, 2007). (http://www.blacksdahistory.org/files/48474371.pdf)

2. F. W. Hale, Jr., *Angels Watching Over Me* (Nashville: James C. Winston Publishing Co., 1996), 160.

3. Laymen's Leadership Conference Constitution Article 2, C. B. Rock, Private Collection.

4. Open Letter from the Laymen's Leadership Conference, July 4, 1961. See also Hale, *Angels Watching Over Me*, 176.

5. Ibid., 170.

6. Hale, *Angels Watching Over Me*, 201.

7. From here on, "Black union conferences" will be referred to as "Black unions."

8. The General Conference Archives has an abundance of material on the subject of Black unions, as covered in this chapter.

9. Actions from the Regional Advisory Committee in Miami, April 7–9, 1969. (http://documents.adventistarchives.org/Periodicals/RH/RH19700604-V147-23.pdf)

10. Technically, at the time this position was the vice president of the General Conference for the North American Division. However, Wilson was effectively the NAD president.

11. Neal C. Wilson, "Recent Developments in the Field of Human Relations in North America," *Adventist Review*, June 4, 1970, 9. (http://documents.adventistarchives.org/Periodicals/RH/RH19700604-V147-23.pdf)

12. Neal C. Wilson, "Advisability of Black Unions" (speech, Autumn Council Session, Takoma Park, Maryland, October 13, 1977), 5–7.

13. "Should the church organize black unions in North America?" *Adventist Review*, September 7, 1978, 4–6. (http://documents.adventistarchives.org/Periodicals/RH/RH19780907-V155-36.pdf)

14. See Jocelyn Fay, "Annual Council 1978—major issues among the routine," *Adventist Review*, November 9, 1978, 4–9. (http://documents.adventistarchives.org/Periodicals/RH/RH19781109-V155-45.pdf)

15. Marjorie Hyer, "Adventists Reject Black's Proposal," *Washington Post*, October 20, 1978, 1.

16. Letter to N. C. Wilson from the Committee of Ten, October 16, 1978. C. B. Rock Private Collection.

17. Ibid.

18. Minutes of the General Conference Committee, January 11, 1979, 79–12.

(http://docs.adventistarchives.org/docs/GCC/GCC1979-01.pdf#view=fit)

19. For a good overview of Banfield's involvement in civil rights, see Samuel G. London, Jr., *Seventh-day Adventists and the Civil Rights Movement* (Jackson: University of Mississippi, 2006), 136–149.

20. Concerned Christian Council Meeting Minutes, May 19, 1969. C. B. Rock Private Collection.

21. W. S. Banfield, "The Great Black Union Controversy: Additional Cognitions," February 23, 1978. C. B. Rock Private Collection.

22. Among W. S. Banfield's more widely read articles are: "*Some Observations of the Regional Union Proposal*" (1977); "Events Precipitating the Demise of the Regional Department" (September 12, 1979); "*The Great Black Union Controversy—Additional Cognitions*" (February 12, 1978); "Remarks to the Office of Human Relations (OHR) Advisory Board" (Tuesday, October 9, 1979); "*Suggestions for Improving Race Relations Within the Seventh-day Adventist Church*" (1980).

23. White, who like Canson spent his entire ministry on the West Coast, served for many years as the first Black secretary of the Pacific Union. Though not as structurally connected to the Black churches as Canson, White was in some ways more visible in that his position lent official authority to his vision.

24. Earl A. Canson, "The Pacific Union Conference Regional Department—Fact and Figures, 1975," 2.

25. Canson spelled out his social philosophy in two articles that generated national attention: "*The Pacific Union Conference Regional Department—Fact and Figures*" (1975), and "*How Much Should the Church Be Divided?*" (June, 1978). He also maintained broad literary contact through his editorship of the *Regional News*—a quarterly newsletter regarding activities in the territory he served.

26. Frank W. Hale, Jr., "Commitment vs. Capitulation," *Spectrum*, Spring 1970, 39. (http://blacksdahistory.org/files/40119017.pdf)

27. Among Hale's more memorable addresses on the subject of race relations within the church are the titles "*Human Values and Denominational Policy: An Open Letter to the General Conference and All Seventh-day Adventists*" (July 26, 1962); "*The Task Ahead*" (June 19, 1956); and "Commitment Versus Capitulation, or Where Do We Go from Here?" (January 13, 1970).

28. Martin Luther King, Jr., "I Have a Dream."

29. C. E. Bradford, "An Appeal to the Leadership of the Seventh-day Adventist Church to Give Special Study to the Position of the Negro Seventh-day Adventist in American Society and in the Church," 2, General Conference Archives.

30. Ibid., 6, 7.

31. For instance, "Letter to R. R. Figuhr, President General Conference of SDA" (1/9/1964); "Tithe Percentages and Regional Conferences" (2/8/65); "Facing Reality" (1/8/67); "An Appeal to the Leadership of the Seventh-day Adventist Church to Give Special Study to the Position of The Negro Seventh-day Adventist in American Society and in the Church" (early 1966) and "The Case for Black Unions" (undated). C. B. Rock Private Collection.

32. E. E. Cleveland also made myriad presentations on the subject of race relations,

such as the following: "Brief on Regional Conferences" (April 11, 1968); "Regional Unions" (January 1970); "White Paper on Black People" (April 4, 1976); "Comment on the Paper 'Black Unions: Options and Consequences' by Dr. Betty Sterling" (July 1977); "To the Kingdom" (July 1978); "A Report to the People" (January 1, 1979). "Opinion," a regular editorial in the *North American Regional Voice*, continued Cleveland's leadership role. Articles he wrote for that publication include "Brotherhood in the Black Church" (April 1981); "Reaganomics and the Church" (May 1981); "A Declaration of Principle" (June 1981); "Together We Stand" (August 1981); "The Dilemma of the Middle Class" (September 1981); "*Self-Help*" (November 1981); and "Upside Down" (December 1981). This can be accessed here: http://documents.adventistarchives.org/Periodicals/Forms/AllItems.aspx?RootFolder=%2fPeriodicals%2fRV&FolderCTID=0x012000DDAC5B94CFBD234AB142FC5C311C732700042C85EA7C1C1A4DB8D75C62A7517A6E.

33. E. E. Cleveland to Ron Graybill, March 27, 1979, C. B. Rock Private Collection. Graybill's classic is now available here: http://documents.adventistarchives.org/Books/EGWCRR1970.pdf.

34. Ellen G. White, *The Spirit of Prophecy*, vol. 1 (Battle Creek, MI: Seventh-day Adventist Publishing Association, 1870), 78. (https://egwwritings.org/?ref=en_1SP.78.2&para=141.314)

35. Ellen G. White, *Testimonies for the Church*, vol. 9 (Mountain View, CA: Pacific Press Publishing Association, 1909), 214. (https://egwwritings.org/?ref=en_9T.214.3&para=115.1201)

36. Ellen G. White, *The Southern Work* (Washington, DC: Review and Herald, 1966), 95.

37. Ellen G. White, "Trust in God," *The Gospel Herald*, March 1, 1901, paragraph 20. (https://egwwritings.org/?ref=en_GH.March.1.1901.par.20&para=503.250)

38. E. E. Cleveland to C. D. Brooks, April 18, 1979, Oakwood University Archives.

39. Charles E. Dudley, *Thou Who Hast Brought Us Thus Far on Our Way* (Mansfield, OH: BookMasters, 2000), 297.

40. Ibid.

41. Ibid.

42. Ibid., 303.

43. Charles E. Dudley, Sr., *"Thou Who Hath Brought Us:" The Development of the Seventh-day Adventist Denomination Among African Americans* (Brushton, NY: Teach Services, 1997); *Thou Who Hast Brought Us Thus Far on Our Way* (Mansfield, OH: BookMasters, 2000).

44. Charles E. Dudley, Sr., *The Genealogy of Ellen Gould Harmon White: The Prophetess of the Seventh-day Adventist Church* (Nashville: Dudley Publishing Services, 1999).

45. Banfield, "Events Precipitating the Demise of the Regional Department," September 12, 1979, 2.

46. Hale, "Commitment vs. Capitulation," 34.

47. W. S. Banfield, "Observations on the Regional Union Proposal," August 3, 1977, 1–2. C. B. Rock Private Collection.

48. Earl A. Canson, "How Much Should the Church Be Divided?" June 1978, 8. C. B. Rock Private Collection.

49. Ibid., 9.

50. With the exception of Hale, these men were not trained scholars treating their subjects with the tools of academia. Rather, we should view them as sensitive, experienced, and articulate Christian leaders swept up by the issues of the most exciting socio-religious debate of their generation; or, for that matter, of the century.

51. Canson, "How Much Should the Church Be Divided?," 10–11.

52. W. S. Banfield to C. B. Rock, July 26, 1978. C. B. Rock Private Collection.

53. W. S. Banfield, "Remarks to the Office of Human Relations (OHR) Advisory Board" (Tuesday, October 9, 1979), 2, 3. C. B. Rock Private Collection.

54. Hale, *Commitment Versus Capitulation*, 21.

55. Ibid., 24.

56. E. E. Cleveland, "Regional Union Conference," *Spectrum*, Spring 1970, 43.

57. E. E. Cleveland, "Comment on the Paper 'Black Unions: Options and Consequences' by Dr. Betty Stirling," 6, 7.

58. Ibid., 7.

59. Bradford, "The Case for Black Unions."

60. Cleveland, *"To the Kingdom,"* 13, 14.

61. Helen Beckett, Samuel Coleman, Frank Hale, Jr., and Burrell Scott, "Open Letter to the SDA Regional Constituency" (August 20, 1979), 1.

62. Ibid.

63. Ibid.

64. The Committee of Concerned Laymen, "Upfront: Where Are We Headed?" September 12, 1979, 2.

65. Ibid., 2.

66. Ibid., 4.

67. Ibid., 5.

68. Hale, *Commitment Versus Capitulation*, 25.

69. Ibid., 37.

70. C. E. Dudley, response to "An Open Letter to the SDA Constituency of August 20, 1979." South Central Conference, September 4, 1979, 2, 3.

71. Warren Banfield, "Events Precipitating the Demise of the Regional Department," Chicago, September 12, 1979.

72. Ibid.

73. C. E. Bradford, telegram to C. E. Dudley; see C. E. Dudley, President of the South Central Conference, to D. A. Walker, I. J. Johnson, Arthur Sanders, P. E. Vincent, W. Murrain, W. E. Coopwood, J. E. Merideth, C. B. Rock, and E. E. Cleveland, letter "Re: Territorial Councils Meeting—Atlanta," January 21, 1980. C. B. Rock Private Collection.

# 4
## THE PUSH FOR EQUITABLE RETIREMENT SECURITY, 1998–2000

Little could those who pushed so ardently for Black unions know that the next generation of Black leaders would, years later, credit their efforts as having provided inspiration for the fourth and final major Black Adventist leadership protest of the twentieth century. That, however, according to more than one of those involved, was unquestionably the case. Conducted by the Black President's Council comprised of leaders of the eight existing Regional conferences, it was the most brief but by no means the least significant of Black leadership's endeavors to seek parity.

The Council was led in the late 1990s by chairperson Alvin Kibble, president of the Alleghany East Conference (1989–2002), and secretary Joseph McCoy, president of the South Central Conference (1993–2005). It mounted and succeeded in a protest that, in two years of intensely contested discussions, accomplished what was previously unthinkable—withdrawal of the Regional conferences from what many had regarded as the North American Division's untouchable central retirement system.

A major spur to action was the Council members' realization that while they put into the church's central retirement fund the same percentage of conference tithe (at the time 10.75 percent) as did White-administered conferences, and while the benefits paid to individual White and Black retirees were the same, the plan did not benefit the two groups equally.

More specifically, they thought it was not fair to Blacks as a group for several reasons: (1) the shorter lifespan of Blacks (particularly males) meant that they had considerably fewer retirement years to benefit from the fund;[1] (2) their contribution to the fund was helping to support hundreds of White retirees from dozens of church entities that hired few and in many cases no Blacks at all; (3) many of the latter church entities (e.g., publishing houses, union conference offices, union conference colleges) made no contribution to the retirement fund; and (4) the disparity in "household net worth" between White and Black Americans (often due to intergenerational wealth) meant that although Black retirees received the same retirement dollar amount as Whites, they were, as a rule, less secure when their service ended.

We can best appreciate the effect of this latter factor (intergenerational wealth) when it is known that, as late as 2013, the median White family net worth in the United States was thirteen times greater than that of the Black family.[2] Among the families studied, Whites were five times more likely to inherit than Blacks, and their typical inheritance was ten times greater.[3] Although the reasons for this are admittedly complex, few would deny that the perpetration of racial inequality toward Blacks in America's past—such as Blacks being denied adequate educational opportunities; denied employment due to their hue; earning less than Whites for doing the same job; being rejected for loan applications; or being offered loans with exorbitant interest rates—plays a large role in the discrepancy.

Yet there was another major consideration involved in the protest for a fair retirement system: the historically lax retirement preparations of early and mid-twentieth century Black Adventist clergy. The "any day now!" belief in the Second Coming of Christ, strongly held by Black Adventist ministers and members, influenced their retirement planning. On the other hand, their White counterparts, in the main, were planning for the long term. Thus, in general, Black Adventists' strong belief regarding an "immediate" rather than a somewhat more distant end to this world had more typically obviated their interest in stock market investments, the purchase of houses and land, and other long term investments.[4]

By the 1990s that mindset was changing. As Paul cautioned the Thessalonians to understand that the Second Coming might occur beyond their lifetime (1 Thess. 5:10; 2 Thess. 2:1–4), Black Adventists too began to accept "soon-ness" rather than "immediacy" as the time-frame for Christ's return. One reason is the continuing passage of time. Another is improvement of socio-economic status that has permitted a growing number to engage in long-term investing.[5]

Coinciding with Black Adventism's awakening to the need for personal long-range financial planning was the growing conviction that change in the church's retirement system was not only needed but should be openly addressed. Thaddeus Wilson (1917–1976), senior pastor of the City Tabernacle Church in New York City from 1967 to 1971, is the first known advocate for the idea. Emboldened by what he had gleaned from his recently earned degree in business at Suffolk University in Boston, Wilson made several attempts to convince his conference leaders that they should take action, even if independent of church policy, to improve the church's existing retirement plan. He was, however, widely regarded as espousing a cause that, even if just, had no possibility of succeeding.

At the same time, Charles E. Dudley, then president of the South Central Conference, held a similar view to Wilson and was in a position to change things, and did so. Burdened by the plight of aging retirees in the five-state area that he administered, and, in particular, touched by the plight of their widows who simply could not survive on the 50 percent of their husbands' pension to which the policy had reduced them, Dudley convinced his conference committee to establish a fund that provided up to $500 per month in additional income to retirees.

JOSEPH W. MCCOY, president of South Central Conference and champion of the Regional conference retirement plan. Courtesy of the General Conference Archives.

In spite of the fact that the White leadership of the Southern Union and the NAD rebuked both Dudley and his successor, Joseph McCoy, who continued the plan, they refused to discontinue the conference's retirement supplementation program. Their actions brought welcome relief to a number of struggling retirees. But it produced considerable angst in the upper levels of church administration, where it was assumed that such a breach of practice might lead to attempts at more independent retirement arrangements at the local conference level. They were correct.

The actions of South Central's leadership inspired the other Regional conferences, several of which implemented similar retirement supplementation programs. It was not until 1998 that they abandoned their individual methods of dealing with the problem and unitedly approached the North American Division retirement administrators about their need. The Division responded that it was unable to make the adjustments requested. Convicted, however, of the necessity to move forward, the presidents consulted several of the nation's better-known insurers of non-profit organizations regarding their concerns.

The actuarial advice they received confirmed their perceptions that there were inequities in the system. A critical revelation was that retirement expense as a percentage of salary for an ongoing plan should range from a minimum of 4 percent to a maximum of 15 percent, depending on the industry. It was found that while all but one of the nine Regional conferences were contributing more than 20 percent, only twenty-three of the forty-two White conferences were doing so.

They further found that only 452 of the 12,900 retirees on the NAD plan (4 percent) were Regional conference and Oakwood College retirees. They also learned that Regional conferences were being additionally disadvantaged in that while all NAD conferences were contributing more than was required to care for the retirement needs of their individual fields, Regional conferences had, between the years of 1996 and 1999 *alone*, contributed approximately 43 percent of the entire amount needed to fully care for *all* Regional conference and Oakwood College workers throughout their retirement years in perpetuity. These additional revelations stiffened the Regional conference presidents' resolve, causing them to accelerate their determination to find relief, whether within or without the system. They began heightening their efforts by involving their conference committees and pastors in structuring options for their own separate retirement plan.[6]

NAD leadership, apprised of the Black leaders' continued activity and the challenges posed by the withdrawal of the Regional conferences from the church's plan—not the least of which was the loss of revenue—formally reacted. They arranged a meeting of the Regional conference presidents, chaired by the General Conference president, even though it was an NAD issue. The meeting was held at GC headquarters on January 4, 2000, with the president, secretary, and treasurer of the General Conference; all nine NAD union presidents; and all nine Regional conference presidents. The Black presidents, whose summons to attend the meeting was received on December 26, 1999, met all day on January 3 of the new year in preparation for what they knew would be a difficult session. They agreed to have only three spokespersons—Kibble and McCoy, their two leading officers, as well as Norman Miles, president of the Lake Region Conference. The meeting, on January 4, as much a threat to major schism as was the aborted January 14, 1980, meeting of protesting Black unionists, was polite but tense. The decisive moment of the meeting came when GC president Jan Paulsen asked what they (the Black presidents) would do if institutional pressures were brought to bear to stop their efforts. Miles, ever the academic and statesman, replied calmly but firmly, "Mr. President, when a bus is going in the wrong direction there are only three options: keep going, turn around, or get off!"[7]

Impressed by both the merits of the Black presidents' case and their resolve to move forward, Paulsen, in one of the most meaningful though unheralded decisions of his tenure, agreed that the matter deserved further study. His wise and moral action led to the appointment of Mardian J. Blair, a recently retired and highly respected health system administrator, to chair a consultant committee to study the matter and render a report. The results of the committee's investigation, presented a few months later, confirmed and, in fact, strengthened the Black presidents' position.

## REGIONAL CONFERENCE RETIREMENT PLAN

Armed with the independent analysis of various insurance agencies, fortified with the findings of the Blair report, convinced that the NAD's pending change from a defined benefit to an employee contribution plan would further disadvantage Black retirees, and having no evidence of the church's willingness or ability to make an accommodation, the Black presidents acted. They settled with the Mutual of America Life Insurance Company in an arrangement providing superior benefits with considerably less costs, covering all present and future qualifying retirees. They agreed among themselves, however, to sign official documents only after allowing the NAD an opportunity to officially approve their severance from its plan.

The NAD, in turn, indicated a willingness to do so but with the requirement that the presidents "place back" into the NAD fund $25,000,000 to assist in refunding the gap created by their withdrawal. The presidents agreed (and as of 2017 were nearing completion of that obligation). NAD approval was voted at its Year-End Meeting in October, 2000. The presidents finalized documents with Mutual of America in December of 2000 with eight of the nine Regional conferences participating. Its operation began on January 1, 2001.

Withdrawal from the plan, though formally voted, was not without pain for all parties involved. Repercussions were felt by (1) NAD leadership, who, having unsuccessfully tried to prevent Regional conference withdrawal, found themselves accused of weakness for "allowing" Black leadership to succeed; (2) NAD retirement fund administrators who faced the difficult task of replacing lost revenue and otherwise restructuring as a result of Regional conference withdrawal; and (3) Regional conference presidents, who were labeled as disloyal and told by more than one White church leader that "they would pay" for their actions.

While it cannot be proven, many in the Adventist Black community believed that the 2005 transfer of African American Ella Simmons from her post as provost and vice president for academic administration at La Sierra University to a General Conference vice presidency, a move unprecedented in terms of gender and ministerial and administrative backgrounds, was a reaction to the Regional conference retirement development. Black leadership recognized it as an astute political maneuver—a means of honoring the tradition of promoting an African American to the office of a General Conference vice president, but doing so in a manner that, while obviously ignoring traditional requisites for such a high GC position (i.e., an ordained male for the North American Black leadership group, sometimes referred to as the Black Caucus), left them without reasonable grounds for complaint.

I admit to feeling conflicted, at first, regarding her election. On the one hand, it was I who had noted her technical abilities and people skills a few years earlier and had successfully pushed to include her as a lay member of the General Conference executive committee. I admit to experiencing a good deal of satisfaction in helping to position a female, and an African American, at that, to membership in that august assembly.

On the other hand, when GC president Paulsen called me shortly before the church's 2005 General Conference session in St. Louis to get my opinion of Simmons serving as a vice president of the General Conference, I was torn. I knew that Black Adventism was, as is the case at every General Conference session, on high alert regarding selection for this position. In fact, since Peterson's election in 1962, it has been for them the most anticipated action of every GC session.

I knew further that versions of the "pay back" narrative mentioned above were stoking the concerns of Black attendees. I also knew that a strong recommendation for Simmons would not be helpful to their hopes of seeing another individual with Black Caucus connections elected as a GC vice president (there had not been one since my retirement in January 2002). However, sensing the improbability of someone from those ranks being nominated (whether for reasons connected with the retirement protest or not), and excited about the prospects of having a qualified female serve at this level of responsibility, I recommended her highly.

Happily, the decision has proven extremely beneficial to the world church. Simmons has provided invaluable service not only as an academic administrator but also as a glowing symbol of racial and gender capability. Meanwhile, two of the Regional conference presidents leading out in the retirement protest were called to broader responsibilities. Alvin Kibble, in 2001, was elected as a vice president for the North American Division. Alex Bryant, in 2008, was elected the Division secretary.

ALVIN KIBBLE, vice president of the North American Division and chair of the Black Caucus. Courtesy of the General Conference Archives.

The operation of the retirement plan is administered from the Office for Regional Conference Ministry on the campus of Oakwood University. It serves approximately 600 employees, and its investment portfolio has reached more than $200 million. The average retiree monthly benefits range from $2,500 to $3,000, on average, approximately $1,000 more than retirees on the standard NAD plan. The health benefits are the same, but vesting takes place in five years rather than ten, and retirement with full benefits is available after thirty rather than forty years of service.[8]

## OAKWOOD UNIVERSITY AND THE RETIREMENT PLAN

It is no surprise that the employees of the Black-administered Oakwood University had from the beginning coveted the superior benefits of the Regional conference retirement plan. In fact, early on, the school's faculty petitioned to give study to ways in which they could be included. The plan's administrators were amenable to their inclusion. However, although the school's governing board is regarded as autonomous by its major accreditation body, its internal designation as a General Conference institution negated any practical means of disengaging from the program operated by the North American Division on its behalf.

Clearly, the world church could not afford any more defections from its tightly administered retirement arrangement. To do so would have opened the gates for still others to leave, wreaking havoc on the complicated and long-standing retirement system. Having eight of the NAD's fifty-eight local conferences, three levels structurally removed from the GC, break away, was one thing; but to have a GC institution do so would have been structurally impossible without General Conference consent.[9] Furthermore, Oakwood, as all other Adventist educational institutions, was benefiting fully from the fund and not paying into it, which meant that it lacked financial leverage with which to press its desire.

Oakwood University's successful appeal at the 2015 Annual Council to change its governance from the General Conference to the North American Division has opened the door for possible reconsideration of Oakwood's involvement in the Regional conference retirement plan. The move, one that surprised many, did take place in part to open up this possibility, but was not the main reason. The primary consideration was that by the early years of the twenty-first century, the Regional conference appropriation to the school's annual budget had grown to greatly exceed that of the General Conference, historically the major source of the school's financial support. Cumulative appropriation amounts for the years 2005 to 2015 from the General Conference were $13,197,722. The Regional conferences' total for the same period, however, was $61,149,199, or approximately five times greater, indicating that the North American Division had become the major supporter of the school. Also, for all practical purposes, Oakwood was more functionally aligned with NAD schools of higher education than those of the General Conference.[10]

Furthermore, the General Conference's trend of reducing the percentage of financial support for Oakwood, caused by the world church's lessening income and growing responsibilities to other institutions that it has traditionally sponsored (i.e., Loma Linda University and Andrews University), shows no sign of reversal. Additional rationale for shifting the relationship included (1) the felt need for closer affiliation with the other schools of higher education in the nation rather than the two major universities under

General Conference direction; and (2) the fact that structural evolution, produced by "the coming of age" of Regional conferences, had reduced the General Conference to a very small percentage (approximately five percent) of Oakwood's Board membership.

As a kind of "back channel," Oakwood for 110 years provided Black Adventism with special access to church headquarters. The "double bind" of external (societal) oppression mandated by "Separate but Equal" (1896–1954) and internal suppression (Adventism's reluctance to counter society's prevailing atmosphere) made that channel especially important. In many respects this relationship, which by-passed standard local, union, and division conference authority, gave valuable top-down support for numerous initiatives helpful to Oakwood. And even when it did not, Black leaders valued it, because it afforded them the opportunity to at least "vent" to the highest level of church authority.

However, continued development of Black Adventism made the loss of that privileged access inevitable. By the century's end, Black Adventists' condition was far different in character from that of the helpless children of slaves at Oakwood's beginning in 1896, or the marginalized group whose good required establishing a Colored Department in 1909 and appointment of a Black director in 1918, or the surprised petitioners who gathered at McElhany's call to establish Colored conferences in 1943.

The exponential growth of these conferences' memberships and financial ability during the last half of the twentieth century, the dismantling of the General Conference Regional Department in 1978, and, most of all, the establishment of a separate retirement fund in 2000, all signaled Black American Adventism's coming of age and lesser need for a special tie to the church's parent body.

History will recall that it was Oakwood's shift to NAD status in 2015, fueled in part by its hopes of participation in the Regional conference retirement program, that removed the last of Black Adventism's reasons for direct access to world headquarters. However, it was Black leadership's successful retirement protest fifteen years earlier that gave both visible and emotional credence to that arrangement.

Ironically, the full consequences of this loss did not dawn immediately upon Black leadership. They were surprised during the sixtieth session of the General Conference in San Antonio, Texas, in 2015, when General Conference president, Ted Wilson, told them, in essence, that Black membership in the United States (approximately two percent of the world church total), no longer had the right or a reason to bypass union and division leadership channels to reach the General Conference president. He was correct.

Upon reflection, the Black presidents agreed and are content to shed the patronage of yesteryear for the greater psychological and material benefits they and their constituents now enjoy. Meanwhile, a number of pastors in White-administered conferences have expressed interest in joining the Regional conference plan, but no significant movement in that direction has yet emerged. Black retirees in the two West Coast unions would also appreciate its superior benefits but are, by policy, locked into the standard arrangement. And that is bad news for them on two accounts: first, they typically spend their service years with less family financial resources than their White counterparts, and then, when retired, spend their after-years with less retirement income than their Regional conference peers.

Further, the conferences in the Pacific and North Pacific unions find it almost impossible to recruit and retain accomplished pastors from the nine Regional conferences—a distinct disadvantage in terms of talent infusion.

In balance, this final protest by Black Adventist leaders at the cusp of the twenty-first century was a glowing success. It was achieved with a degree of unified agreement unmatched in the previous protests.

This review of the four major protests lays the groundwork for the next part of this volume which contains my personal views on the discussion to terminate Regional conferences that began shortly after Black Adventists finally attained to something approaching racial parity in the church structure.

**Notes**

1. "The average life expectancy of Black men in 2009 was just 71 (compared to 76 for White men)." Lauren F. Friedman, "Huge Racial Gap in Life Expectancy," *Business Insider,* Jan. 4, 2014. http://www.businessinsider.com/huge-racial-gap-in-life-expectancy-2014-1.

2. Tanzina Vega, "Blacks Still Far Behind Whites in Wealth and Income," *CNN Money,* June 27, 2017. http://money.cnn.com/2016/06/27/news/economy/racial-wealth-gap-blacks-whites/index.html. Accessed July 31, 2017.

3. Amy Traub, with Laura Sullivan, Tatjana Meschede, and Tom Shapiro, "The Asset Value of Whiteness: Understanding the Racial Wealth Gap," February 6, 2017. http://www.demos.org/sites/default/files/publications/Asset%20Value%20of%20Whiteness_0.pdf. Accessed August 21, 2017.

4. This was a difference that I personally came to understand when, at age thirty-seven, I left the familiar circumstances of the Regional conference pastorate to serve the entire Southern Union Conference as Associate Ministerial Secretary. I was genuinely surprised to find that many of my White colleagues enjoyed earnings from business ventures (some done in the names of their wives) and, very early in their ministry, were already considering retirement issues. There are, in fact, several streets near the former Southern Union Conference office in Decatur, Georgia, with names which testify to the enterprising spirit of White Adventist clergy as far back as the 1960s.

5. An example of this dynamic, and a very personal one, is that when Robert L. Bradford, mentioned in the Introduction, who had inspired his son and two grandsons to enter Adventist ministry, died in 1958 after approximately fifty years of service, it was necessary for his descendants to help fund his burial. We were privileged and happy to do so. Should time last, however, the three ministers who followed his lead will need no such assistance.

A critical difference is the changing attitude described above. Another is the improved retirement position of Regional conference retirees. As seen, the family of Bradford's descendants who exited service on the Regional conference retirement plan has a clear financial advantage over the two who did not, even though they both retired at the highest level of the church's pension bracket.

6. Norman K. Miles, "What Is Right and Pleasing?" *Regional Voice* (Special Summer Edition, 2000), 4–5.

7. This was relayed to the author by an attendee of the meeting.

8. Data provided by the Regional Retirement Office, Huntsville, Alabama.

9. As Delbert Baker, Oakwood president, and I, chair of the Oakwood Board at the time, wrestled with ideas of how to overcome the structural barriers to the institution's inclusion in the Regional conferences' retirement plan, we saw none. And, of course, neither did the Board itself, comprised as it was (and is) primarily of union and General Conference personnel who saw such inclusion as structurally untenable and Regional conference presidents who wished for the school to join the retirement plan, but at the time were not prepared to fund either the additional buy-in required or replace the loss of annual GC appropriations.

10. Details provided by the office of the Vice President of Financial Affairs, Oakwood University, Huntsville, Alabama (October 1, 2016).

PART TWO

# THE CHALLENGE AHEAD

# 1
# THE QUESTION

The intensity of racial dynamics that accompanied the various twentieth-century Black Seventh-day Adventist leadership protests in the United States has, with time, diminished. That is largely because in the wake of the defeated Black union appeal, the church wisely, and in some instances very courageously, moved African-American leaders to staff committees and positions on administrative levels above the local conference. That initiative, vigorously championed by Neal C. Wilson during his tenures as president of the Columbia Union (1963–1966), the North American Division (1966–1979) and the General Conference (1979–1990), has reaped dividends in terms of not only reduction of concerns regarding fairness but also infusions of talent that have greatly enhanced the church's mission.

Another reason for the diminishing protests in the church is what Eugene Robinson, in his book *Disintegration: The Splintering of Black America,* identifies as the increased spread of diversity into what was once a monolithic Black social order. According to Robinson, contemporary Black American society, unlike the past, now consists of a number of discretely differing elements:

- a mainstream middle-class majority with full ownership stake in American society
- a large, abandoned minority "left behind" in ghetto poverty
- a small elite with enormous wealth and influence
- two newly emergent groups—persons of mixed heritage and Black immigrants primarily from Africa and the Caribbean.[1]

The African and Caribbean immigration influx in the United States remains small compared to Asian and Latin American groups. However, according to the 2015 government census, Black immigrants in the United States had grown four times the number in 1980. The total in 2015 was 4.2 million, or approximately nine percent of the nation's Black population, and has been rapidly increasing.[2] The infusion of new and varied social understandings and interests produced by this diversification dictates for Black society a somewhat less concerted protest profile.

The cause or differing levels of pain notwithstanding, it is clear that systemic racism in America—resulting from what some theorists label the tyranny of "Anglo-Saxonization" (the idealizing of preferred phenotypes, i.e., color and facial features)—remains a prevalent paradigm. This reality, along with feelings of entitlement, the raw exercise of power, and the reluctance of the privileged to yield their advantage, is fundamental to America's continuing racial dilemma.

Ellen G. White was prescient in addressing this matter when she wrote as early as 1899, "The relation of the two races has been a matter hard to deal with, and I fear that it will ever remain a most perplexing problem."[3] In spite of this recognition, and for some because of it, the question, "Why do we need Regional conferences?" has emerged.

For many, the standard responses to this question—that is, continued racial insensitivity and Regional conferences' success—are increasingly less satisfying. It is especially difficult to make the case about racial indignities when all of the denomination's institutions (e.g., churches, schools, hospitals) are desegregated. To date, there have been ten Black union presidents; a Black president of the Review and Herald Publishing Association; Black chairpersons of several hospital, college, and university boards; and a Black female president at Pacific Union College. As of this writing, one of the six general vice presidents of a denomination that has thirteen world divisions is a Black American female, and the North American Division itself has a Black executive secretary, two Black general vice presidents, and several department directors.

As for the successful growth of Regional conferences, the questions are: Do the ends justify the means? Do we not have, as many perceive, a segregated form of governance, thereby making a negative statement to the world and thus impeding our mission? And is it fiscally responsible for this form of organizational overlap to continue when, as often reported, so many local conferences, both White and Black, are struggling financially? Further, if some of the Black and White local conferences in South Africa, of all places, can be structurally united, why cannot those of the North American Division? Also, logically for some, since there will be no racially designated enclaves in heaven, should we not begin that arrangement here?

Such doubts have surfaced in many quarters: (1) very noticeably among young African-American professionals whose distance from the Civil Rights era and its aftermath, coupled with their acceptance and success in corporate America, make them especially susceptible to the illusion of a color-blind society; (2) socially liberal Caucasian Adventists who are genuinely embarrassed and are willing to sacrifice position and privilege to effect organizational fusion; (3) persons of African heritage who have migrated here and cannot understand (until they have been here long enough to undergo the African American-experience) the sensitivities of those whose roots sink deeply into the blood-soaked soil of American history; and, (5) very disturbingly, recent converts who see Black conferences as contradictory to the trends of modern society, not to mention the ethic of love and brotherhood taught by Christ.

Even more significantly, members and pastors of Regional conferences, particularly the millennials and their children for whom the term "whatever" expresses a dwindling sense of racial angst (except when shocked by extreme incidents of physical brutality), frequently question their necessity. These questions are fair and require credible responses, both sociological and theological. Not to provide them is to further delegitimate Regional conferences in the minds of a growing percentage of the church's membership and needlessly prolong the debate regarding their presence.

Given the emotional and material investment of Black Adventism in the creation and highly successful operation of Regional conferences over seventy years, it is extremely doubtful that the lack of additional arguments in their favor will spell their demise. However, without them, they will remain to many as: (1) public embarrassments to a church already tasked with preaching a day of worship unpopular with many; (2) anachronistic reminders of the days of "Separate But Equal"; (3) unnecessary stumbling blocks to true fellowship and the state of unity necessary for the outpouring of the Latter Rain; and (4) illegitimate appendages fastened to the church by a selfish and unforgiving minority.

## Notes

1. Eugene Robinson, *Disintegration: The Splintering of Black America* (New York: Doubleday, 2010), 5.

2. Monica Anderson, "6 Key Findings about Black Immigration to the U.S.," Pew Research Center, April 9, 2015. http://www.pewresearch.org/fact-tank/2015/04/09/6-key-findings-about-black-immigration

3. Ellen G. White, *The Southern Work* (Washington, DC: Review and Herald, 1966), 83. https://egwwritings.org/?ref=en_SWk.83.2&para=139.354

# 2
## THEORETICAL REPLIES

An adequate response to the question of the continued viability of Regional conferences involves reasoning both theoretical and practical. In this chapter, answers will be explored both on the sociological and theological fronts.

## THE SOCIOLOGICAL RESPONSE

A number of sociological factors when once clarified will assist in understanding the need for Black conferences. While they were all at work in the history chronicled above, their roles deserve individual examination. Below is an exploration of the factors that are paramount: Desegregation vs. Integration, Cultural Pluralism, and Self-determinationism.

### Desegregation vs. Integration

A critical sociological factor illumining the need of structural accommodations in the United States is the distinction between a desegregated society and one that is in the narrow sense integrated. A huge element of the problem is that it is not Webster's broad definition of integration as "the bringing of different racial or ethnic groups into free and equal association" that pervades society today; rather, it is the more limited view as assimilations—or, in the not uncommon extreme, the homogenization of cultures—that most generally prevails. The brutal truth is that long decades of integrationist efforts employing the latter emphasis has, by many accounts, retarded the effective accomplishment of the former.

Not that the integrationist thrust has proven totally impotent—it has not. In fact, "formal integration," the kind that assimilates Blacks and Whites at the level of secondary relationships (association in public transportation, public assembly, and the work place), is now the norm. However, "informal integration," the assimilation of the masses at the level of primary relationships, or the arena of personal choice in the private sector, is not the norm. The population still chooses by a wide margin to build families and affiliate in clubs and other voluntary associations (such as churches) that reflect one's ethnic heritage. In this sense, desegregation is objectively sustainable as law while integration is not. There are no sanctions, government or otherwise, capable of holding together in private those who do not wish such a relationship.

A nation proclaiming equal justice should not tolerate discrimination. On the other hand, adults divinely granted the power of choice should not, and cannot, be forced into warm personal relationships. Under freedom's grand provision, desegregation—the absence of barriers to access and opportunity—is appropriately a mandate. But integration, or private, personal relationships with individuals of other cultures, is always an option, not a dictate.

We can accept the consequences of this reality without tension when we remember that the opposite of segregation (exclusivity) is not integration, or assimilation, as many often assume, but *desegregation* (equal access). The latter is the true promise of democracy—not the blending of lives or even cultures.

Desegregation functions as a superior strategy for Black social progress, because it envisions the right of participation without suggesting the inevitability of physical, cultural, or personal merger. It says, "The door is open, all are allowed, come in if you wish, but neither of us need feel guilty if you don't. You may function within the cultural milieu of your choice—that is not a problem. It is neither anti-American nor anti-Christian for you to work and/or worship here. However, excluding another because of color or race is both."

The term "integration" routinely conjures for many Whites fears of economic displacement, cultural contamination, and racial amalgamation. Desegregation also causes trepidation for some; but because its dominant appeal is fairness, not displacement, it speaks less threateningly to the advantaged class.

Martin Luther King, Jr.'s view of desegregation as "eliminative" (indicating the removal of legal and social prohibitions), and integration as "creative" (indicating the aggressive, more productive means of assimilation),

*Theoretical Replies* 169

illumines this point.¹ It is true that integration, not desegregation, was the dominant theme of the Civil Rights Movement that King championed. But an objective analysis of the movement's results reveals that desegregation, not integration, has been its more enduring consequence. Nevertheless, because the quality of relationships occurring from private (voluntary) integration are more binding than those provided by broad-scale desegregation (the mandated "involuntary" public kind), some insist that private integration should be the mandated strategy.

What is lost in this kind of thinking is not only desegregation's superior appeal to both Whites and Blacks, but that the cross-cultural dynamics of desegregation are, themselves, a sure and effective means of integration. It is further helpful to keep in mind that social (i.e., "public") desegregation is in the United States a massive reality, but private (i.e., "personal'") integration is not, nor need it be for the functioning of a socially stable society. The fulfillment of America's promise of "liberty and justice for all" does not require assimilation. Desegregation's open access with its potential for unforced relationships is adequate. It is especially liberating to admit that efforts at forced integration (e.g., busing) have been counterproductive to racial harmony and to realize that it is the unforced kind (integration as a derivative of desegregation) that constitutes the genuine article.

Those visionary Black leaders who strive for a culturally assimilated society, and the more militant ones who, in view of White America's 300-year economic advantage, dream of just reparations, would both do well to be guided by the more tangible results of desegregation. For the former, it is because Black Americans have, as history shows, proven indissoluble in the nation's cultural melting pot, and the latter because reparations, while merited, are not doable except when expressed in the compensatory benefits of such set-asides as affirmative action, a provision now seen by many Whites and some Blacks as reverse discrimination.

Those well-meaning social scientists who point to the lower test scores of Black students and deem integrated studies—that is, the presence of White students in primarily Black classrooms or Blacks in largely White schools—as the key to Black academic improvement, also err. That is because, as demonstrated by the fact that White students in the North generally score higher than Whites in the South, it is environmental factors, not genetics, that make the difference. While integration as described above is rightly valued, it is "fixing," not "mixing," that America's sprawling Black metropolises most urgently need.

## Cultural Pluralism

The second and kindred element of the sociological undergirding of Regional conferences is an acceptance of the fact that America's social construct is that of cultural pluralism, not cultural homogenization. The presence of Black America as a distinct subculture within the nation is anchored in two bedrock realities. The first, as already noted, is Black America's resistance to melting in the pot or crucible declared by Ralph Waldo Emerson and others as America's social destiny.

It is doubtful that these thinkers had citizens with African blood in mind or any other of the ethnic groups whose color and features differed from Anglo-Saxons. Whether or not they did, it is a fact that virtually all of the ethnic groups obviously distinguished by color and/or culture that have ever existed in America have, to a large degree, retained their distinctive identity.

Many have interpreted certain highly profiled societal events and trends as evidence of modern America becoming a "post-racial" society, one in which centuries of color prejudice, the grading of human worth and status on the basis of skin tone, is at last ending. One reason for this growing optimism is the increase of interracial dating and marriage.[2] The apparent increasing numbers of mixed couples seems to support such a conclusion. According to the 2010 Pew Research Center Report developed from the U.S. Census Bureau's 2008 American Community Survey, eleven percent of Blacks who marry in a given year do so with White partners, a significant increase in mixed marriages since the courts struck down the last of the nation's miscegenation laws in 1967.[3] But it is also true that only "4.6% of all married Blacks in the United States were wed to a White partner, and 0.4% of all Whites were married to a Black partner."[4]

An even more sobering realization for those who think that mixed marriages presage the dawn of a "color-blind" society is the fact that the children of White and Black couples, unless fair enough to pass as White and choose to do so, are viewed as Black, not White (e.g., President Barak Obama, baseball icon Derek Jeter, and actress Halle Berry). Objective reflection reveals that while intermarriage is, indeed, society's ultimate expression of racial togetherness, its very byproduct or offspring are, by their social designation, an indication of a continuing racially-defined pluralistic society. Studies do reveal that the percentage of Blacks whose features allow them to pass for White is greater than commonly believed.

That many do so is not surprising given the obvious advantages of being White in America and the fact that choosing Blackness subjects them to a life of double curiosity, inquisitive wonder in White society, and guarded speculation among other Blacks. Another reason offered for "post-racial" optimism has been the ascendance to high political office of a growing number of African Americans, the most obvious of which is the nation's presidency. That, of course, is another welcome and needed development. However, evidence that it has not significantly altered the nation's racially pluralistic structure appears in the fact that rarely does a Black politician get elected to office from any other than a majority-Black voting constituency. In all of United States history, out of a total of 1,970 senators, only ten have been African Americans. Of that number, two were appointed and eight elected. The fact that in 2017, of the 100 elected senators presently in office, only three are Black, hardly supports the belief that color no longer matters or is decreasing in importance.[5] Further, as revealed by the two-term presidency of Barak Obama, there is little or no correlation between high-profile Black political presence and the blurring of distinctions in our racially-pluralistic society. In fact, in his case, it may have even sharpened the recognition and deepened the divide.

Doug McAdam and Karina Kloos, Stanford University professors, comment on this latter reality in their book *Deeply Divided: Racial Politics and Social Movements in Post-War America*:

> ... nothing in the 40 years between Nixon's first election in 1968 and Obama's ascension to the White House in 2008, could have prepared us for the extreme racial attitudes and behaviors exhibited by the GOP during Obama's time in office. It is hard to imagine a starker rebuke to all those who wanted to believe that, with the election, the country had finally put its troubled racial past behind it. Far from the imagined post-racial society Obama's election was supposed to herald, we find ourselves living through the period of greatest racial tensions and conflict since the 1960s and early 1970s.[6]

Most Blacks believe that Obama's lesser plurality of 5,867,152 votes in 2012 compared with his stronger 9,550,193 plurality in 2008, and the tepid poll approvals during his second term are due, more than anything else, to the stout resistance of Congress to numerous initiatives that would have helped those described as angry, deprived middle-class White Americans, and reduced doubts propagated by uber-conservatives in the media concerning Obama's birth, schooling, religion, veracity, courage, and love for America.

But as obvious as has been the crass political and emotional resistance to the nation's first Black president, the greatest reminder of the culturally pluralistic nature of American society is the growing "left behind" of the Black community. This group, much of which remains behind by choice as well as by circumstance, is neither integrated or desegregated. They are locked together in the inner core of such major cities as Atlanta, Baltimore, Birmingham, Cleveland, Detroit, Gary, Jackson, Memphis, New Orleans, Newark, Oakland, Philadelphia, Richmond, St. Louis, and Washington, DC.

According to the government census, the United States has 950 cities and townships with populations between 25,000 and 100,000 in which Blacks comprise more than fifty percent of the population, the majority clustered in the difficult circumstances of what is commonly called "the hood."

The failure of most liberals, White and Black, to factor into their hopes of a color-blind society this reality, and the obvious improbability of integrating this increasingly isolated mass of humanity into the mainstream of society, is unfortunate. It suggests either a naive unawareness of facts or, as is often the case, a stubborn denial rooted in a well-meaning but harmful sense of community.

Another reason to doubt Black America's cultural absorption is the strength of its ethnic solidarity. While the social and legal constraints placed upon the Black community by White America are largely responsible for the endurance of Black culture, it is also true that a major factor behind Black resistance to assimilation is the strong internal attraction of the culture itself. Black Americans, in the main, wish neither to forget nor abolish their distinctiveness.

Ethnic solidarity, the companion reality to racial identity, is a prominent reason for Black America's reluctance to melt into majority America. As with all minority people groups, the cultural conditioning of their community (the instilling of folkways and mores) is so deeply ingrained that, while not indissoluble, it is for all practical purposes not eradicable. The result is that its members not only interpret life through the lens of their ethnic reality, but they usually find their greatest comfort and assurance in the company of those of like culture.

I began to appreciate this social dynamic more fully when attempting to deal with a situation on the campus of Oakwood College during my presidency there. The problem was that our bourgeoning international student body and our American-born contingent did not relate as freely as we administrators thought they should. It was not surprising that the students from various countries in Africa, the Caribbean, and Latin America, as well as those from Canada and Australia, found common cause in the very active and popular campus International Club. What caused a number of students, faculty, and administrators a good deal of angst was the seeming social divide between this group and the much larger number of African-American students.

The most obvious way this gap manifested itself was that Black Americans regularly ate on one side of the cafeteria and international students on the other. Thus I decided that would be a good place to begin correcting the situation. I made an appeal to the student body in Wednesday chapel for them to intermingle more. For a day or two it worked—or so it seemed. A number of students from both sides made a conscious effort to sit with those on the other side of the room. But it did not last. The "Hello, my name is, where are you from?" activity was interesting. But beyond that, it did not provide the students enough common ground for the conversational intimacy during meals that they had formerly enjoyed or, in fact, needed given the rigors of their work and study schedules. They tried and I tried; but in spite of their efforts and mine, within a few days the former patterns returned.

When they did, I noticed that not only were the Americans congregating on one side of the cafeteria and the international students on the other, but also that on the American side the configuration was decidedly regional—the Pine Forge Academy graduates and others from the East Coast, those from the Chicago vicinity, and those from the West Coast (particularly the Californians) all tended to sit together in separate areas. And on the international side, matters were even more stark. Not only did students from West and East Africa tend to sit in different areas, but they did so by country: Kenyans with Kenyans, South Africans with South Africans, Liberians with Liberians, and Nigerians with Nigerians. I continued to explore means of fostering camaraderie between the various people groups on campus. But as an eye witness to the strength of the pull of cultural solidarity, I never again felt impelled to alter the very natural and affirming fellowship the students were enjoying.

I also learned during itineraries that took me to seventy-three countries during my combined thirty years of church administration that it is universally the case that humans prefer to speak to, listen to, and worship God in innate and familiar ways. Congregations that understood English still preferred to have my sermons translated into their native tongue, and the translators themselves often prayed in their mother tongue. That is because it is the inner sanctum of the soul that shelters our most sacred memories and symbols, and we humans enjoy our "God encounters" in the surroundings where we hear Him most clearly and know Him best.

I have further observed that group consciousness or common identity is for Black Adventists, in comparison to other Black Protestant Christians, especially real and meaningful. Its strength is guaranteed (1) by the social distance historically sustained (forced and voluntarily) from Whites in the church; (2) by their theological and social distance from other Black Christian groups, almost all of whom see them as a politically and socially withdrawn, quasi cultish threat to their traditions; and (3) by the treasured spiritual and social ties created and pervasively maintained by life at and around Oakwood University.

The point to keep in mind is that a non-diversified culture is a necessary condition for a non-diversified worship profile. Clearly, given the dynamics reviewed above, the Seventh-day Adventist membership in North America does not, in the main, qualify in this regard. Wishing it were so, or declaring it to be so, or programming as if it is so, does not make it so. The vast majority of Christian congregations in the United States remain primarily, and often entirely, either Black or White. A main reason is that ethnic solidarity, a seemingly inescapable social reality, dictates with a stern hand a people's preference for worship.

## Self-Determinationism

A third sociological perspective critical to the undergirding of Regional conferences is an informed and firm regard for the principle of "self-determination." It is important to view this position as founded not on the premise of White insensitivity, but, as demonstrated above, on the consequence of the very natural tendency to share one's space with one's own tribe, who are typically identified by such characteristics as ancestry, marriage, residence, politics, skin color, and other physical traits.

That tendency, very evident in the Black community, has since slavery served as a critical force in the life of a people who have at periods striven mightily for inclusion while at the same time assiduously nurturing their distinctiveness. Thus, even today, Du Bois's dictum of "twoness" remains a vital truth. It should also be recognized as the basis of the double challenge facing the Black community—the brain drain that occurs when its best and brightest gravitate to the general society on one hand, and the absence of representation in the broader society when its "talented tenth," as Du Bois labels qualified Black leadership, remains cloistered in their local cultural environment.

For a minority group not to be at the table when overarching policies regulating their existence are established is to risk decisions detrimental to their well-being. Yet not relating realistically to the specific wants and needs of one's own community has its distinctive disadvantages. Regional conferences have continued to meet this latter need very effectively; the Negro Department, however, caught in the cross hairs of opposing views during the Black union debate, has long since been abolished. Even when their proposed sequel, Black unions, did not materialize, Regional conferences still functioned with stunning success.

An overview of the membership growth of Regional conferences reveals that in late 1944 at the conferences' beginnings, Black membership in the North American Division was 17,891, or nine percent of NAD's total membership of 226,906. However, by the end of 1977, it had reached 20 percent, 23 percent by 1985, and 25 percent by 1995. By 2016, the membership had grown to 324,719, roughly 26 percent of NAD's total 1,184,395 believers.[7]

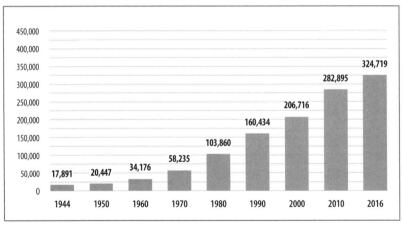

FIGURE 1. Regional Conferences' Membership Growth, 1944–2016.

Further evidence of Regional conferences' effectiveness appears in the fact that "in 1944 the tithe from the Black constituency was $511,000. It grew to $18 million in 1977, $40 million in 1984, $69 million in 1990 and to more than $90 million in 1995."[8] From there it increased to $128 million in 2000, $145 million in 2004, $170,092,400 in 2014, and $184,027,830 in 2016, or 18 percent of NAD's tithe total. This amount exceeds all but three of the church's thirteen world divisions (North America, South America, and the Inter-American Divisions). Additional indication of the value of these conferences is that they started with 233 congregations, but by the end of 2016 that number had blossomed to 1,215.[9]

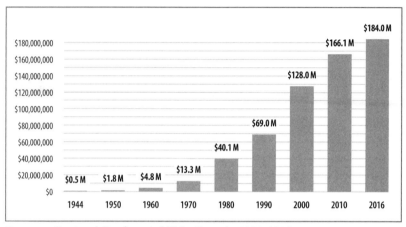

FIGURE 2. Regional Conferences' Tithe Growth, 1944–2016.

Consider the following: The nine Regional conferences now operate the Office for Regional Conference Ministry, a coordinating office in Huntsville, Alabama, from which they process their own retirement program; produce their own quarterly magazine, *Regional Voice*; support their own evangelistic telecast, "Breath of Life"; give major funding to their own institution of higher learning, Oakwood University; plan their own youth congresses and lay witness programs; and facilitate an annual year-end ministerial workshop, Pastoral Evangelism and Leadership Council (PELC), that draws 800 or more pastors and other church employees—almost all from the Black conferences and Black churches of the West. This record of institutional and organizational vigor makes it understandable that talk of merging Regional conferences into state conferences, or dismantling them altogether, usually meets with a less-than-enthusiastic response from their directors and constituents.

That Black Adventism has experienced such exponential church growth under Regional conference direction is not surprising. As demonstrated by the church's mission program around the world, with the exception of areas where intense tribalism necessitates a "neutral" presence, indigenous leadership is more effective than the expatriate kind. Indigenous directors are better equipped to provide such benefits as appropriate planning, informed counseling, accurate evaluation, inspirational modeling, and heightened morale—the exact physical and tangible variables so essential for minority group progress.

Nevertheless, some argue that since obvious progress has been made with respect to "formal" integration (workplace association) in various institutions in the church as well as in general society, and since current civil law both within and without the church makes access to congregational membership (a function of "informal" integration) available to all, the denomination no longer needs racially-driven accommodations.

They believe that similar or even greater good will accrue from dismantling or merging Black conferences, thus placing full confidence in the "melting pot" rather than the "flower garden" model of worship and association. But they need to keep the following points in mind. First, with the exception of what Eugene Robinson terms the "Transcendent Elite," the spiritual needs of all other segments of the Black community—the abandoned "left behind," the mainstream middle class, and the Newly Emergent—are, as a rule, most meaningfully met not by the liturgy of an alien culture but that which expresses the understandings and feelings inherent to the group in which they have been acculturated. Second, as proposed above, communities formed by such grouping are most effectively served by indigenous leadership. Third, as demonstrated below, when significant numbers of Blacks venture to join a White congregation, the Whites tend to leave and either migrate to other White churches or begin again in a new location.

However, we should not simplistically describe the phenomenon colloquially labeled "White flight" as a function of raw racism. What brings Blacks into White churches is demographic relocation. As neighborhoods change from White to Black, so do schools and churches. One cannot judge Whites harshly for moving to other, usually more affluent and safer neighborhoods. After all, Blacks who are able to do so also leave themselves.

None of the above suggests that Regional and White-administered conferences and congregations would not benefit from engaging in any cross-cultural exchange. The races have much to learn from one another. Nor is it to suggest that Regional conferences should possess total autonomy within the main body of the church. They are rightly subject to the higher levels of denominational authority. What it does mean is that their needs are best met within the understandings of "modified" self-determination, or the ability of representative agents to administer, in the garb of the cultures they serve, the policies of the body politic.

Self-determinationists should never forget that interracial association has high potential for reducing stereotypes and increasing racial harmony. But again, sustained racial association in the Adventist church at the personal level is rare on a large scale. That is true not only within the pattern of church attendance, as discussed earlier, but also in a more telling manner within Adventist colleges and universities. This is because as with local congregations, when the Black presence at a school becomes predominant, or nearly so in spite of the good intentions of most faculty and staff, the schools either close—as have numerous boarding academies and the church's college in Massachusetts—or begin to function as Black institutions, as does its well-known university in the nation's capital.[10]

Observers correctly ascribe such changes to financial, student, alumni, and demographic-related considerations. However, the resulting lost opportunities for racial association and hence racial understanding are no less real. Black Adventists' passionate dedication to Oakwood University, with its goal that as many Adventist Blacks as possible have the opportunity to go there, is also a significant factor.

Human nature, aptly described by Reinhold Niebuhr as collectively immoral, has in American social history consistently manifested itself as innately tribal, hence selfish.[11] The human tendency to reflexively engage in "intra-group" bias is understandable in terms of group sociology. We do "see and think about the world through the lens of group affiliations."[12]

These instinctive and in some cases culturally ingrained biases can be, and are, overcome by some. However, reinforced by racial stereotyping and systemic discrimination, they linger as implicit if not explicit racism. Because of this pervasive reality, self-determinationists cannot depend upon the moral sensitivities of the majority for understanding and remedying the needs of the Black community. Although recognizing legislative negotiations as necessary, they decry the role of the "eternal petitioner." They see assimilation (racial blending) as a legitimate individual choice but hold little faith in attempts at massive acculturation. And while they admire the claims of *agape* (self-sacrificial love), they regard four centuries of "cross time" as more than enough for any minority to endure.

Self-determination builds its own nationhood, handles its own funds, and respects its own culture. Rejecting the notion that Blacks were thought to be—even should be—an indistinguishable part of America's "melting pot," it values the "flower garden" motif instead. As a result, self-determinationists do not agree that there is, or need be, or even can be, such a thing as a "colorless society" or that the removal of descriptors such as African, Spanish, Asian, and White Americans is a logical or worthwhile pursuit. Accepting what history has revealed about Black/White relations, they waste no time or energy on social projects that attempt to disprove the ancient Aristotelian logic that "birds of a feather flock together." But self-determinationists also understand that likeness of class sometimes trumps likeness of color and binds individuals of different races in a fellowship outside their racial mainstream. Such cross-cultural identification is both legitimate and welcome. Furthermore, self-determinationism rejects all vestiges of racial exclusivity and welcomes the strangers within its gates as "Sisters and Brothers."

Further, self-determinationsim sees the "fatherhood of God" and the "brotherhood of man" as essential tenants of race relations and demands that it be allowed to sit at the table of humanity with all its cultural differences as a power among other powers. Aware that in the larger arenas of deliberation it will usually be outnumbered and often outvoted, it believes that the needs of its communities are better served as usually out-voted units with political vitality than as a diffused, unorganized, patronized minority. Regional conferences bring together what would otherwise be isolated, powerless fragments of Black Adventism into political entities that can and do give accurate expression to its needs.

Thus, while it is true that Regional conferences began, in part, because of racial indignities, it is not true that their continued presence ignores obvious progress in this regard or clings to feelings of animosity because of past hurts. They exist today, in part, because in spite of social progress in America in general and in the church in particular, Black America remains a distinct cultural reality with specific needs. That the cultural distance between Whites and Blacks within the Seventh-day Adventist church is just as real as that of society as a whole is verified by the pervasive pattern of "White flight" by White Adventists all across the land,[13] and by the choice of most Blacks to congregate together even when they have the option to establish membership elsewhere. To pretend that such realities do not exist, or that they are fading away, is not realistic.

## SUMMARY OF SOCIOLOGICAL OBSERVATIONS

It is quite popular in some quarters to say that the love of God transcends culture; and of course it does. However, it does not do so by suddenly dissolving group distinctions. That requires time—often centuries. Rather, it does so by equipping varied cultures to hold identical doctrinal beliefs while employing differing methodologies for mission. Segregation (exclusivity) is indeed sinful, and so is the attempt, even in the name of unity, to deprive minority cultures of structural accommodations vital to their psychological and missional well-being.

Those of both cultures who, in spite of the reality of Black and White social distance in America and the glowing achievements of Regional conferences, wish to dissolve cultural distinctions are to be admired for their motives but not for their practicality. It is not helpful to ask an ethnic minority of any stripe, especially one of color, to relinquish accommodations essential to their well-being for arrangements that assume attitudes and conditions that do not exist. Love that "will not let one go" is appropriate in outreach for those we seek to save. But it is a cumbersome weight upon the backs of those already saved who are seeking freedom to save others.

The elimination of Regional conferences would place Black Seventh-day Adventists in double jeopardy: (1) weakening political ties with each other; and (2) continued soft, or more likely non-existent, social relationships with their White counterparts at the local congregation level. The results would be a retarding of mission not unlike that experienced by the United Methodist Church that decades ago disbanded its Black structural accommodations, called Central Jurisdictions, only to experience a decline in Black membership, leadership, income, and enthusiasm. Their experience, and the fact that most American Blacks who are Christian belong to one of the seven Black-administered denominations, is a further reminder that, at root, the issue is not one of order or even unity, but of fellowship.[14]

The fact that the two North American Division unions lacking Regional conferences (the Pacific and the North Pacific Unions) found it necessary to structure accommodations for their Black members clearly affirms this. Although called Regional departments, not conferences, they are directed by *Black* leaders who counsel *Black* personnel and churches, supervise *Black* workers' meetings, conduct *Black* camp meetings, chair *Black* mission committees, administer funds designated for *Black* congregations, and conduct separate caucuses for *Black* delegate sessions at constituency meetings for the purpose of planning and recommendations—in short, function as a Black cultural segment within the main conference structure.

That is not to say that a people cannot, if they must or choose, survive under non-indigenous leadership. We see this demonstrated by the fact that the nine Regional conferences contain approximately 140 non-Black congregations, among them Caucasian, Hispanic, Korean, Brazilian, Portuguese, Asian, and Indonesian. In addition, the predominately Black congregations of Regional conferences have thousands of Whites and the other ethnic groups within their membership. And there is a growing number of Blacks attending White churches, an increasing number of whom are, in my opinion, justifiably "turned off" by the excessive sound and demonstration characterizing so much of Black worship today.

These, however, are the exception. We should expect that as long as America's overwhelming social patterns dictate for its Black minority a differing social culture, the need for structural accommodations in their church life will be necessary.

## THE THEOLOGICAL RESPONSE

As critical as are the sociological understandings to the existence of Regional conferences, the theological aspects are even more important. That is because it is theology, not sociology, that must ground the church's convictions and shape its values. No justification, not even that of "mission particularity"—the notion that evangelistic strategy is most effective when geared specifically for and implemented by members of that group—is conclusive without an understanding of the theological assumptions chiefly responsible for the church's historic social conservatism. It is, after all, the church's cluster of socially conservative theological positions that more than any other element determine the discomfort of many regarding Regional conferences and which, more broadly, function as a deterrent to creative social arrangements.

The truth is that those who defend the continued existence of Regional conferences are hard-pressed to justify them by traditional Adventist theological emphases. It is not that Scripture does not support their existence, but rather that the socially conservative convictions derived from the church's highly conservative theological assumptions do not. That is because Adventism's interpreters of Scripture have, in the main, done so through the lens of their particular cultures and not those of the racially oppressed. Consequently, what they have given us is sound doctrine with biased delivery—correct commandments but narrow hermeneutics.

## Contributing Belief Patterns

We can observe this phenomenon of correct identification of doctrine but social naiveté with regard to everyday application in a number of belief patterns. Chief among these are radical determinism, extensive free will, the miracle motif, socially lacking eschatology, extreme ecclesiology, and the righteousness of God.

### Radical Determinism

The notion of "radical determinism," that is, the view that all solutions lie in God's hands and that He will step in and settle matters in time, is a fundamental premise of Christian social conservatism. An illustration of how this attitude is formed is seen in the unfortunate way that some are informed by Ellen White's description of the Civil War Battle of Manassas, also known as the Battle of Bull Run. White, who fell into vision during a conference at Roosevelt, New York, on August 3, 1861, related that she was shown a detailed account of how, in this pivotal fight, the Northern troops miraculously escaped certain annihilation. Understanding the successful retreat of Northern forces as an act of God intended not only to spare their lives but also to preserve the cause of right, she wrote:

> I had a view of the disastrous battle at Manassas, Virginia. It was a most exciting, distressing scene. The Southern army had everything in their favor, and were prepared for a dreadful contest.... The Northern men were rushing on, although their destruction was very great. Just then an angel descended, and waved his hand backward. Instantly there was confusion ... and a precipitate retreat commenced. This seemed wonderful to me.
>
> Then it was explained that God had this nation in His own hand, and ... had the Northern army at this time pushed the battle still further in their fainting, exhausted condition, the far greater struggle and destruction which awaited them would have caused great triumph in the South. God would not permit this, and sent an angel to interfere. The sudden falling back of the Northern troops is a mystery to all. They know not that God's hand was in the matter.[15]

It is not difficult to see how an awareness of such remarkable historical events can lead to a presumptuous reliance upon acts of divine intervention. However, God's usual *modus operandi* is not that of overriding natural consequences but of preparing and strengthening His people to perform courageously in everyday encounters.

A highly revealing study of militancy among Black ministers and laity conducted by Gary Marx during the Civil Rights Movement demonstrates how this element of social conservatism functions. Marx found that when pressed for reasons for their hesitancy to become involved in social protest, his sample of Black ministers and laity most often reflected the belief that God would take care of things in His own time. Examples included: "I don't go for demonstrations. I believe that God created all men equal and at His appointed time He will give every man his portion, no one can hinder it." And, "You can't hurry God. He has a certain time for this to take place."[16]

Unless stimulated by a colossal tragedy or highly emotional event, Christians both White and Black are slow to contest social evil at its source. They will often provide welfare relief, but seldom go after the thief who wounds the victim—the corporate robber-barons in large manner responsible for societal injustice and disadvantage.

Other such studies on the correlation between theological and social conservatism confirm a clear inverse relationship between the two: the stronger the belief system, the weaker the response to social injustice in the assumption that it's all in God's hands—He will correct matters in His own time.

**Extensive Free Will**

Another influence on Christian social conservatism is the idea of "extensive free-will" which holds that individual status in society is entirely the function of one's inner strength, and that every person can "make it" if properly motivated and sufficiently energetic. The exaggeration of concepts of "rugged individualism"—the idea of pulling oneself up by the bootstraps—along with the current trend of what is labeled the "prosperity gospel," all contribute negatively to the social good. It simply is not true that everyone has either the talent or the opportunity to climb out of restrictive circumstances to heights of success. Judging one's social standing to be the sure consequences of his or her willingness to exercise willpower overlooks factors of raw ability, health, competition, timing, societal openness, and other critical factors in the formula of success.

Research by Rodney Glock and Charles Y. Stark led them to describe the harm done to the disadvantaged by the notion of the "invincible free will":

> The results of our ... analysis lend themselves to the following interpretation: a free-will image of man lies at the root of Christian prejudice toward

Negroes and of attitudes toward the civil rights movement; it also underlies the rejection of programs underwritten by the church and the government to improve the situation of minorities. The simple fact seems to be that a great many church people, because they believe men are mainly in control of their individual destinies, think that Negroes are themselves largely to blame for their present misery. It is not that these Christians condone the social forces that deprive black people, but rather that they simply do not recognize the existence of such forces in the world. They do recognize that Negroes are collectively disadvantaged. But the conclusion that logically follows from their theology is that this disadvantage must be the result of a racial shortcoming.[17]

Further evidence that the notion of an extensive free will is antithetical to social liberalism appears in the following:

> To the extent that Christian theology and institutions support a radical view of individual freedom and accountability, their members can be expected to reject the very premises upon which the battle against prejudice and discrimination rests. For if the disadvantaged condition of minority groups is proof of their unworthiness, how can people be expected to support measures to help them?[18]

The notion of a free will capable of limitless achievement remains a primary source of America's justification for private wealth as well as attitudes of racial superiority. But many of society's disadvantaged have neither straps nor boots and remain crushed beneath the circumstances perpetuated by the very ones, Black and White, who disdain them.

## The Miracle Motif

A third primary theological influence toward social conservatism is the "miracle motif"—the belief that since conversion is the key to brotherly love, the church's effort should not involve attacking societal evils but of saving sinners who, once converted, will then reflect Christ's likeness. Otherwise stated, it is the belief that since conversion is the key to brotherly love, the church's effort should focus only on saving sinners, who, once delivered, will live out the principles of Christian charity.

Joseph Bates (1792–1872), a cofounder of the Seventh-day Adventist church and early on a vocal critic of slavery, in later years shifted to a similar viewpoint:

> Some of my friends that were engaged in the temperance and abolition cause came to know why I could not attend their stated meetings as formerly, and argued that my belief in the coming of the Saviour should make

me more ardent in endeavoring to suppress these growing evils. My reply was that in embracing the doctrine of the Second Coming of the Saviour, I found enough to engage my whole time in getting ready for such an event, and aiding others to do the same, . . . further I could not see my duty in leaving such a great work to labor single-handed as we have done, when so much more could be accomplished in working at the fountainhead, and make us every way right as we should be for the coming of the Lord.[19]

The notion of converting the advantaged majority as prerequisite for granting freedom to the disadvantaged minority is neither scriptural nor logical. Nevertheless, it remains an effective barrier to social concerns in theologically conservative religious denominations such as Seventh-day Adventism.

## Socially Lacking Eschatology

Also contributing to the church's socially conservative posture is its often misapplied eschatology. Adventism has progressed beyond most of the sectarian characteristics that accompanied its emergence in the middle of the nineteenth century. It is no longer largely withdrawn from society, hostile to government, and mostly poverty stricken. However, it has not lost or abandoned its stated expectation of the soon return of Christ that was the theological hope of deliverance from the troubled world into which the church was born.

As demonstrated by the content of its preaching and music, the church's eschatological fervor is not as pronounced as it once was. Nevertheless, it is still the overarching tenet—and that is as it should be. The problem, however, is that apocalyptic eschatology, or high expectation for the future kingdom of glory, without proper concern for the present kingdom of grace (the kingdom of God on earth), guarantees passivism in matters of social concern.

Inadequately informed apocalypticists downplay or even ignore social action. For them, the immediacy of the Second Coming and the dawning of eternal peace nullifies any need to engage in social reform. Their subconscious—and, for some, "conscious"—conclusion can be summed in the saying, "The hour is too late, the problems are too great, if we can just wait—it will soon be over!"

Such Christians live in the paralyzed posture of what Gilbert Murray describes as "the sad philosophy of those who knowing how short time is . . . do not undertake to build what they cannot finish or employ those materials fit for use in a structure that would require many generations or unlimited time for its completion."[20] Put another way, these believers render asunder what God has put together—glowing expectation of future bliss and active concern for present reality, concepts forever wed by the Master's command, "Occupy 'til I come!"

## Extreme Ecclesiology

Another of the church's theological components responsible for its social conservatism is what has proven to be its overly protective regard for its societal image. One example of how this position has contributed to the church's social conservatism is its unfortunate response to a warning Ellen White made near the end of the nineteenth century:

> At the General Conference of 1889, resolutions were presented in regard to the color line. Such action is not called for. Let not men take the place of God, but stand aside in awe, and let God work upon human hearts, both white and black, in His own way. He will adjust all these perplexing questions. We need not prescribe a definite plan of working. Leave an opportunity for God to do something. We should be careful not to strengthen prejudices that ought to have died just as soon as Christ redeemed the soul from the bondage of sin.[21]

Her advice, given in the climate of post-Civil War bitterness, was very sound. But following it into the more socially liberal atmosphere of the sixth and, for some, even the seventh decade of the twentieth century and beyond, was not.

Another example involves the exaggerated response to the prophet's advice that "so far as possible, everything that would stir up the race prejudice of the white people should be avoided. There is danger of closing the door so that our white laborers will not be able to work in some places in the South."[22] While her comment made in the wake of the nation's 1896 "Separate but Equal" law was clearly justified, it has, along with similar Ellen G. White statements, and even some from the Bible itself, been misused as an excuse to tolerate social injustice. By failing to take into account the qualifier "in some places in the South," church leadership both accommodated and participated in the exaggerated timidity (better stated, racism) practiced by White Adventist congregations in much of the country well into the 1970s.

It is true that beginning with its 1961 public pronouncement regarding racial intolerance, the church has from time to time issued statements avowing racial justice and inclusivity. However, there have been cases of unthinkable human rights violations in which the church's attention was far from appropriately focused in this regard. For example:

- Mass kidnappings of girls in Africa
- Mass drownings of desperate immigrants seeking refuge in Europe
- Mass assassinations in the Middle East
- Mass shootings and horrific hate crimes in the United States highlighted by the burning of Black churches in the South

Most shocking was the massacre of nine Black worshippers in Charleston, South Carolina, two weeks before the beginning of the Seventh-day Adventist church's ten-day quadrennial session in San Antonio, Texas, in 2015. The church made no public statement during this gathering either of regret or concern.

But if this lack of response by General Conference leadership is indicative of their social malaise, so is the failure of its delegates, Black and White, to protest the church's deafening silence. Meanwhile, the toll of Blacks repelled from church membership because of its unnecessary caution, and of Whites who have lost faith in the church because of its continued silence regarding oppressive social practices, is incalculable.

The primary public relations concern today is no longer, "What will the public think if Blacks are admitted into White fellowship?" Or, as some think, "What are the consequences, as seemingly manifested by the existence of Regional conferences, of the appearance that Blacks are *not* welcome?" But rather, "What is the responsibility of the church in taking a stand against social evil?" That is why, for Black Adventists, the essential question is, "Which is more damaging to mission, the perception of racial segregation held by those who view Black conferences as such, or the loss of the structural leverage that is so essential for effective witness in our communities?"

**The Righteousness of God**

While all of the above factors have worked to suppress social activism in the Seventh-day Adventist Church, none has been more effective than its incomplete portrayal of God's righteousness. The unbalanced emphasis of conservative Protestantism upon God's righteousness as His antiseptic, do-no-evil, "burning fire" purity (Heb. 12:29) does not square with the many biblical texts that give even greater emphasis on His righteousness as meaning His regard for equity in human relations. No less than sixty of the 145 "justice verses" in the Old Testament present this aspect of divine righteousness. The books of Job, Psalms, Proverbs, Isaiah, Jeremiah,

Amos, Micah, Zephaniah, among others, all speak eloquently of God's righteousness as demonstrated by His justice.

This unity appears as early as Genesis 18:19 where God trusts Abraham to direct his family in "righteousness and justice." It is heard in Deuteronomy 32:4, which states, "for all His ways are justice, a God of truth and without injustice; righteous and upright is He." It sounds in Psalm 89:14: "Righteousness and justice are the foundation of Your throne." And it is proclaimed in Isaiah 28:17 when God announces, "I will make justice the measuring line, and righteousness the plummet."

What we see in these verses is not simply God being described as justice, but, just as meaningful, justice being portrayed as God. It is not righteousness and justice functioning in happy companionship, but rather their being inextricably interwoven. Furthermore, it is compensatory justice that is usually portrayed—the kind serving as correction for past or present injury, exploitation, or violation of rights. It is not merely legal or retributive; rather, it is God's righteous regard for the economically deprived, the politically oppressed, and the socially marginalized.

God's antipathy for injustice, often declared before He came in the person of His Son, rang clearly in His promise to "lay waste" the inhabitants of Jerusalem, because "He looked for justice, but behold, oppression" (Isa. 5:7). It sounded in His Messianic declaration, "For I, the Lord, love justice; I hate robbery" (Isa. 61:8). And it thundered in His judgment upon Israel when He said, "I hate your feast days . . . take away from Me the noise of your songs. . . . I will not hear the melody of your stringed instruments. But let justice run down like water, and righteousness like a mighty stream" (Amos 5:21–23). And it burned in his acidic wish upon one who is guilty of exploitation: "Let the iniquity of his fathers be remembered before the Lord, and let not the sin of his mother be blotted out. Let them be continually before the Lord, that He may cut off the memory of them from the earth; because he did not remember to show mercy, but persecuted the poor and needy man, that he might even slay the broken in heart" (Ps. 109:14–16).

All of this reflects the creed by which Christ lived while here on earth. It is seen in His association with the downcast and outcasts; in His parables such as that of the importunate widow or the forgiven debtor who wouldn't forgive; in His scathing rebukes upon the Jewish ruling class; in His demand that the rich young ruler sell all that he had and give to the poor; in His cursing the deceptive, space-wasting, good-for-nothing fig tree; in His overturning of the tables of the price-gouging, robber baron money-changers;

and by His publicly denouncing Herod, ruler of Peraea and Galilee, puppet of the Romans, and murderer of John the Baptist as a "fox." We are not surprised then that Christ's own description of His ministry was in regards to acts of righteousness—to "preach the gospel to the poor . . . heal the brokenhearted, to proclaim liberty to the captives and recovery of sight to the blind, to set at liberty those who are oppressed; to proclaim the acceptable year of the LORD" (Luke 4:18). While here, He practiced what He had for millennia preached—the justice quality of righteousness. Christ's was a proleptic theology, one whose earthly manifestations anticipated heavenly forms—a process often called "doing the kingdom now!"

It is ironic that it was precisely because of Christ's righteousness (His performing the works of justice) that the Jewish leaders judged Him as being unrighteous. And it is also ironic that conservative Protestant theology (of which Adventism is a derivative), influenced by Augustine's theory of private goodness and more recently by the Protestant ethic that equates material prosperity with personal salvation, correctly condemns Christ's opponents yet blindly repeats their glaring error—the removal of social injustice from the category of evils that God has commissioned the church to combat.

No less an authoritative source than *The Seventh-day Adventist Bible Commentary* articulates this position:

> *"The kingdom Jesus came to proclaim was not of this world" (see John 18:36). He never commissioned His disciples as agents of social justice, important as that may be, nor did He at any time attempt to adjudicate between men (see John 8:3–11). Like the prophets of old (Micah 6:8, etc.). Jesus clearly set forth the principles that should govern a man's relationships with his fellow men . . . but left the administration of civil justice exclusively to the duly appointed civil authorities.*[23]

But, of course, Jesus did adjudicate between individuals. Consider His resolution of the tension between the woman found in adultery and her guilty accusers in John 8; between Mary who bathed His tired feet in love and insidious Judas in John 12; between His ambitious, feuding disciples in Matthew 20; and, by clear example, the separation of His disciples and those of John in John 3. Furthermore, in addition to tasking His disciples with the preaching of the gospel in Matthew 28:18–20, Jesus assigned them the work of adjudication (Matt. 16:19) and promised to ratify in the supreme council of heaven whatever decisions they made on earth.

To be clear, all of this is not a directive to pastors and church boards to attempt to administer civil disputes. The church is not established to arbitrate, negotiate, or "settle the temporal affairs of the people."[24] That is the province of government, the secular arm of human affairs referred to by Paul as "God-authorized," hence worthy of the believer's respectful obedience (Rom. 13:1–7). It is evidence, however, of Christian responsibility to condemn injustice and seek peace not by silence but by active interjection on behalf of those purposely disadvantaged.

Additionally, Paul's directive to respect and submit to government is not an injunction to blind obedience "no matter what." It is clear from Acts 5:29 that when the commands of the secular arm of human affairs conflict with those of the sacred Word, it is the latter that we must obey. Nor does Paul's, "Therefore whoever resists the authority resists the ordinance of God" (Rom. 13:2) suggest individual or corporate silence when it is obvious that unjust laws and the systems and individuals responsible for them need correction.

Those who regard Ephesians 6:5 as calling for unconditional obedience to earthly powers, no matter how vile, do not pay proper attention to the cultural dynamics of New Testament times. These include the reporting of Christ's well-fed crowds as consisting of a specific number of men "beside" women and children; of Paul's advice that women not speak in church or pray with their heads uncovered; and his honoring the institution of slavery, all admonishments very few Christians find applicable today.

It was precisely such uninformed and, most often, selective scriptural literalism that prompted German Adventists' shameful cooperation with the ungodly politics and policies of Nazism. German Adventism's misguided acquiescence to social injustice is bared in the book *The Silent Church: Human Rights and Adventist Social Ethics* by Zdravko Plantak, previously chair of the religion department at Washington Adventist University, in one of his more telling observations:

> Adventists failed in numerous ways in regard to the Nazi regime. . . . When some Adventists refused to salute the Swastika flag and to use the Hitler greeting, the President of the East German Conference . . . argued that it was bad for the church's image. He concluded that "under no circumstances did any Adventist have the right to resist the government, even if the government prevented him from exercising his faith. The resistance would be unfortunate because it would mark Adventists as opponents of the new state, a situation that should be prevented."[25]

In May of 2005, Adventist German and Austrian church leaders, in commemoration of the sixtieth anniversary of the conclusion of World War II, issued what they announced as an apology for Holocaust actions. The expression of regret, however, while stating genuine sorrow for victims of Nazi cruelty, falls short of tapping the true source of Adventist lethargy with regard to social injustice: insufficient interpretation of biblical categories of the role of government and the church's relationship to secular rule.[26]

Civic rule is indeed God's design for the directing and protecting of the masses in the conduct of their secular activities and the guarantee of freedom of worship for the believer. However, He dictates neither its forms nor its officiants. Rulers come to office via human means—votes, royal bloodline, and radical, often murderous revolution—not celestial selection. They are vested and voted by human processes and are therefore subject to human critique. The question for the church is not whether social involvement is godly, but when and how to critique or even resist unjust authorities.

In addition to the stinging rebukes that He rendered against the Jewish rulers of His day, our Lord gave formidable critiques of existing earthly kingdoms. He did so by contrasting His spiritual kingdom with the political kingdoms of His day and by His example of sacrificial servanthood (e.g., Matt. 20:25–28). However, to have overtly attacked Roman rule would have been to abort His mission. He would have died as a crusading revolutionary overwhelmed by the might of Rome, not (as was prophesied and infinitely more meaningful) as the courageous Redeemer crushed by the sins of humanity.

We should further note that the prophets were not, as intimated above, passive conduits of the "principles of proper relationships." They served as corrective agents when rulers abused their God-given power, as witnessed when Nathan upbraided David, Samuel stood down Saul, and Elijah called out Ahab and Jezebel. The prophets not only condemned the injustices of individual Israelites and often the nation, but also the atrocities of non-Israelite individuals and nations around them.

Were not Joseph in Egypt and Daniel in Babylon godly arbiters of social affairs? And if anyone protests that they were especially emboldened by personal authority from God, what do we make of the prophet's words:

> Dear youth, what is the aim and purpose of your life? ... Have you thoughts that you dare not express, that you may one day stand upon the

summit of intellectual greatness; that you may sit in deliberative and legislative councils, and help to enact laws for the nation? There is nothing wrong in these aspirations.[27]

If some argue that Joseph and Daniel served as individuals, not as representatives of the organized body of believers, thus indicating God's approval of individual protest but not the corporate kind, what are we to make of His instruction to His people Israel to remove from the face of the earth whole tribes and nations whose primary evil was profound injustice upon others? And how do we respond to the fact that it was what the *Seventh-day Adventist Bible Commentary* interprets as the "protest" of the Greek-speaking believers in Acts 6:1–6 that produced the first major organizational change in the early Christian church?[28] Also in this regard, should not the body of Christ in our day reason that a people who on principle vote against and boycott operations guilty of physical evil (e.g., prohibition and tobacco) act likewise toward politicians, propositions, and businesses guilty of social evil?

The theologians who dutifully taught us the Isaiah 58:12–14 truths of our being "the repairer of the breach, the restorer of paths to dwell in," as well as the blessings received if one will "turn away your foot from the Sabbath," did us no favor when they failed to stress properly the preceding verses (1–11) that emphasize God's disdain for injustice. Before promising the Sabbath-keeping reward to "ride on the high hills of the earth" (v. 14), God pledged that removal of the yoke of oppression (vv. 6–10) would give His people light in darkness, satisfaction in drought, and unfailing resilience (vv. 10–11).

Rightly understood, the justice aspect of God's righteousness reveals Him as a Ruler who is intrinsically fair and quintessentially just—a God who values goodness above goals, people above policy, mercy above methodology, actuality above appearance, pragmatics above cosmetics, freedom above formality. As such, clarity in this belief has more potential for defining and underpinning the rationale for granting structural accommodations to disadvantaged minorities, especially those of significant size and social difference, than any other theological tenet.

## Historical Directives

Another important aid to understanding Adventist social conservatism is appreciation for the way that prominent spokespersons of both the early Christian church and the Reformation lent credence to Christian and, by way of inheritance, to Adventist social passivity. Also to be considered are the consequences of the lack of significant contribution to prevailing Adventist theological thought by minority theologians—more specifically, the almost total absence of writings of Scriptural exegesis by Black Adventist authors.

### Early Christian Tradition

That Adventist theology is weak in concepts of social and political freedom is, in retrospect, not surprising. The church, after all, in significant ways is part and parcel of the thought of the early centuries of Christianity. The Seventh-day Adventist Church did not arrive on the scene in the middle 1800s untouched by the socially conservative thought of the early church fathers. Christian social conservative thought traces as far back as the early believers' interpretation of Christ's instruction not to let the left hand know what the right one is doing (Matt. 6:3) as meaning restraint from all public acts (even the merciful kind), and Paul's advice to "mind your own business" (1 Thess. 4:11) as intending absolute separation of public and private duty.

But it was the writings of the early churchman Augustine of Hippo (AD 354–430), the converted philosopher known as the father of modern Christianity, that contributed most enduringly to the foundation of Christian social thought. Among his teachings that encouraged social reticence was his admonition that in the face of intractable tyranny the Christian should "bend . . . lest we be broken," and his attitude of "homo moriturus," which cast human experience as a doomed chain of mortal succession and his belief in contemplation, or "thinking," as the highest form of action.[29]

This last idea, borrowed from Aristotle (384–322 BC), who taught that the highest mode of action was not simply "thinking" but "thinking about thinking," was particularly effective in discouraging activism of any kind among believers. For him, thinking anticipated the happy day of untroubled study and worship in an afterlife free from competing thoughts of conflict and labor.

But, of course, Augustine was not alone in leading early Christianity away from social activism. Before him, Tertullian (c. 160–220), known as the father of Latin Christianity, had boldly proclaimed, "No matter is more alien to us [Christians] than what matters publicly."[30] And also contributing significantly was Thomas Aquinas (1225–1274), among the most influential theologians in Christian history, who taught that the common needs and cares of life—what came to be known as the "vita activa"—were akin to those of brute animals.

## The Protestant Reformation

Ironically, strains of Reformation theology also influenced Adventists toward social conservatism. One need look no further than to the thought of Martin Luther who, according to Reinhold Niebuhr, was perversely indifferent to tyranny.[31] Luther's one-sided emphasis on Paul's "Let every soul be subject to the governing authorities. For there is no authority except from God" (Rom. 13:1) allowed him to reject the demand of the German peasants for the eradication of serfdom, because it "would make all men equal and so change the spiritual Kingdom of Christ into an external worldly one." He further stated, "Some must be free, others serfs, some rulers, others subjects."[32]

Another of Luther's contributions to the Reformation's socially conservative thought was his claim that "it is a malicious and evil idea that serfdom should be abolished because Christ has made us free. This refers only to spiritual freedom given to us by Christ in order to enable us to withstand the Devil."[33]

Yet another of Luther's positions that resulted in later Christian passivism was his forceful defense of government authority and opposition to peasant rebellion in his treatise *Against the Robbing and Murdering Hordes of Peasants* (1525): "Since they [the peasants] are now deliberately and violently breaking this oath of obedience and setting themselves in opposition to their masters [the political authorities].... Therefore let everyone who can, smite, slay, and stab [the peasants], secretly or openly.... It is just as when one must kill a mad dog."[34]

In his book, *The Nature and Destiny of Man*, Niebuhr comments on Luther's contribution to social pessimism or pacifism as follows:

> Even without this particular error, the Lutheran political ethic would have led to defeatism in the field of social politics. Its absolute distinction between the "heavenly" or "spiritual" kingdom and the "earthly" one, destroys the tension between the final demands of God upon the conscience, and all the relative possibilities of realizing the good in history.[35]

Niebuhr's summary view of the Reformation's sustained contribution to Christian conservatism is that both the defeatism of Lutheranism and the obscurantism of Calvinism "failed to relate the ultimate answer of grace to the problem of guilt to all the immediate and intermediate problems and answers of life. Therefore it [the Reformation] did not illumine the possibilities and limits of realizing increasing truth and goodness in every conceivable historic and social situation."[36] When one adds to this the fact that many of Luther's followers interpreted his "Righteousness by Faith," a concept that he promoted as a spiritual goodness available without works, as license for social passivity, Niebuhr's dour conclusions shed helpful light on the issue of Christian social conservatism.

## Lack of Minority Literary Impact

Given the influences to social conservatism bequeathed to modern-day Protestantism by the early church fathers and the Protestant reformers, the social activism of so many pioneer Adventists is all the more remarkable. The fact that their ethic soon gave way to one that was and has remained distinctly socially pessimistic may be attributed to a number of factors. A primary one is the social background of the writers who formulated Adventism's tenants.

As the church transitioned beyond its early days of a loosely organized group focused upon a few fundamental beliefs to needed institutionalization and more expanded doctrinal development, that transition occurred without contributions from the disadvantaged in society. Consequently its theological expressions, in the main, remained unaffected by the needs of the society's marginalized and did not readily identify with their condition. To the contrary, they often have the effect of supporting current social systems no matter how oppressive.

An obvious demonstration that it makes all the difference through whose sociological lens the Word gets interpreted is seen in the fact that much of White American Christianity justified slavery for 300 years and Jim Crow segregation for another 100 years. Society's advantaged and disadvantaged read about the Exodus from two very different points of view. The advantaged have a harder time identifying and portraying the Israelite bondage and suffering with the same passion and clarity than those whose experience more closely mirrors that of the Hebrews. Expressed another way, Adventist theology is highly Eurocentric, shaped almost exclusively by White European, American, and Australian theologians.

That the church's Black minority has contributed so little to the denominational theological direction is not the fault of White Adventism. Much of it is a consequence of Black leadership's failure to recognize, cultivate, and support credible theological scholarship. The Black Adventist ministry, in some ways victimized by its preaching prowess and focused on the more immediate results of public evangelism, being unable to imagine that society with all its ills would last long enough to permit lengthy years of academic preparation, has, until recently, failed to produce major works of bonafide theology.[37]

The failure, however, has not been absolute. Despite formidable impediments to theological endeavors, a number of Black writers have provided thoughtful works in the area. The most prolific Black Adventist writer to date, E. E. Cleveland, produced fifteen books, most of them referenced elsewhere in this study, attractively wedding Adventist theology with the Black experience.

Other Black Adventists have engaged in serious theology on the written page: Charles E. Bradford, *The God Between* (1984), *Timothy and Titus* (1994), and *The King Is in Residence* (2017); Roy Adams, *The Sanctuary Doctrine: Three Approaches in the Seventh-day Adventist Church* (1981), *The Sanctuary: Understanding the Heart of Adventist Theology* (1993), *The Nature of Christ* (1994), and *The Wonder of Jesus* (2007); Keith Burton, *The Blessing of Africa* (2007) and *Laying Down the Law* (2013); Pedrito Maynard-Reid, *Rich Wisdom* (1989) and *Poverty and Wealth in James* (2004); Randy Maxwell, *"Weight" on the Lord* (1986), *If My People Pray* (1995), *Bring Back the Glory* (2000), *Steps to Christ-Like Living* (2001), *Let Not Your Heart Be Troubled* (2002), *On Angels' Wings* (2014), and *Boot Camp for the Last Days* (2016).

Black Adventists have also contributed theological insights in other literary media. The *Adult Sabbath School Quarterly*, a vital theological medium studied worldwide, has had almost a dozen Black-authored study guides (quarterlies): "Stewardship in Its Great Aspects" by O. A. Troy (the first Adventist of any color to earn a doctorate of theology), 4th Quarter 1959; "The Final Conflict" by E. E. Cleveland, 4th Quarter 1963; "Christian Social Behavior," coauthored by C. D. Brooks, 1st Quarter 1971; "God's Way of Setting Men Right" by L. B. Reynolds, 2nd Quarter 1972; "The Church—Home at Last" by E. E. Cleveland, 2nd Quarter 1981; "Jesus Our Mediator" by C. E. Bradford, 4th Quarter 1984; "Living for His Coming" by C. B. Rock, 3rd Quarter 1991; "Pillars of Our Faith" by Joel Musvosvi, 3rd Quarter 2001; "The Wonder of Jesus" by Roy Adams, 2nd Quarter 2008; "Growing in Christ" by Kwabena Donkor, 4th Quarter 2012; and "Christ and His Law" by Keith Burton, 2nd Quarter 2014.[38]

Besides these, several Blacks have contributed to the *Seventh-day Adventist Bible Commentary* and the upcoming Bible commentaries being produced by Andrews University and Pacific Press. Also bearing mention is the extensive theology that Black Adventists have forged in theses and dissertations, a good deal of which are now freely available on the Digital Commons@Andrews University.[39]

Also available is a plethora of periodical articles in which Black Adventists have engaged in theology. *Message Magazine, Ministry Magazine,* and the *Adventist Review* have been particularly receptive in this regard. Most of these works can be accessed for free by doing searches on the SDA Periodical Index and accessing the articles at the General Conference Archives website.[40]

It is of particular importance, in concert with the purposes of this study, to observe the number of Black Adventist authors whose writings relate specifically to social (racial) justice. The precursor to all such manuscripts, Frank Loris Peterson's classic book, *The Hope of the Race,* was published in 1943 by the Pacific Press. While Peterson does not, in this work, directly challenge the systems that perpetuate social evil as do the later Black writers, he does so in several chapters by illumining the promises of God as having special import for his long-suffering people.

Among Black Adventist authors who have followed him with books addressing social justice both in and out of the church but, as most titles indicate, in a more direct and forceful way, are E. E. Cleveland, *The Middle Wall* (1969) and *Free at Last* (1970); Jacob Justiss, *Angels in Ebony* (1975); Tim Dennison, *Sex, Race and Grace!* (1981); Louis B. Reynolds, *We Have Tomorrow* (1984); Richard Williams, *They Stole It but You Must Return It* (1986); Frank W. Hale, Jr., *Angels Watching Over Me* (1996); Keith Burton, *The Faith Factor* (2005); Ganoune Diop, *Portraits of Freedom and Fellowship* (2001); Clarence Hodges, *This Far by Faith* (1998); Alven Makapela, *The Problem with Africanity in the Seventh-day Adventist Church* (1996); Samuel G. London, Jr., *Seventh-day Adventists and the Civil Rights Movement* (2009); Emory J. Tolbert, *Seventh-day Adventism and the Civil Rights Movement* and *Race and Culture in America* (1986); L. Alex Swan, *When Whites Riot* (1973) and *The Politics of Riot Behavior* (1980);[41] and Delbert Baker, ed., *Telling the Story* (1996).

Adventist scholar Bertram Melbourne, former dean of Howard University Divinity School, in his article "Black Seventh-day Adventists and Theological Directions," printed in the book *Perspectives: Black Seventh-day Adventists Face the Twenty-First Century* (1996), identifies a number of Black writers whose major theses or papers have contributed also in this vein. Those whom he highlights are Lorenzo H. Grant, "Ethical Rationale and Model for Meeting the Growing Needs of the Regional Work"; Walter

B. T. Douglas, "Liberation Theology and Theologies of Liberation"; Calvin B. Rock, *A Better Way* (1970); and Pedrito Maynard-Reid, *Poverty and Wealth in James* (1987).[42]

Melbourne summarized his own conclusion regarding the social aspect of the gospel in these words:

> While it is true that the gospel is not all social, there is a social dimension that must not be ignored. The gospel must not be so other worldly that it is of no earthly good.... Recognition by the church that it has a role in the social order to do what Jesus did in His ministry will assist in seeing that injustice in any form is not tolerated in the Christian community.[43]

And he continues:

> Analysis reveals that a social justice agenda characterized the early church and the early Advent movement. Micah's poignant question "What doth the Lord require of thee, but to do justly, and to love mercy, and to walk humbly with thy God?" (Micah 6:8) is representative of the early pioneers of the Seventh-day Adventist Church, who were involved in the antislavery and abolitionist movements as well as the Underground Railroad. Shouldn't we be also concerned about social justice? Shouldn't our voices be heard against injustice? This is not just a liberal agenda; it is God's agenda for His people: "These ought ye to have done, and not to leave the other undone" (Matt. 22:23).[44]

In addition, Melbourne calls for Black theologians to see and transmit Scripture through the lens of the oppressed without condescending to a cultural religion in this way:

> I believe that we cannot continue to embrace a Eurocentric theology. However, proclaiming an Afrocentric theology could be interpreted as reverse discrimination. I would suggest a Christocentric theology, and by this I am not pulling Christ down into a human problem as the Corinthian Christians did. Like Paul I am seeing Christ as the one who gives meaning and legitimacy to any doctrine or theology; He must be the center and focus of any meaningful dialogue.[45]

More recent offerings of significance than those listed by Melbourne include Winsley Benjamin Hector's 2012 Claremont School of Theology dissertation titled "Racial Reconciliation, Privilege, and the Debate within the Seventh-day Adventist Church in the United States on the Future of the Regional (Black) Conferences"; Gregory J. Allen's *Christ Has Welcomed You* (2017); and John Thompson's (ed.) *The Enduring Legacy of Ellen G. White and Social Justice* (2017).

Given the number of Black authors noted, it is fair to ask why their minority interpretations have not had greater influence on the church's socially conservative thinking. The following reasons would seem to apply: (1) the far greater percentage of works by Black authors address general doctrinal statements rather than social issues; (2) very few works dealing with social concerns (perhaps through no fault of the publishers) have been printed by Adventist publishing houses, and therefore enjoyed the wide exposure provided to the Adventist public; and (3) most of the authors of both emphases (general doctrinal concerns and that of social issues) have done so without the capacity for understanding original biblical languages and therefore lack both the depth and the credibility required for full acceptance in the academic or, for that matter, general public.

It is, however, gratifying to note that the number of individuals fitting the last description is growing. Their submissions tend to fit what Melbourne has identified as Black theology, the increasing effort of Black theologians and those of related disciplines to prepare first-hand commentary on biblical text. This branch of theological endeavor has roots in the decision of fifty-one Black clergy at a 1966 interdenominational Bible conference in Atlanta, Georgia, to promote biblical interpretation through the sociological grid of the oppressed.

The results of this effort are especially helpful in contextualizing Scripture by demonstrating its relevance for the real-life situation of the hearer. Minus the effects of critical contextualization (e.g., preserving the truth in the gospel while taking into account cultural difference), minorities are subjected to perhaps well-meaning but nonetheless imperial, and therefore unfulfilling, interpretations of the Word. The directives outlined are helpful not only as guidance in principles of structural arrangements but also for Black worship form and liturgy as well.

It is neither strange nor wrong, given their differing cultural history, that the liturgical preferences of White and Black worshipers often differ. The challenge for Black Adventists is that while they do not readily resonate with the typical worship practices of their White counterparts, there is a dearth of theological instruction helpful for fusing Adventist doctrine with their cultural orientation. The result is a vacuum that has given rise to a brand of celebratory singing and instrumental music distinguished by volume and repetition generally void of doctrinal reference and conducive of theatrics and emotional display.

Given the pervasive and enthusiastic endorsement of parishioners and pastors alike, it is questionable whether this trend can be easily reversed. However, to the extent that it is addressed (and it should be), it will be the work of Black scholars whose experience in the Black community and whose academic tools equip them to relate to the Black condition in the light of divine revelation—in other words, who will speak to the issue within the framework of Black theology.

A few African-American Adventist scholars have attempted to address this need, particularly as concerns the matter of music. One is James Richard Doggette, Sr., who did so in his Claremont School of Theology, Doctor of Ministry project "Emotion and Rationality in African American Seventh-day Adventist Worship" (1992). Another is Errol T. Stoddard who devoted his two-volume work, *The Silent Shout* (2001; 2016), to the subject. Both speak to the good of "celebratory worship" and the need for what Doggette terms a neo-Pentecostal approach as the solution for worship that is "rational enough to be accepted by traditional Adventists yet emotional enough to be appreciated by traditional African-Americans." "By creatively integrating the truth of Seventh-day Adventism with the rhythm of African American Christianity, and emotion with rationality," Doggette concludes, "the resulting product would be a neo-Pentecostal worship style that would be both attractive to the Black masses and faithful to Seventh-day Adventist tradition."[46]

Eurydice V. Osterman, professor of music at Oakwood University, has authored two books dealing with this critical aspect of worship in the Black Adventist community.[47] In each volume, Osterman, who makes generous use of both Scripture and the writings of Ellen White, arrives at conclusions different from that suggested by Doggette and Stoddard. Osterman does not disagree with their notion of Black Adventism's need for a musical form that incorporates fundamental Adventist doctrine with legitimate Black cultural expression. However, she does not see the solution as requiring a radical reduction of the use of traditional Christian music: anthems, hymns, Negro spirituals, and gospel songs of the non-jazzy, heavy metal type. Which is to say she is critical of what she terms a "non-discriminatory" embrace of what has come to be known as "praise worship." Among her more incisive comments are:

> Unfortunately for some, heritage music is considered to be that which is currently produced by today's African American musicians.... The *contemporary*

*style* of these musicians is really a fusion of today's popular sounds.... Black heritage music really begins with the spiritual.[48]

[T]hus many believe that they are filled with the Holy Spirit when in reality, they are physically responding to the sound stimulus that secretes a hormone that makes them feel that way...... Artificial stimulants in worship are like empty calories—they satisfy for the moment but provide no nourishment for spiritual growth and development.[49]

... [T]hus was born the praise song, many of which were characterized by a rock/hip-hop beat, very loud volume, and profuse syncopation to jump start and induce the enthusiasm of the congregation.... Attention is shifted to the musician.... Hymns that expressed a yearning for the promised land have been replaced by hymns yearning for peace and a more comfortable and abundant life in this world.[50]

Additional Black Adventist writings on worship music include Alma Blackmon's "Black Seventh-day Adventists and Church Music" and Mervyn Warren's "Black Seventh-day Adventists and Worship" *in Perspectives: Black Seventh-day Adventists Face the Twenty-first Century* (1996), as well as Pedrito Maynard-Reid's *Diverse Worship: African American, Hispanic, and Caribbean Perspectives* (2000).

Black Adventist preaching, which also (in many instances) today assumes a message and manner undistinguished from other forms of Protestantism, is likewise a fertile field for Black Adventist theological endeavor. Several Black Adventist authors have provided helpful insights in this area, including Charles E. Bradford, *Preaching to the Times* (1993); Calvin B. Rock, "Black SDA Preaching: Balanced and Binding or Betwixt and Between" (*Ministry*, September 2000); Peter J. Prime, *The Gospel of Love and Real Evangelism* (2009); and Mervyn A. Warren, *Black Preaching: Truth and Soul* (1977) and *Ellen White on Preaching; Insights for Sharing God's Word* (2010).

Additional scholarship in these two critical aspects of worship is arguably Black Adventism's most urgent need. One reason is that both forms of proclamation—music and preaching—like all art not only reflect the level of a people's culture but are highly determinative in shaping their understanding and commitment. Another reason is that while a significant percentage of more educated Blacks regard the dominant brand of celebratory preaching and musical offerings a thing to be endured, a growing number of others are moving their membership, tithe and all, to churches with a more traditional worship style (Anglo congregations in White conferences). They are not completely satisfied there, but they regard "less" enthusiasm in praise preferable to the "more" of most Black congregational worship. Their exodus is extremely disquieting to Regional conference directors, especially in view of the loss of revenue. However, without serious attention to the cause, the trend will predictably widen with increasingly negative consequences. Their leaving will likely not doom Black conferences, but it is certain to modify their character and restrict their potential.

Regional conferences have been successful because they have responded to people's needs with remnant faith and reverent fervor. Continuing in that tradition is critical to maintaining the "cantus firmus "or "true church" melody (persona) that God's people are called to project. A specific challenge in this regard, not uncommon to their sister (White-administered) conferences, is balancing the truth that, when fishing for souls, it is, indeed, necessary "to catch them before you clean them," with the equally critical imperative to "clean them before they are accepted into the body!"

Another challenge, one especially pertinent to the Black sector, is that of defining the balance between David's call to come before God with loud instruments of praise (Ps. 150) and Habakkuk's enjoining to "keep silence before Him" (Hab. 2:20). Again, the answers to be credible for Black believers must be provided by Black Adventist scholars themselves. They alone understand the two separate and demanding components: the innate cultural longings (needs) of Black culture and the peculiar (true church) doctrinal concepts of Adventism. That Black writers, as shown above, sometimes disagree regarding the proper liturgical form or forms this union suggests can be confusing. But it is vital that the quest for agreement be continued and credibly expressed.

To lack proper guidance in this matter is to risk a convert's answer to the query: "Into what then were you baptized?" (Acts 19:3) as being not a separate denomination, but a faith quite different from that which, through a century of struggle, protesting predecessors dared to develop and defend. As demonstrated by the discussion above, by the very nature of needs inherent to its community and culture, Black theology is mandated to consideration of micro as well as macro matters of Christian concern.

Perhaps the most meaningful contribution to Christian thought of the latter kind, its "types modality," likens the enslavement of Blacks in America to Israel's bondage in Egypt. This view holds that just as Israel was enslaved by an evil oppressor and eventually freed by God through Moses, Aaron, and Miriam, so through a series of deliverers (Harriet Tubman, Thurgood

Marshall, Martin Luther King, Jr., and others) African Americans have been released from bondage here in the United States.

It further holds that as Israel retained its distinctiveness after the Exodus, so have African Americans maintained theirs. It also affirms that Black Americans, having no physical land of promise as did the Israelites and thus confined to the land of the oppressor, a land in which they have suffered widespread physical and social abuse, urgently and understandably require distinctive means of addressing their cultural needs.

Black theology affirms that without such arrangements the Black community is doomed to wander in a political no-man's land, culturally distanced from the advantaged class while at the same time bereft of structures essential to healthy functioning within their largely separate community. Black theology differs from traditional Protestant theology in that it deals with the "isness" of America's social realities, not the "oughts" of the nation's expressed dreams. It takes into account the fact that Blacks have not been assimilated into Emerson's social melting pot, and that theirs is not nor has ever been "one nation, under God indivisible, with liberty and justice for all." Instead of living in denial, Black theology shines the light of the gospel upon the real, existential situation and prescribes for the disadvantaged what they need for spiritual and social betterment.

Further, Black theology looks with reasonable suspicion upon the White moderate who, in the words of Dr. King, "... is more devoted to 'order' than to justice; who prefers a negative peace which is the absence of tension to a positive peace which is the presence of justice; who constantly says 'I agree with you in the goal you seek, but I can't agree with your methods of direct action'; who paternalistically feels he can set the timetable for another man's freedom; who lives by the myth of time and who constantly advises the Negro to wait until a 'more convenient season.'"[51]

There are, however, cautions to be observed with respect to the Black theological tradition. The first is that of anointing any ethnic group, other than the one that was prior to the stoning of Stephen, as God's chosen people. While there are significant parallels between Israel's experience and that of Black Americans, they are not to be taken to extremes.

Second is the danger also common to some Black theologians of radicalizing elements of Scripture in ways that type all White Americans as racially biased. That, of course, is not true. From the time of the Quakers, who first brought to slaves the liberating news of the true God, to the Abolitionists whose efforts shattered the foundations of slavery, to the 185,000 White Union soldiers who died in the Civil War, and to the marchers and martyrs who served in the Civil Rights Movement, concerned White citizenry has sacrificed to assist Black Americans in their progress.

Third is the mistake of some Black theologians who seek to make God the Lord of the poor only. Scripture makes it clear that He is already now and will someday soon be formally crowned "Lord of all."

Fourth, to be truly authentic, Black theology, while decrying racism, must be careful to avoid the danger of ethnocentrism (validation by comparison with other groups) or even fully trust in what Leslie Pollard identifies as "ethnorelativism" (the assumption of equality with all other groups). That is because ethnocentrism is guilty of the sin of self-centeredness and ethnorelativism which, "while appealing, falters because humans, as Scripture asserts, are powerless to fully extricate themselves from the hold of their own self-service (see Rom. 1–3; 7:21–25)."[52]

Fifth, while it is correct to reject the notion that social freedom is something to be had only in the world to come, it is a lethal error—in fact, heresy—to elevate its present opportunities as remotely comparable to the believers' "eye has not seen, nor ear heard, nor have entered into the heart of man" (1 Cor. 2:9) joys to come.

## The Ellen White Exception

This discussion has noted the insensitivity of mainline Adventist authorship with regard to social freedom. However, we must recognize a notable exception: the literary corpus of Ellen G. White. C. D. Brooks, pastor, evangelist, and, for several decades, member of the board of trustees of the White Estate, provides one of the clearest comments about the contrast between White's social posture and that of latter-twentieth-century church leaders:

> Something dreadfully negative has happened to us. Though we have a heritage of justice and courage from our Adventist pioneers, we seem to have forgotten it. Our present blandness is simply out of keeping with the heroic facts of our past.... The reasons... include the fact that our thinking is clouded by misconceptions and misrepresentation, and the fact that section six in volume nine of *Testimonies for the Church* has wrongly become a tool for widening discrimination and broadening existing prejudice...
>
> The truth, then, is that a change toward moral blandness has come about despite the steadfast humanitarianism of the church's prophet. To a tragic degree our church has been shaped by the unenlightened views of a

selfish society. We have not been as willing to fight for brotherhood as we have been to attack the tobacco industry and to battle with lawmakers who hint at Sunday legislation.[53]

Regardless of whether Ellen White had African ancestry, as a significant percentage in the Black Adventist community believe, her childhood sufferings qualified her to empathize with the plight of society's wounded and their need to resist oppression.[54] Unfortunately, some view her otherwise, largely because of statements such as one that appears in *The Desire of Ages*:

> The government under which Jesus lived was corrupt and oppressive; on every hand were crying abuses, . . . extortion, intolerance, and grinding cruelty. Yet the Saviour attempted no civil reforms. He attacked no national abuses, nor condemned the national enemies . . . not because He was indifferent to the woes of men, but because the remedy did not lie in merely human or external measures.[55]

Another declares, "Let God have the matter of condemning authorities and governments wholly in His own keeping."[56] And a third one reads:

> Again and again Christ had been asked to decide legal and political questions. But He refused to interfere in temporal affairs. He knew that in the political world there were iniquitous proceedings and great tyranny. But His only exposure of these was the proclamation of Bible truth. . . . He refused to become entangled in personal disputes.[57]

But these and similar expressions become consistent with the strong biblical emphasis on justice when we remember the following: First, protest against government abuses by Christians in either Christ's time or in the days of the embryonic Adventist church would have triggered such sanctions as to abort their witness and, in fact, their very existence. Second, Christ's purpose to establish not a physical kingdom or "state-church" government as the Jews desired, but a spiritual kingdom in which matters of the soul superseded matters of the body, always guided His relationship to Rome. Third, while the church should try to avoid being seen as an enemy of the state, Christian social pacifism should have its limits, as demonstrated by the servile silence of German Adventism in the Third Reich. Fourth, the fact that North American Seventh-day Adventism was one of the last denominations in the country to publicly affirm the nation's Civil Rights Act indicates that there was, and reoccurring events show that there still is, need for reconciling our social justice posture and the biblical injunction to be "the head and not the tail" (Deut. 28:13). Fifth, the fact that entanglement in political affairs would hinder the church's pursuit of ultimate realities does not dictate for it silence regarding injustice. All matters political are indeed social but not all matters social are political.

The 2015 *Seventh-day Adventist Church Manual* addresses the issue of political involvement in language that, while low-key, is surprisingly activist given the church's history of tepid social involvement:

> While our highest responsibility is to the Church and the gospel commission, we should support by our service and our means, as far as possible and consistent with our beliefs, efforts for social order and betterment. Even though we must stand apart from political and social strife, we should always, quietly, and firmly, maintain an uncompromising stand for justice and right in civic affairs, along with full adherence to our religious convictions....[58]

Sakae Kubo, at the time an Andrews University Seminary professor, in his memorable worship address "In Christ There Is No East Nor West" on Saturday, June 13, 1964, in the school's Pioneer Memorial Church, moved away from the "always quietly and firmly" position of the *Manual* to a decidedly more assertive posture. In language consistent with the church prophet's condemnations of social injustice, Kubo stated:

> If it [the church] is to serve its function, it must be a voice crying in the wilderness and not a mere echo of the secular mores and standards of worldly society. It is a sad commentary on the church's witness when it cannot speak out boldly on the Biblical message of love and brotherhood for fear it might be political.[59]

Giving further validation to the activist nature of Ellen White's social ethic is her repeated use of the "types" modality (referenced above) very prominently employed by Black theologians in their portrayal of African Americans' sojourn in what she derisively labels as this "so-called Christian nation."[60]

Her language, paralleling closely that of Black theologians, includes the following:

> When the Hebrew people were suffering cruel oppression under the hand of their taskmasters, the Lord looked upon them, and He called Israel His son. He bade Moses go to Pharaoh with the message, "Israel is my son, even my firstborn."... He says, "Let my son go, that he may serve me: and if thou refuse to let him go, behold, I will slay thy son, even thy firstborn."... God cares no less for the souls of the African race that might be won to Him than He cared for Israel.[61]

And again:

> But the Hebrew nation is not the only nation that has been in cruel bondage, and whose groanings have come to the ears of the Lord of hosts. The Lord God of Israel has looked upon the vast number of human beings who were held in slavery in the United States of America. . . . God spoke concerning the captivity of the colored people as verily as He did concerning the Hebrew captives, and said, "I have surely seen the affliction of my people . . . and have heard their cry by reason of their taskmasters; for I know their sorrows; and I am come down to deliver them."[62]

Such statements do not, as intimated earlier in addressing the tenants of Black theology, provide African Americans with a superior covenantal relationship with God. That is clear from the "whosoever will" New Testament appeal to every nation, kindred, tongue, and people. They do, however, demonstrate the prophet's keen identity with society's disadvantaged; speak to the fact that those who oppress their fellow humanity, as with the case of the Egyptians, unfailingly incur the wrath of the just and merciful God; and confirm that within the theological strain for which the "types modality" is paramount, there is good to be gained.

Other evidence of Ellen White's distance from social conservatism appear in her appeals to social rights vs. social wrongs; her disdain for social caste and social inequality;[63] her calls to social sympathy and social kindness; and, very significantly, her notion of restitution (reparations) for Black enslavement.[64] This latter principle, that of compensation or redress for past wrongs, is very pronounced in her writings. She could not be clearer than when stating:

> The Lord demands restitution from the churches in America. You are to relieve the necessities of this field. . . . . . The Lord calls upon you to restore to his people the advantages of which they have so long been deprived.[65]
>
> The Lord wrought in freeing the Southern slaves; but He designed to work still further for them as He did for the children of Israel, whom He took forth to educate, to refine, and ennoble.[66]
>
> The Lord would have His people who love Him to know [that] the converted colored men and women who love God and try to do His will are His property, of as much value in His sight as the white who have not endured the same embarrassments that the colored race have, however educated and talented they may be. Let the white people who ignore the color of the skin be sure to show their appreciation of the same by making their own peace [and] gratitude offerings to God, and by teaching those who are

not so highly favored that they will help, that they will restore to them as far as they can what has been lost through the years of privation and slavery.[67]

And, it should be added, her justice categories speak not only for Blacks, but also to every socially disadvantaged segment of society, be it Native American, immigrant, or the group of females that in spite of modern enlightenment is still striving for parity in society worldwide. Which is to say that what the church needs is not scholarship that focuses narrowly on Regional conferences, but that which will more broadly free the church from its penchant for social conservatism: scholarship that will counter the traditional portrayals of our Lord as a passive bystander to Roman oppression; the apostle Paul as advising cooperative obedience and silent suffering under government atrocities; and Ellen White as the cautious seer of a "Better Way," a way which for the fearful has never come and which for the brave has indeed arrived but which, as this discussion reveals, requires informed understanding.

## SUMMARY OF THEOLOGICAL RESPONSE

Several things should be considered by the Adventist Church, as with all Christian denominations whose theological undergirding have led them to a conservative relationship to the cause of social justice.

Micah's regard for that which is good (Micah 6:8) begins with "doing justice." While his companion injunction "love mercy" clearly allows for active participation in the struggle against social evil, "doing justice" is an even more formidable command to action. One can, by assisting the wounded with lifesaving tourniquets and needed aid, assume that one has fulfilled "loving mercy": not so with "doing justice." Both commands are absolute in character and divine in principle. The connotation of "loving mercy" does in fact have meaning for the prevention of injustice as well as assistance for its victims. However, it is in the more robust and prophetic tone of "doing justice" that we sense its other noble aspects: both the identification and apprehension of agents of social evil.

It was not just God's final judgment upon the perpetrators of injustice that David had in mind when he wrote, "He will bring justice to the poor of the people; He will save the children of the needy, and will break in pieces the oppressor" (Ps. 72:4). That the identification and apprehension of oppressors is, in the meantime, doing justice is witnessed in Amos 5:7–12 and throughout the chapter in his scathing rebukes upon those "who turn justice into wormwood, and lay righteousness to rest in the earth"; they are the ones who "tread down the poor and take grain taxes from him . . . afflicting the just and taking bribes; diverting the poor from justice." And, most instructively, it is emphasized repeatedly in Christ's unmasking of the insensitive, self-serving leaders of His day (see, e.g., Matt. 23:23–33; John 2:14–16).

An additional activity suggested by the prophetic call for "doing justice" is that of social advocacy or protest, an obligation traditionally disavowed by most conservative religionists. However, Proverbs 31:8, 9 is clearly instructive here: "Open your mouth for the speechless. . . . Open your mouth, judge righteously, and plead the cause of the poor and needy." Isaiah speaks to this constituent element of justice with the admonishment "learn to do good; seek justice, rebuke the oppressor, defend the fatherless, plead for the widow" (Isa. 1:17). And again, when condemning those who countenanced injustice by turning away from oppression, he chided, "Your hands are defiled with blood, and your fingers with iniquity; your lips have spoken lies, your tongue has muttered perversity. No one calls for justice, nor does any plead for truth" (Isa. 59:3, 4).

Among the legitimate ways that the Christian can protest are voting for proper officials and issues, writing letters and signing petitions to influential individuals, lobbying to influence legislation, boycotting firms and products that prey upon the oppressed, and even marching in peaceful demonstrations for justice. The church does not transform itself into a political body when it engages with society in this way.

"Pastor," the church secretary addressed me over the phone, "someone just called saying that they saw you on TV marching with protestors around one of the corporate headquarters here in Detroit. Can you imagine that?"

"Yes," I replied, "it was I."

"Oh, no," she responded in disbelief. "We are not supposed to do that. We are not supposed to fight!"

"But I wasn't fighting," I replied. "I was marching and singing and praying with factory workers and their sympathizers in behalf of the workers' better wages."

Attitudes about social responsibility have broadened somewhat since that exchange half a century ago. Unfortunately, however, the social fear and reluctance reflected in that conversation with one of the most saintly members I have known remains an effective barrier to practical gospel witness.

The correct social posture of the church is not a precise duplication of the actions of Paul, or even so recent a figure as Ellen White. This truth becomes abundantly evident when we remember that while the prophets often strained against the cognitive boundaries of their time, they still addressed social and political issues within the cultural perspectives of their era. Though they often pushed the envelope of societal understandings, as when Paul asked Philemon to treat Onesimus, his slave, as a brother, they did not and could not speak to the audiences of their day in the behavioral reasoning of future generations. In Paul's case, he did not—could not—conceive of a slave-less society.

The social directives of the biblical writers come to us not as absolute commands but as illustrations of how eternal principles work out within specific historical incidents. Those same principles must be lived out in our post-modern society as bravely as they were by people who could not have imagined our complex world.

The capacity and need for succeeding generations of Christians to implement more fully social principles that former generations upheld to the best of their more limited ability is reflected in the concept of "middle axioms" developed by English social theorist J. H. Oldham. Ethicist Paul Ramsey, in his book *Basic Christian Ethics*, illumines this concept: "'Middle axioms' are intended . . . 'to define the directions in which, in a particular state of society, Christian faith must express itself. They are not binding for all time, but are provisional definitions of the type of behavior required of Christians at a given period and in given circumstances.'"[68]

The list of social evils against which Ellen White wrote and spoke included slavery, intemperance, exploitive child labor, gender discrimination, economic disadvantage, dissolved families, educational limitations, and the abuses of organized capital and labor. Her example reminds us that the proper question for each era is not what did the prophets say or do, but what would they say or do given their principles were they alive today. As Niebuhr further reminds us, individuals of piety and good will do not just duplicate the "then and there" but rather with confidence in God's purposes and commands respond appropriately to the "here and now."[69]

Those who read about Christ's decision to keep aloof from earthly governments and not attack Rome should remember that in addition to the suicidal consequences to His own program, and to that of believers throughout history who would have followed His example, much of society's injustice comes not from government but from "private" institutions. Jesus did boldly attack those. He did so by crying out against unjust wealth (Matt. 19:21–26), authority (Luke 11:46), rewards (Matt. 23:35), and obstruction of justice (Luke 11:52). His attacks against unjust clergy, land owners, tax collectors, day laborers, bankers, teachers, managers, and lawyers profoundly demonstrated His aversion to injustice that He had so often proclaimed through prophets before assuming human flesh.

While it is true that the solution for injustice does "not lie in merely human and external measures," and that "to be efficient, the cure must . . . regenerate the heart," sufferers need relief whether or not their oppressors are converted.[70] Which is to say that the immediate role of justice is not to convert the perpetrators but to relieve the oppressed. Furthermore, to say that the cure does not lie "merely" in human or external measures is to acknowledge that it does lie "partly" there and that believers should confront injustice to the best of their ability.

We are not surprised then, as seen in Ellen White's contrast with the apostle Paul on the issue of civil disobedience (e.g., his position to return the runaway slave versus hers not to do it), that a latter-day prophet might differ in approach from an earlier one. Her clear mandate to defy the unjust Fugitive Slave Law of 1850 reads: "The law of our land requiring us to deliver a slave to his master, we are not to obey; and we must abide the consequences of violating this law. The slave is not the property of any man."[71] White's category of "civil disobedience," seen in both her charge not to return the runaway slave and in her praise of the German princes for their defiance of government authority at the Diet of Spires (1529), has biblical precedent as well.[72] This includes the practical measures employed by the parents of baby Moses (Ex. 2), the rescue measures taken by Rahab in saving the spies (Josh. 2), and the actions of Paul and Silas (Acts 4 and 19). Such biblical events remind us that when the principles of the two realms—the earthly government and the heavenly one—clash, we must obey the latter, the consequences notwithstanding. Comparing Ellen White's response to social evils with that of Christian spokespersons who pre-dated her clearly demonstrates this principle. While her early church and Middle Ages predecessors were greatly restricted in their freedom to speak out against political and social evils, the more socially liberal climate of her day freed her to do so, and she did so boldly.

Contrary to much conservative theological opinion, the church's charter does not provide a choice "between satisfying *physical* hunger and *spiritual* hunger, between being healed and being eternally saved, between being lifted up from deprivation and alienation and being offered eternal life. Neither must the church in its mission be caught between false choices."[73] These are not separate agendas. The gospel does not function as a visionary desire or abstract principle—it has hands and feet to use in restoring wounded humanity into the freedom and image of God. Christian mission and Christian duty are not antithetical or even merely complementary events—they are synonymous activities to pursue in the light of human reality.

As demonstrated by the similar social interaction between Whites and Blacks on the West Coast of America where there are no Regional conferences, and that where they do exist, eliminating them would not automatically improve brotherhood.[74] The reality is that as long as major differences in social culture exist at the local level, clearly discernable association patterns will also exist.

Further, since group association to a large extent results from cultural factors not related to racism, no matter what we might do, we will still need specific administrative mechanisms. Even when factoring in racism, the core of the issue is not whether various groups love each other, but, given the fact that distinctive cultural associations will continue to persist, thus requiring some kind of minority administrative structure, the question remains: What is the most productive form of administration possible?

**Notes**

1. Martin Luther King, Jr., "The Ethical Demands for Integration," *Religion & Labor* (May 1963): 1, 3–4, 7–8.

2. This discussion is dealing with Black and White couples, not intermarriage among other races.

3. "One-in-Seven New U.S. Marriages Is Interracfial or Interethnic." http://www.pewsocialtrends.org/2010/06/04/ii-overview-2

4. Roland G. Fryer, Jr., "Guess Who's Been Coming to Dinner? Trends in Interracial Marriage over the 20th Century," *Journal of Economic Perspectives* 21 (Spring 2007): 71–90.

5. United States Senators, "African American Senators." https://www.senate.gov/pagelayout/history/h_multi_sections_and_teasers/Photo_Exhibit_African_American_Senators.htm

6. Doug McAdam and Karina Kloos, *Deeply Divided: Racial Politics and Social Movements in Post-War America* (New York: Oxford Press, 2014), 281.

7. See "2017 Annual Statistical Report," General Conference Archives, 18–19. http://documents.adventistarchives.org/Statistics/ASR/ASR2017.pdf

8. Delbert W. Baker, "Regional Conferences: 50 Years of Progress," *Adventist Review* (November 1995), 14. http://documents.adventistarchives.org/Books/TTS1996.pdf

9. Statistics shared with the author by the Office of Regional Ministry, Huntsville, Alabama. See also Delbert Baker, "Regional Conferences: 50 Years of Progress," and Office for Regional Conference Ministry, "Within Our Regional Conferences: . . . Every Kindred Tongue and People," 2005, Oakwood University Archives.

10. The two higher-education institutions referenced are Atlantic Union College in South Lancaster, Massachusetts, and Washington Adventist University in Takoma Park, Maryland.

11. See Reinhold Niebuhr, *Moral Man and Immoral Society: A Study in Ethics and Politics* (New York: Charles Scribner's Sons, 1932).

12. Daniel A. Yudkin and Jay Van Bavel, "The Roots of Implicit Bias," *The New York Times* (December 9, 2016), 8. https://www.nytimes.com/2016/12/09/opinion/sunday/the-roots-of-implicit-bias.html

13. Examples are Takoma Academy, Atlantic Union College, and Washington Adventist University (in the East), and Golden Gate, Lynwood, and San Fernando Valley Academy (in the West). It is also the case with churches, such as the Takoma Park, Sligo, Silver Spring, and Pennsylvania Avenue (in the East); the 54th Street, Westminster Good Samaritan, Hollywood, Grand Avenue, and Los Angeles Central (in the West); and the Belvedere, Grand View, Marietta, and Stone Mountain, Georgia (in the South). The phenomenon, of course, repeats itself many, many times throughout the rest of the country. The fact that the once all-White Florida Conference is now more than 50 percent non-White and the Greater New York Conference, once predominantly White, is now except for a dwindling remnant entirely non-White, further accents the depth of this trend.

14. Alfonzo Greene, Jr., "Black Regional Conferences in the Seventh-Day Adventist Church (SDA) Compared with United Methodist (Black) Central Jurisdiction/Annual Conferences with White S.D.A. Conferences, from 1940–2001," PhD diss., Loyola University Chicago, December 2009, pp. 206, 284. http://ecommons.luc.edu/cgi/viewcontent.cgi?article=1159&context=luc_diss

15. White, *Testimonies for the Church*, vol. 1 (Mountain View, CA: Pacific Press Publishing Association, 1868), 266–267. https://egwwritings.org/?ref=en_1T.266.3&para=116.1308

16. Gary P. Marx, "Religion: Opiate or Inspiration of Civil Rights Militancy Among Negroes?" *American Sociological Review* 32.1 (February 1967): 70.

17. Rodney Stark and Charles Y. Glock, "Prejudice and the Churches," in *Religion in Sociological Perspective: Essays in the Empirical Study of Religion*, ed. Charles Y. Glock (Belmont, CA: Wadsworth, 1973), 95.

18. Ibid., 96.

19. Joseph Bates, *The Autobiography of Elder Joseph Bates* (Battle Creek, MI: Steam Press, 1868), 261. https://egwwritings.org/?ref=en_AJB.261.2&para=1086.1050

20. Quoted in H. Richard Niebuhr, *The Responsible Self: An Essay in Christian Moral Philosophy* (New York: Harper and Rowe Publishing, 1963), 90.

21. Ellen G. White, *The Southern Work* (Washington, DC: Review and Herald, 1966), 15. https://egwwritings.org/?ref=en_SWk.15.1&para=139.63

22. White, *Testimonies for the Church*, 9:214. https://egwwritings.org/?ref=en_9T.214.3&para=115.1201

23. F. D. Nichol, *The Seventh-day Adventist Bible Commentary* (Washington, DC.: Review and Herald, 1956), 5:796.

24. Ellen G. White, *Christ's Object Lessons* (Hagerstown, MD: Review and Herald, 1969), 254.

25. Zdravko Plantak, *The Silent Church: Human Rights and Adventist Social Ethics* (New York: St. Martin's Press, 1998), 18. Sadly, many non-Adventist scholars have written on Adventists during the Nazi regime, also rendering a negative verdict of our church. For example, see Christine Elizabeth King, *The Nazi State and the New Religions: Five Case Studies in Non-conformity* (New York: Edwin Mellen Press, 1982), 89–119.

26. See Mark A. Kellner, "Europe: German, Austrian Churches Apologize for Holocaust Actions," Adventist News Network, August 15, 2005. https://news.adventist.org/en/all-news/news/go/2005-08-15/europe-german-austrian-churches-apologize-for-holocaust-actions

27. Ellen G. White, *Messages to Young People* (Washington, DC: Review and Herald, 1958), 36. https://egwwritings.org/?ref=en_MYP.36.1&para=76.134

28. F. D. Nichol, *The Seventh-day Adventist Bible Commentary* (Washington, DC: Review and Herald, 1956), 6:188.

29. Augustine, *De Catecizandis Rudibus*, xiv, 20. https://archive.org/details/liberdecatechiza00augu

30. Cited in Hannah Arendt, *The Human Condition*, 2nd ed. (Chicago: The University of Chicago Press, 1958), 74.

31. Reinhold Niebuhr, *The Nature and Destiny of Man* (Louisville, KY: Westminster John Knox, 1996), 2:195.

32. Martin Luther, *Works* (Weimar ed.), 18:326. Quoted in Reinhold Niebuhr, *The Nature and Destiny of Many* (New York: Charles Scribner's Sons, 1964), 2:193–194 #15.

33. Martin Luther, *Works* (Weimar ed.), 18:333. Quoted in ibid., 194.

34. Martin Luther, "Against the Robbing and Murdering Hordes of Peasants," in *Luther's Works*, ed. Robert C. Schultz (Philadelphia: Fortress, 1967), 46:50.

35. Reinhold Niebuhr, *The Nature and Destiny of Man*, 2:195.

36. Ibid., 204, 205.

37. A fine exploration of Black Adventist theology is Bertram Melbourne's "Black Seventh-day Adventists and Theological Directions" in *Perspectives: Black Seventh-day Adventists Face the 21st Century*, ed. Calvin B. Rock (Hagerstown, MD: Review and Herald, 1996), 47–58.

38. The full suite of Adult Sabbath School Quarterlies can be downloaded here: http://documents.adventistarchives.org/SSQ/Forms/AllItems.aspx

39. https://digitalcommons.andrews.edu

40. SDA Periodical Index (https://www.andrews.edu/library/ASDAL/sdapiindex.

html); General Conference Archives (http://documents.adventistarchives.org/default.aspx).

41. Benjamin Baker, *Black Authors Anthology*, Department of Archives and Statistics, General Conference of Seventh-day Adventists, Tacoma Park, Maryland.

42. Ibid.

43. Bertram Melbourne, "Black Seventh-day Adventists and Theological Directions," in *Perspectives: Black Seventh-day Adventists Face the 21st Century*, ed. Calvin B. Rock (Hagerstown, MD: Review and Herald, 1996), 49.

44. Ibid., 56.

45. Ibid., 57.

46. James Richard Doggette, Sr., "Emotion and Rationality in African American Seventh-day Adventist Worship," DMin diss., Claremont School of Theology, May 1992, 84.

47. Euyrdice Osterman, *What God Says about Music* (Huntsville, AL: Awsahm Music, 1998); *Worship: From Praise Him to Praise Hymn* (Bloomington, IN: Xlibris Book Publishers, 2015).

48. Osterman, *What God Says about Music*, 31, 32.

49. Ibid., 58.

50. Eurydice V. Osterman, *Worship: From Praise Him to Praise Hymn*, 38.

51. Martin Luther King, Jr., "Letter from a Birmingham Jail," April 16, 1963.

52. Leslie N. Pollard, "Leaders, Race, and Ethnicity: Temple or Vehicle?" in *Embracing Diversity: How to Understand and Reach People of All Cultures*, ed. Leslie N. Pollard (Hagerstown, MD: Review and Herald, 2000), 16–17.

53. C. D. Brooks, "The Church and the Black Dilemma," *Insight* Magazine, Oct. 27, 1970.

54. See Benjamin Baker's "'They Lived Near the Bridge Where We Went Over:' Ellen White and Blacks," *Spectrum* 42, no. 2 (Spring 2014), 45–52.

55. Ellen G. White, *The Desire of Ages* (Mountain View, CA: Pacific Press, 1940), 509. https://egwwritings.org/?ref=en_DA.509.3&para=130.2488

56. Ellen G. White, *Testimonies for the Church*, vol. 6 (Boise, ID: Pacific Press, 1948), 397. https://egwwritings.org/?ref=en_6T.397.2&para=118.2170

57. White, *Testimonies for the Church*, vol. 9, 218. https://egwwritings.org/?ref=en_9T.218.1&para=115.1222

58. *Seventh-day Adventist Church Manual* (Hagerstown, MD: Review and Herald, 2015), 137–138. https://www.adventist.org/fileadmin/adventist.org/files/articles/information/seventh-day-adventist-church-manual_2015_updated.pdf

59. Sakae Kubo, "In Christ There Is No East Nor West," Sermon, Pioneer Memorial Church, Andrews University, Berrien Springs, MI, June 13, 1964.

60. White, *The Southern Work*, 29. https://egwwritings.org/?ref=en_SWk.29.1&para=139.122

61. Ibid., 14.

62. Ibid., 42.

63. Ellen G. White, *Gospel Workers* (Hagerstown, MD: Review and Herald, 1994), 330; Ellen G. White, *Patriarchs and Prophets* (Boise, ID: Pacific Press, 1989), 534.

64. White, *The Southern Work*, 94–96. https://egwwritings.org/?ref=en_SWk.94.2&para=139.408

65. Ibid., 95.

66. Ibid., 42.

67. E. G. White to Brother and Sister Hughes, August 1, 1903, Letter 304, 1903. https://egwwritings.org/?ref=en_Lt304-1903.3&para=7649.9

68. Paul Ramsey, *Basic Christian Ethics* (Louisville, KY: Westminster/John Knox Press, 1950), 349–350.

69. H. Richard Niebuhr, *The Meaning of Revelation* (New York: The MacMillan Company, 1941), 42.

70. White, *The Desire of Ages*, 509.

71. White, *Testimonies to the Church*, 1:201, 202. https://egwwritings.org/?ref=en_1T.264.2&para=116.1298

72. Ellen G. White, *Acts of the Apostles* (Boise, ID: Pacific Press, 2005), 68, 69.

73. Jan Paulsen, "Is Social Service Our Mission?" *Adventist Review* (August 31, 1989), 19, 20. http://documents.adventistarchives.org/Periodicals/RH/RH19890831-V166-35.pdf

74. W. S. Lee, "Integration and the Regional Department" (c. 1974).

# 3
# REPLIES OF PRACTICAL REASONING

The sociological and theological responses notwithstanding, there remains the need for a practical address to a number of "bottom-line" questions often asked concerning the continuing existence of Regional conferences.

## THE HEAVENLY IDEAL

"But," many ask, "what about preparing for heaven where there will be no racial divide—should we not establish that pattern now? Are we not as a people to shape what we do in light of the ideal?" I believe that E. E. Cleveland gives the correct answer:

> When I hear of the word, "ideal," I always wonder just what the person is talking about. Does he mean the "ideal" for heaven, where there is a perfect society and an all-wise, all-powerful God to judge and enforce; or does he mean the "ideal" for the earth, where imperfect men control the work of God who are neither all-wise nor all-powerful . . . ? It is obvious that there will be no need for conference presidents, union presidents, division presidents, or even a president of the General Conference in heaven, for Jesus will be the all-wise controller of all men's destinies . . . we are not planning for heaven when we talk about subdivisional organizational facets. We are talking about down here! It seems that men get confused on this issue and speak platitudes that apply in heaven [but] that bear little or no relationship to the actual situation that we are faced with on earth.[1]

Otherwise stated, we earthly stewards err when we superimpose the just social conditions of glory upon present sinful circumstances and function "as if" heaven has already begun. Social action, guided by the word of God, does not fall prey to utopian idealism. Bonhoeffer's concept of "acting in correspondence with reality" is helpful. He observed:

> For the responsible man the given situation is not simply the material on which he is to impress his idea or his programme by force, but this situation is itself drawn in into the action and shares in giving form to the deed. It is not an "absolute good" that is to be realized; but on the contrary it is part of the self-direction of the responsible agent that he prefers what is relatively better to what is relatively worse and that he perceives that the "absolute good" may sometimes be the very worst.[2]

## THE PRINCIPLE OF UNITY

"But," others query, "Given the principles of unity expressed in John 17:10–21, Galatians 3:28, and elsewhere, as well as Ellen White's counsel that we 'press together,'[3] is it really biblical to be separated this way [the present conference arrangement]?" The answer is that a pejorative use of the word "separate" in this matter, as in so many other situations, is not warranted. All separation is not negative. For example, separation is not only helpful but strategically necessary in matters affecting gender, age, and our military branches.

This reasoning finds support from Acts 13:2 in which God instructs the Antioch prophets and teachers, "Now separate to Me Barnabas and Saul for the work to which I have called them." The leadership then anointed the two men not to a different cause but to a more efficient way of supporting their common goal of gospel outreach. If one can accept this interpretation along with Paul's observations regarding the relationship within the church of its varied elements—the circumcised and uncircumcised, slave and master, bound and free, Jew and Gentile—as a recognition of legitimate plurality within Christian community, it will more likely relieve some of the concerns about the existence of Regional conferences.

In *The Church*, Hans Küng speaks to this point when he discusses the two major organizational forms seen in the New Testament: the Jerusalem-Palestinian form observed in the book of Acts, and the Corinthian-Gentile form addressed in Paul's various epistles. His conclusion is: "It is not necessary for this diversity and variety to breed dissentions, enmity and strife ... unity is only endangered by co-existence which is neither co-operation nor support, but basically a hostile confrontation. It is not the differences in themselves which are harmful, but only excluding and exclusive differences."[4]

Regional conferences are not segregationist: they do not refuse membership to others. As pointed out previously, one significant proof is that the nine Black conferences incorporate approximately 140 non-Black congregations: Caucasian, Hispanic, Asian, as well as thousands of individual non-Black members in their churches. Rather than being separatist, they are, in the truest sense, inclusive: a legitimate and an effective means of nurturing a historically separated people (at the local church level) into the spiritually united, worldwide remnant church.

The factor that allows culturally diverse parts to live in harmony without discrimination on the one hand, or the destructive illusion of social amalgamation on the other, is love, a principle that fosters relevant accommodation within a united whole. It does so by what the apostle regards as "radical subordination" of each to the other, and functions as the "bound freedom" of all of its parts.

## THE WAY THINGS LOOK

"But," others ask in genuine concern, "Does not the existence of parallel conferences make a negative statement to the onlooking public?" The answer is, "Yes, it does, for some." But not to those who understand that in all socially pluralistic bodies, the higher yields of structural accommodation, though uncomfortable for some, far exceed that of the "one size fits all" arrangements that retard forms of mission especially valuable to large and vibrant minorities.

Rightly ordered, the church's most pressing concern is not that of societal opinion or public relations—it is not the optics of the form that matters more, but rather mission effectiveness. Its structural arrangements will most accurately reflect the righteous principles of God's Word when they provide minorities both the freedom to witness within their socially separate communities and the authority to represent themselves in the general councils of the church.

Instead of modeling, as it often does, the politically motivated bureaucratic forms about it or of shrinking from the label of difference, the church should, at the risk of being misunderstood, courageously plan in those ways that focus gospel mission above societal opinion. It is a badge of honor that Seventh-day Adventists have, in various ways (i.e., Sabbath observance, dress, and diet), historically done so. Identifying right gospel principles and developing appropriate church structures, though they be misunderstood by some, is a gospel necessity.

## THE NEED TO KNOW EACH OTHER BETTER

"But we need to know each other better, and how can that happen as long as we have Regional conferences?" many thoughtful inquirers of both races will ask. The answer begins with the recognition that social relations between the races are no more binding where Regional conferences do not exist (the two West Coast unions) than where they do. In other words, "member interaction" across ethnic lines is no more personal in Altadena than in Atlanta, in Las Vegas than in Long Island, in Portland than in Pittsburg, in Tucson than in Tulsa. Nor have churches described as "All Nations" proven to be the answer. They may prosper initially but inevitably, over time, become identified by whatever ethnic group (as a result of immigration in and migration out) becomes dominant. Contributing to the seeming irreducible reality of this phenomenon is the fact that the rate of "other kind" ethnic immigration (judged by language and/or color) into the group determines how quickly the majority "original kind" will move away. Clearly, merging or dissolving Regional conferences is not the answer to bringing people closer together at the congregational level.

The answer to a more intimate relationship pattern at the congregational level is neither of the above, but rather pastoral and church board leadership with determination to plan jointly in ways that will initiate meaningful intergroup contact. These include joint evangelistic endeavors, prayer meetings, mission trips, federations, Easter and Christmas music festivals, social outings (particularly involving younger individuals and families), and the celebration of Communion, including the Ordinance of Humility. Such activities wisely planned would foster genuine fellowship without interrupting the specific mission of Regional conferences. And there is always, of course, forging friendships on the personal level.

## THE NEED FOR RECONCILIATION

"But what about reconciliation?" some inquire. Would not, they reason, the issue of Regional conferences and racial dissonance of which they are a reminder be resolved if White and Black leaders of goodwill united in genuine efforts to reconcile their differences?

Black leaders understand that many of their White brothers and sisters do genuinely desire closer relations between the two groups. However, given the usual implications associated with reconciliation (e.g., mutual confession of guilt, mutual apology, mutual desire to restore relations lost because of offensive speech or action), Black leaders do not see it as applicable to either their past or present.[5]

The protest appeal that led to Regional conferences is more accurately described not as evidence of a fractured relationship, but rather the cry of a suffering people for freedom from structural bondage. Their creation more closely parallels Israel's miraculous escape from Egyptian bondage, for which reconciliation had no meaning, than Jacob's measured escape from his brother, where reconciliation did have meaning. Black leaders see themselves as innocent of any behavior requiring apology or confession. Their doctrinal beliefs have never wavered and their association patterns with White believers have always been open and friendly; while they have repeatedly sought equitable privileges and controls, they have, in the main, done so within the bounds of respectful debate and appeal.

Regional conference leaders, in my estimation, do not see themselves as in an adversarial relationship with White Adventism. And why should they? They are disappointed by some White attitudes, as that displayed by the refusal of White North American Division leadership at the 2009 NAD Spring Counsel to pray publicly for recently inaugurated U.S. president Barak Obama. However, they have not, nor have they ever, as a body reacted to such attitudes of recrimination and retaliation.

As reflected in the mission emphasis of Kinney's 1889 appeal and clarified in McElhany's 1944 urging that they be immediately established, Regional conferences are not, nor have they ever been, retaliation for racial slights. Racism had much to do with their need to exist, but mission at the local church level was the main factor for their creation and remains so today.

That Regional conferences have also served as a training ground for leaders who have ministered in both the North American and international arenas of church administration is an additional benefit of no small consequence. Given that Black leaders and their committees are (1) in charge of the administrative needs of Black congregations at the local church level (except in the two West Coast Unions); (2) well pleased with the missional results that their indigenous leadership is providing; (3) well integrated at the other levels of church administration; (4) content, for the most part, with White local church acceptance, when sought; (5) aware that Black and White relationships are as warm in those areas that *have* Regional conferences as in those that *do not*; and (6) unaware of actions on their part or that of their predecessors that cast them in the role of a feuding, or alienated wing of Adventism, the cry for reconciliation as generally understood lacks true meaning.

Reconciliation, in this context, does not mean organizing summits structured to promote fusion of cultures and denial of diversity. Rather, reconciliation means White Adventists apologizing for past indignities, and Black Adventists, in turn, forgiving and experiencing a cathartic relief of suspicions or even animosities that some may hold.

This later dynamic was clearly observable at the Cassopolis, Michigan, June 2015 seventieth-anniversary celebration of the Lake Region Conference. On that historic occasion, Don Livesay, White president of the parent body, the Lake Union Conference, surprised and sobered the large and appreciative congregation with a courageous statement of apology:

> So as we celebrate 70 years of Lake Region—the progress, the mission, the tens of thousands of people brought to the Lord who may not have ever heard the message, children educated, the expansion of the message and mission of God's remnant people, I come to you with my fellow officers ... with a heart that compels us to not only bring our joy in the success of the Lake Region but also to bring a personal and an official apology to our brothers and our sisters of the Lake Region Conference on behalf of the Seventh-day Adventist church of the Lake Union.
>
> We apologize with sorrow for the failures of the Church in regard to race for individuals disrespected, for the lack of time taken to understand, for the mistreated, the leadership marginalized, and for students of our colleges who were only able to sit with Black students in the cafeteria, for Lucy Byard, and for the slowness, reluctance and the stubbornness to do the right thing. We are sorry that we as a Church did not rise above the sins of society that day, and we are sorry for the lack of progress our Church has made in the last 70 years in the establishment of the Regional work.[6]

Lake Region Conference president, R. Clifford Jones, responded in part:

> Mr. President, on behalf of the officers, the departmental directors, pastors, Bible instructors, principals, teachers, all of our committee members from the Executive Committee on down, and on behalf of the constituency of the Lake Region Conference: I'd like to say that we accept your apology. And as you stated, an apology is good but let's work aggressively and vigorously and intentionally now to eliminate this surge of racism that is so prevalent and pervasive in our lives, yet even in our Church. Let's work to that end.[7]

Andrews University's president, Andrea Luxton, provided another example of genuine reconciliatory action from White church leadership during that institution's 2017 Black history programing. In response to the demand of Black student leaders for an apology not only for present but historical racial indignities, President Luxton and her team of top administrators did, in fact, apologize for what they called "the systemic racism it [the school] has perpetuated on its campus" since its origin in 1874.[8] She not only led her team in apology, but she pledged to institute a number of programs designed to foster cultural sensitivity and provide needed sounding boards for the school's minorities, perhaps the most practical of which was the creation of a new, fulltime position: vice president for diversity and inclusion.[9]

The Livesay-Jones exchange and the Luxton response offer helpful templates for improved race relations in the North American Seventh-day Adventist church. More than a simplistic formula of "live and let live," it is a conversation initiated by the historically advantaged part of the church acknowledging its culpability that at the same time requires from the historically disadvantaged a spiritual grace—the willingness to forgive. And as importantly, while it pledges a united effort to combat racism and to improve relations, it does not, nor should it, nor can it, annul the proven wisdom of indigenous leadership in distinctive minority communities.

### Notes

1. E. E. Cleveland, "Comment on the Paper 'Black Unions: Options and Consequences' by Dr. Betty Sterling," 5.

2. Dietrich Bonhoeffer, *Ethics*, ed. Eberhard Bethge (New York: The MacMillan Company, 1955; reprint 1995), 224.

3. Ellen G. White, *Selected Messages,* vol. 2 (Hagerstown, MD: Review and Herald), 69. https://egwwritings.org/?ref=en_2SM.69.4&para=99.384

4. Hans Küng, *The Church* (New York: Image Books, 1976), 356, 357.

5. For a detailed review of these and other important reconciliation connotations, see Winsley Benjamin Hector, "Racial Reconciliation, Privileges, and Debate within the Seventh-day Adventist Church in the United States on the Future of Regional (Black) Conferences," PhD dissertation, Claremont School of Theology, 2012.

6. "Apology by Don Livesay on behalf of the Lake Union Conference," June 20, 2015. http://www.lakeunion.org/uploaded_assets/100358

7. Ibid.

8. Marcos Paseggi, "Andrews University Takes Bold Steps to Foster Racial Conciliation," *Adventist Review Online*, February 2, 2017. http://www.adventistreview.org/church-news/story4844-andrews-university-takes-bold-steps-to-foster-racial-reconciliation.

9. Ibid.

# 4
# CONCLUSION

A summary of the dynamics revealed in this review of the four major twentieth-century protests of Black Adventist leadership, with its justification for continuing the major structural accommodation that they produced, leads to a number of instructive conclusions.

One is the tendency of religion to resist change. Religion is by its very nature a conservative enterprise. Its "sacralization" of forms as well as beliefs assures for its functions an aura of divine approval. The result is that change or difference, if not properly informed, suggests disrespect for one's traditions, for one's teachers, and, most troubling of all, toward one's God.

Also there is a significant difference between "cultural pull" and "racial bias." The former, shaped by the circumstances of one's birth and socialization, will, if unspoiled by racist attitudes, allow one to function as an equal among other cultures. The desire to hold to the legitimate comforts of familiar folkways and traditions is not something to condemn. This tendency, ingrained by nature, can be, and is at times, modified by education and/or cross-cultural association, but should not be regarded as wrong when expressed in matters of marriage, residence, or place of worship.

Racial bias, however, is the result not of "cultural pull" but of "cultural push"—a learned belief in racial superiority based on skin tone, accent, and other physically observable features. Always culpable, it is never capable of producing harmonious co-existence. Racism is a factor that can influence how Blacks and Whites associate, both in public and in private. However, it is a mistake to regard it as *the* reason why individuals of common ethnicity choose, especially in the matter of worship, to do so among their own ethnic group.

Another conclusion is that religious bodies almost always function within the social constraints of the government under which they reside. Even when their governments are manifestly socially oppressive, groups that claim to have a prophetic mission are seldom prophetic in addressing social evil. Change usually occurs when and if their governments initiate it, and even then conservative religionists tend to follow "afar off." In matters of social justice it is most often God's civil, not His sacred, order that leads the way.

Yet another conclusion, and in the light of this study one of the most essential, is that the conservative nature of religion notwithstanding, the Word of God contains the seeds of freedom that over time inexorably germinate into protest against unjust social restrictions. It is impossible to be truly affected by the redemptive aspects of Scripture and not long for social as well as spiritual freedom.

We have seen this principle of gospel enlightenment most dramatically portrayed in the various resistance efforts of slaves who heard the gospel. They took up arms, created the celebrated Underground Railroad that often used church buildings as stations along its routes to freedom, and also sparked the Civil Rights Movement, itself driven by the courageous sacrifices of stalwart Christians, both Black and White.

And not to be forgotten is the heroic loyalty of Black American Seventh-day Adventists who, in spite of racial challenges, have not only increased their membership percentage but dramatically elevated their place within the various service channels of the denomination. We can best appreciate this when we remember that Black Adventists have always faced a double challenge. They have from without endured the usual criticisms heaped upon Adventists as cultish and apolitical, and from within suffered racial slights not known to their counterparts in the seven Black-administered denominations that comprise the majority of African-American Christianity.

Happily, the relations between the two races both within the nation and the church are not as difficult as when addressed by the church prophet in her somber June 5, 1899, statement on the subject: "The relation of the two races has been a matter hard to deal with, and I fear that it will ever remain a most perplexing problem."[1] But as the country's current political debate demonstrates, it still remains, as she warned, "a most perplexing problem"—a problem, as has been noted, that is best resolved by awareness of the sociological dynamics of group relationships and the knowledge and application of the illumining, healing, empowering light of Scripture.

None of the above suggests that Regional conferences should be exempt from evaluation or, as is the case with all other church units, scrutiny with respect to increasing organizational effectiveness. It is rather to say that to naively declare their work done, and tout their dissolution as a necessity for racial harmony, is far too simplistic and controversial a premise from which to pursue racial concord.

Viewed in this manner, Regional conferences—Kinney's precocious concept, Humphry's pressing contention, Dykes's professional conclusion, Peters's prayerful calculation, McElhany's pronounced conviction, and Dudley's persistent passion—will retain their reason for being. Far from being divisive, or an embarrassment or duplication of effort, they will remain an arresting display of the "unity in diversity" modeled in Scripture and manifest throughout God's wondrous creation.

**Note**

1. Ellen G. White, *Testimonies for the Church,* vol. 9 (Boise, ID: Pacific Press, 2002), 214.

# PART THREE

# APPENDICES

# A NOTE ABOUT THE APPENDICES

The trim size of this book made it impossible to provide readable photo-reproductions of the primary source material included in these appendices. Thus, all of the documents have been transcribed and re-created using standard typography. For some of the older documents and letters, some effort has been made to present the information in a format similar to the way it appeared in the original. Letters from more recent times have been presented in a common business-letter format. Thus, there may be some minor differences between the original and the transcription here in matters of paragraph indentation and spacing. In some cases, obvious errors in the original documents have been noted by using the standard [sic] formulation, or corrected by putting information in brackets: [ ].

Every reasonable effort has been made to ensure the word-for-word accuracy of these documents. However, researchers doing further work where the information from these documents may be relevant are best advised to access the originals, according to the information provided below.

The original forms of the documents represented in these appendices are housed in the following locations:

1. The Collected Poems of Langston Hughes, ed. Arnold Rampersad (New York: Alfred A. Knopf, 2004), 281.
2. General Conference Archives
3. Oakwood University Archives
4. Oakwood University Archives
5. Oakwood University Archives
6. General Conference Archives
7. Private Collection of C. B. Rock
8. Oakwood University Archives
9. Oakwood University Archives
10. Oakwood University Archives
11. General Conference Archives
12. Arna Bontemps-Langston Hughes Letters 1925–1967, selected and edited by Charles H. Nichols (New York: Dodd, Mead & Co., 1980), 18, 19.
13. Private Collection of C. B. Rock
14. Private Collection of C. B. Rock
15. Private Collection of C. B. Rock
16. Private Collection of C. B. Rock
17. Oakwood University Archives
18. Private Collection of C. B. Rock
19. Private Collection of C. B. Rock
20. Private Collection of C. B. Rock
21. Private Collection of C. B. Rock
22. Private Collection of C. B. Rock
23. Private Collection of C. B. Rock
24. Private Collection of C. B. Rock
25. Private Collection of C. B. Rock
26. Private Collection of C. B. Rock
27. Private Collection of C. B. Rock
28. Private Collection of C. B. Rock
29. Private Collection of C. B. Rock

# APPENDIX 1

## "FROM BEAUMONT TO DETROIT: 1943" BY LANGSTON HUGHES

In the following poem, Langston Hughes, prominent African-American poet, references two of the cities in which major racial conflicts were engaged in 1943. In it, Hughes gave voice to the dark dismay of Black veterans of both World Wars.

Looky here, America
What you done done–
Let things drift
Until the riots come.

Now your policemen
Let your mobs run free
I reckon you don't care
Nothing about me.

You tell me that hitler
Is a mighty bad man.
I guess he took lessons
From the ku klux klan.

You tell me mussolini's
Got an evil heart.
Well, it mus-a been in Beaumont
That he had his start–

Cause everything that hitler
And mussolini do,
Negroes get the same
Treatment from you.

You jim crowed me
Before hitler rose to power–
And you're STILL jim crowing me
Right now, this very hour.

Yet you say we're fighting
For democracy.
Then why don't democracy
Include me?

I ask you this question
Cause I want to know
How long I got to fight
BOTH HITLER—AND JIM CROW.

# APPENDIX 2

## W. H. BRANSON LETTER TO UNION CONFERENCE PRESIDENTS

December 23, 1953

Union Conference Presidents
Chairmen of Sanitarium and
College Boards

Dear Brethren:

The matter of non-segregation is still coming more and more to the front and just now, as you know, the whole question is in the hands of the Supreme Court; that is, the question as to whether segregation shall be declared illegal. Whether or not the Court finds that segregation is not in harmony with the laws and constitution of this country, it is everywhere evident that the old segregated lines are rapidly breaking down and that one organization after another is declaring themselves for integration so far as education and medical institutions are concerned.

You will recall that just prior to the Autumn Council a large group of our leaders from North America, including all union presidents and a number of institutional chairmen met together and studied this matter at considerable length. It was agreed as a result of this discussion, that Seventh-day Adventists should not hold back any longer in this matter, but should step into the ranks of those religious organizations that are declaring themselves in favor of non-segregation in our schools and sanitariums.

Near the end of the Autumn Council, Brethren Torrey, Rebok and I had [E]lder Moseley call together a small number of our colored leaders who were in attendance at the Council and we discussed the matter with them. We appraised them of the discussion that had taken place in the large group that met prior to the Council, and told them that it had been agreed that we should begin to work toward non-segregation in our schools and medical institutions. We explained that this would come gradually and that all the institutions would perhaps not deal with this matter simultaneously, but one after another would fall in line as their boards had opportunity to give the matter careful consideration and to plan for it. It was really touching to see their reaction. Many tears were shed by these colored brethren and they promised their full and hearty cooperation with the chairmen of institutional boards where this matter was given favorable consideration.

We explained to them that if immediately after some institutions took action to open its doors to colored patients, nursing students or college students there should be immediately a large influx of colored people, it might greatly jeopardise [sic] our efforts to gradually work into a non-segregation program. They recognized this and said they would use good judgment and would try to select the very finest of their young people to take advantage of such an arrangement if and when it was made, and that they would not give large publicity to the matter among their people until the whole thing was worked through smoothly.

I have just received a letter from Elder C. E. Moseley, Jr., secretary of the Negro Department of the General Conference, a copy of which I am attaching to this letter. I am sure you will appreciate the wonderful spirit shown by Brother Moseley in writing this note to me and you will know from this that we will have his full cooperation in working out the program.

We would greatly appreciate it if during the present winter the various board chairmen would bring the matter to the attention of their respective institutional boards and endeavor to get some favorable action so that in 1954 this new program can go into effect in most of our institutions. The Southern Union, we understand, is also working actively on this and one of the Florida sanitariums is, we believe, the first of our institutions in the south to take a definite action to open its doors for colored patients and possibly colored nursing students. I think we will gain immeasurably by pressing into this program rather than lagging behind and waiting until we are the very last of the religious groups to do so. In the southern states it may be easier for some of our sanitariums to take an advance [sic] step in this matter before our colleges do, but I am sure that before much more time has passed, we will be able to work out the program even for our educational institutions in the south and certainly we should be able to do it quickly for our institutions in the north and west.

We shall greatly appreciate your kind cooperation in this matter.

Sincerely your brother,

/s/ W. H. Branson,
President

# APPENDIX 3

## C. E. MOSELY, JR., LETTER TO W. H. BRANSON

November 5, 1953

Elder W. H. Branson
Office

Dear Elder Branson:

This statement of heartfelt appreciation more than implements the verbal expressions made to you on the evening of October 28th. It formally records the fading of a shadow over our work for the Lord, and the emerging of an era of light and hope.

Your information to us that the fields are committed to a study of untrammelled integration in Seventh-day Adventist institutions of education and health lit our faces with a new hope. Our hearts thrill, with Heaven and you, over the fact that our great church which has more to offer of Christianity than all churches, will no longer lag behind other Christian bodies, in removing the shadow that allbut [sic] hid the Christ from view of some of our darker brothers. And while we are not unmindful of the pressures of adversity which your efforts will surely face, we congratulate you on the wisdom of a quiet, unheralded, and steady method, even if of gradual application. Full and uninhibited Christian fellowship and full spiritual guidance are enjoyed by the believers only when the reproach of discrimination and segregation hinders none.

We reaffirm our loyalty to the church, our respect for the leaders, and our undying faith in the triumph of truth, love, and right, and in the great Spiritual outpouring which may now weld all true Christians into one family in Christ.

Very cordially yours,

C. E. Mosely, Jr.

# APPENDIX 4

## OWEN A. TROY LETTER TO W. H. BRANSON

October 13, 1954

Elder W. R.[H.] Branson
Takoma Park
Washington 12, D. C.

Dear Elder Branson:

It brought a great deal of joy to our hearts when you and Elder Rebok called a number of us together at the 1953 Autumn Council to inform us of the decision of the General Conference officers and the institutional heads to open our institutions to all of our people irrespective of racial background.

Most of us were unaware of any further effort on the part of our leaders through the subsequent months until we gathered in San Francisco for the General Conference. Then we learned that in March you had written a letter relative to "racial segregation" to the union and local conference presidents and business managers of S. D. A. institutions.

One of our Regional conference presidents had obtained a copy of your letter from one of the other local presidents in his union, which he brought with him to San Francisco. After contacting your secretary, you were very kind to grant her permission to give me several copies of your letter. Elders Peters, Peterson, and Reynolds received copies and read your letter for the first time. They, like all of us who have had the privilege of reading this Christian masterpiece, were deeply moved by the contents of your forthright presentation.

Through the months, your letter has been handled with sacred regard. Occasionally, among our workers, I have made available the contents of the letter in order to let them know the position that the real leaders of our denomination take. Typical of the courage and cheer which your letter brings is the case of Elder G. N. Banks, former superintendent of the Liberian Mission, now stationed in Stockton, California. He said that he wished he had known of this letter sooner so that he could have been able to rejoice several months earlier.

The purpose of my letter to you, Elder Branson, is to let you know just how much what you have written means to us. For us, in a minority group, it represents a sort of unwritten "emancipation proclamation". Many of us have read the pronouncements of other denominations along these lines, but never has any denomination made a stronger and a more clear-cut statement of belief than the one made by you. God gave you wisdom and courage to draft this document. Of course, it will require decision and even patience to carry out the Christian ideals set forth in your epistle; but the principles are right, they are Christian, and God's people can be counted on to follow His leadings.

May God strengthen you day by day to perform the work committed to you, and may the day soon come when the Christian principles enunciated so clearly in your letter will be adopted throughout the field.

Kindest Christian greetings!

Very cordially yours

/s/ Owen A. Troy
Departmental Secretary

cc: Elders R. R. Figuhr, D. E. Rebok, F. L. Peterson, C. E. Moseley

# APPENDIX 5

## C. M. KINNEY'S STATEMENT

*Nashville, Tenn., S. D. A. Camp-ground*
*Oct. 2, 1889*

Elder R. M. Kilgore: Now, Bro. Kinney, we are ready for your statement.

C. M. Kinney: It is probable that my ideas may be a little different from what has been expressed by some. But they are mere suggestions, and I would be extremely glad if there were no necessity to carry them out.

In the first place, a separation of the colored people from the white people is a great sacrifice upon our part: we lose the blessing of learning the truth—I have reference especially to general meetings. The colored people as a class are in need—

Eld. K.: What kind of separation do you refer to?

C. M. K.: I refer to the separation in the general meetings; that is, for them to have a different camp-meeting. It would be a great sacrifice upon the part of my people to miss the information that these general meetings would give them; and another thing, it seems to me that a separation in the general meetings would have a tendency to destroy the unity of the Third Angel's message. Now, then, this question to me is one of great embarrassment and humiliation, and not only to me, but to my people also.

There are four thoughts that suggest themselves to my mind that should be considered in the solution of this question: the first is that the course that shall be taken shall be pleasing to God; second, that a position will be taken that will not compromise the denomination; third, that the position that is to be taken will be to the best interest of the cause; fourth, that a position will be taken that will commend itself to the good judgment of the colored people, that they may not be driven from the truth by our position on this question. Now, these are questions that seem to me should be considered in the solution of this matter. I am glad to state first that the Third Angel's message has the power in it to eliminate or remove this race prejudice upon the part of those who get hold of the truth.

Eld. K.: That is clearly demonstrated, at least to a great extent, as I learned on the camp-ground here.

C. M. K.: Second, that the Third Angel's message is to go to all nations of people; that it cannot take hold of them if there is some obstacle in the way, and that the truth of the Third Angel's message will enable us to remove that obstacle. The colored-line question is an obstacle; in other words, the very presence of the colored people in church relation and in our general meetings is an obstacle, is a barrier that hinders the progress of the Third Angel's message from reaching many of the white people.

Now, I wish to present 12 propositions, which, to my mind, would be a complete or perfect solution to the difficulty:

1. A frank understanding between the two races on all questions affecting each. This would avoid much trouble that would otherwise occur.

2. That colored laborers shall have no special desire to labor among white people, except an occasional invitation where to accept would cause no trouble.

3. That the colored brethren do not interfere with the outside interest among the white people; the minister in charge of such work to be judge of such interference.

4. Where the two races cannot meet together without limitation in the church, it is better to separate.

5. That missions be established among them, thus raising up separate churches. White laborers giving their time exclusively to this work. I realize the difficulty of white laborers attempting to labor for both classes in the South, for if they labor for the colored people they will lose their influence among the white people; but in laboring among the colored people exclusively that difficulty is obviated.

6. That in view of the outside feeling on the race question, and the hindrance it makes in accomplishing the work desired among the whites, the attendance of the colored brethren at the general meetings should not be encouraged, yet not positively forbidden. If they do attend let there be a private, mutual understanding as to

the position they should assume on every phase of the meeting. I would say in this connection that in my judgment a separate meeting for the colored people to be held in connection with the general meetings, or a clear-cut distinction, by having them occupy the back seats, etc., would not meet with as much favor from my people as a total separation. I am willing, however, to abide by whatever the General Conference may recommend in the matter, and advise my people to do the same.

7. In those churches where there are two or more let them remain until an effort can be made to raise up a church among them; then have them to unite with it.

8. Until there is enough to form a conference of colored people, let the colored churches, companies or individuals pay their tithes and other contributions to the regular state officers, and be considered a part of the state conference.

9. That the General Conference do what it can in educating worthy colored laborers to engage in various branches of the work among them, when such can be found.

10. That Christian feeling between the two races be zealously inculcated everywhere, so that the cause of separation may not be because of the existence of prejudice within, but because of those on the outside whom you hope to reach.

11. That when colored conferences are formed, they bear the same relation to the General Conference that white conferences do.

12. That these principles be applied only where this prejudice exists to the injury of the cause.

# APPENDIX 6

## ACTIONS OF THE AUTUMN COUNCIL OF THE GENERAL CONFERENCE COMMITTEE

September 24 to October 2, 1929
Columbus, Ohio

Much time was devoted by the delegates and special committee to studying the needs of the good and growing work that is carried on by our colored brethern [sic] in North America.

A commission appointed at the time of the spring meeting of the Committee had met a few days prior to the Council, and had formulated plans and recommendations relative to the future conduct of the Negro work. These recommendations were submitted through the Plans Committee, and after full and free discussion, were adopted as follows:

### ORGANIZATION

"1.a. That the General Conference Committee select one of our representative colored ministers to fill the office of secretary of the Negro department.

"b. That this secretary locate in Washington, having his headquarters at the General Conference office.

"c. That in giving general supervision to the colored work throughout North America, he work under the counsel of the General Conference Committee, as do all other General Conference departmental secretaries.

"2.a. That in each union conference where there are as many as 500 colored believers, except in the Southeastern, Southern, and Southwestern, a Negro Secretary be elected, this secretary to be a member of the union conference committee.

"b. That the union secretary, together with the secretaries of the Southeastern, Southern, and Southwestern Union Conferences, be invited to attend such Autumn Councils as the local conference presidents may be called to attend. Thus they would receive the encouragement to be gained by contact back to the colored churches in their fields the world around.

"c. These secretaries, together with the union secretaries of the Southeastern, Southern, and Southwestern Unions, and such other persons as the General Conference may appoint, would form the General Conference Negro Department advisory committee, to counsel over matters pertaining to the colored work.

"d. These secretaries would work under the direction of the union conference committees. When laboring in a local conference, they would work under the counsel of the local conference president, just as all other union departmental secretaries do.

3. The primary responsibility of these secretaries would be to build up the colored constituencies:

"a. By holding evangelistic efforts when advisable.

"b. By assisting evangelists with their efforts when advisable.

"c. By helping to train young preachers and workers.

"d. By helping to foster real soul-winning work in each of the churches and conferences.

"e. by co-operating in all lines of departmental and church activities.

"4. That where the colored constituency in a local conference is sufficiently strong and is represented by a colored minister of experience, we recommend that he be made a member of the local conference committee.

"5. That the Negro work in the Southeastern, Southern, and Southwestern Union Conferences be organized on the following basis:

"a. That the Negro committee of the union conference be composed as follows: The president of the union conference; the secretary-treasure [sic] of the union; the president of each local conference; the Negro union secretary; the Negro Missionary Volunteer, educational, and home missionary secretary, where there is such a secretary; and the Negro evangelist of each local conference; said committee to have full administrative charge of the colored work.

"b. That the Negro committee of the local conference be composed as follows: The president of the conference; the secretary-treasurer of the conference; the colored evangelist of the conference, and two Negro members to be elected.

"We recommend, 6. That in conferences receiving appropriations for their colored work, the proportionate share of local conference administrative expenses be on a ratio of one-third to the colored and two-thirds to the white work, this calculation to be based on a practically equal constituency of white and colored membership, and that where the proportion of constituency varies from that of equality, either up or down, the proportion of administrative expenses be varied on the same ratio up or down."

# APPENDIX 7

## REJECTION LETTERS

Union College
Harvey A. Morrison, President
College View, Nebraska

Friday
August 22
1919

Dear Mr. Jervis:

According to your request, I am sending you a catalog giving full information in regard to our school. We do not have a Junior Ministerial Course. Many students work a portion of their way.

In your letter you do not state whether or not you were colored. In making application to enter, this should be done. It is not our policy generally to receive colored students outside our own territory unless there is some very special reason why this should be done. Ordinarily we do not have colored students in our school, even from our own territory.

Most sincerely,
Harvey A. Morrison

Mr. J. E. Jervis
Rolling Fork, Mississippi.

COLLEGE OF MEDICAL EVANGELISTS
Clinical Division
WHITE MEMORIAL HOSPITAL

Boyle & Michigan, Boyle Heights
LOS ANGELES CALIFORNIA

January 8, 1929

Mrs. Baryl Holness
3336 Market St.
Oakland, Calif.

My dear Mrs. Holness,

    At the Executive Faculty Meeting, held the other day, it was voted that we do not see our way clear to adopt you to the nurses' course because of your nationality. We have had some difficulty in training students of your nationality before. While they have done very excellent work in many ways, yet many complications have arisen in connection with their training which, we feel, would not have arisen in Institutions and Schools of Nursing farther north.

    I sincerely hope you will be able to enter some other training school, and regret very much that we are not able to accept you here.

Yours truly,

Martha E. Borg, R. N.
Director of School of Nursing.

# APPENDIX 8

## H. J. KLOOSTER LETTER TO GEORGIA R. HARRIS

EMMANUEL MISSIONARY COLLEGE
(Incorporated)
Berrien Springs, Michigan

Office of the President       Dec. 11, 1938

Miss Georgia R. Harris
2160 North Capitol Avenue
Indianapolis, Indiana

Dear Miss Harris:

Your letter of December 1 has been received. In a careful reading of your letter I observe that there are several statements that are not in harmony with facts as they pertain to this institution. I shall first endeavor to place before you the situation as it exists here in order that there may be no misunderstanding as to the program that is carried on on [sic] our campus.

Your letter states that segregation of negro from white students occurs in the dining hall, worship room, and religious services of the institution. The fact is that our negro students have their own tables in our dining room, but as far as all public servies [sic] are concerned, they are at liberty to sit anywhere they choose as is true of all other students. Furthermore, as far as race prejudice is concerned on this campus, I must state emphatically that there is no race prejudice against the negroes in this institution, either on the part of the staff or on the part of our white students. Had there been such prejudice, it would have been a simple matter to exclude negroes from the campus of this institution.

On the contrary, we have dealt more liberally in the admission of our colored students under the present administration than has been the case at any previous time in the past history of the institution. Objective evidence in support of this statement is found in the fact that a larger number of negro youth have been admitted in the last two years than has been the case at any previous time in the history of the institution. Certainly this does not indicate a race prejudice.

Moreover, on repeated instances when applications have been under consideration, we have chosen to take colored students who needed employment on our campus and have rejected white students who needed employment, at the same time giving preference in employment to colored students. I know that this is the truth because I have been primarily responsible for the decision as to who should or should not be admitted to the institution. Obviously in the face of this attitude on our part toward the negro students your accusations of race prejudice seem to us to be beside the point.

It is true that separate tables are provided for the colored students in our dining room and this is done in the belief that our colored young people should find their social contacts with their own people.

Your letter indicated that in several points "the rights and privileges" of the negro yourth [sic] are not equal with those of the white students. Let me assure you that our colored students have every right and every privilege that is accorded to the white young people of this institution. We are as emphatic in the belief that our white young people should find their social contacts among white young people as that our colored young people should find their social contacts among their own young people. This is in no sense based upon the assumption of superiority on the part of either race, but rather upon the belief that the social co-mingling of the races would eventuate in greater embarrassment that [sic] is already experienced. The validity of this position has already been demonstrated on more than one occasion in the conduct of our school work where this principles has not been observed.

At the recent Fall council held in Battle Creek, Michigan, President Moran of Oakwood Junior College met with the secretary of our Department of Education and with the presidents of our senior and junior colleges and requested at that time that the lower division negro students applying to our senior colleges should be directed to Oakwood Junior College rather than to be accepted in our four-year institutions, and further request was made that the senior class of Oakwood Junior College each year be allocated to the various senior colleges established among us and that provision for their admission be worked out by President Moran in consultation with the presidents of the senior colleges concerned. The suggestion met with general approval on the part of our school men and it is my opinion that this policy will shortly become operative throughout our schools.

I wish, however, to make clear that the iniatiative [sic] in making this request was made by President Moran and it is at his instnace [sic] that the plan has received favorable consideration. It is my frank opinion that there is an unwarranted amount of sensitiveness on the part of our colored youth towards this whole question of race consciousness and race prejudice. We have opened the doors of this institution to our negro youth in an attempt to meet the upper division needs of our colored students. We have tried to give them every reasonable advantage in employment and have not discriminated against them in any particular compared with our white students.

May I point out to you that the continued agitation on the part of this group after having been given the consideration which has been shown them on this campus can result only in closing the door of opportunity to them, and this in my judgment would be most unfortunate. I hope that you and the negro youth with whom you may be acquainted and with whom you may discuss this problem will be helped in your understanding of the situation with which we are confronted and that you will cooperate in the maintenance of the type of program that will make possible the continuance of an open door of opportunity our [sic] our negro youth. It will take much of the spirit of tolerance, and forebearance [sic] must be exhibited by all parties to the problem if a satisfactory solution is to be found.

May I thank you for your letter and assure you that I have appreciated your frank statements though I must point out to you that your letter does not adequately represent the situation as it exists on this campus.

Please be assured of my interest in our colored youth and of my sincere desire to make available to them in full measure the opportunities of Christian education afforded by our own school system as far as it is within my power to do so.

With kindest wishes, I am

Very cordially yours,
H. J. Klooster (signed)
President

# APPENDIX 9

## GEORGIA R. HARRIS LETTER TO J. L. MORAN

2160 North Capitol Avenue
Indianapolis, Indiana
January 30, 1939

The President's birthday

Dear President Moran:

How delighted to hear from you. Sorry immensely, however it had to be on such an unpleasant mission. I always like to hear from you.

President Moran it would be the last desire of my life to embarrass or chagrin you publicly. The newspaper article with all its harrowing train of events following after it was not intended to place you in this position at all.

Yes, President Moran, Mr. Klooster did tell me everything you read. I'll send you the original copy. When you have read it please send it back.

If I have said one word amiss about you I'm willing to go the limit (The same as was used before, the press) to rectify it. I can truthfully say I am not responsible for what was said about you. I did'nt [sic] know it was to be said. I am definitely responsible for the publishing of the information concerning the segregation. I am wholeheartedly opposed to it and am fighting it.

I did not write the article. An S. D. A. did not write it.

There are others beside myself who are a part of the protest. I do not have the permission to use their names. There are about fifteen ohters [sic], scattered about the country, that's how the "coast to coast" phrase enters in.

In an attempt to clear himself, another has mixed this affair up with his personal work. That was not our object. We are afterthis [sic] segration [sic] at E. M. C. The one who is responsible is linking others with it who are not resonsible [sic] for. Among these are Elder Troy and several teachers of Shiloh. This is not true. I was sorry when I saw all of the [sic] write up about you. If it is false I am surethe [sic] limit of our rectification and apologies will be the sky.

If this is not sufficient information I shall be very glad to send you more. Please let me know the mistakes of the article. I mean the mistakes in detail.

The letters in origination follow these.

Thank you very kindly for the stamped envelop [sic]. I trust you are getting along nicely. I am a thousand per cent for you and am sorry for the hurt and harm you have sustained, it was not maliciously done.

Very sincerely yours in the Christian service,

(Miss) Georgia R. Harris

# APPENDIX 10

## H. J. KLOOSTER LETTER TO J. L. MORAN

EMMANUEL MISSIONARY COLLEGE
(Incorporated)
Berrien Springs, Michigan

Office of the President      February 13, 1939

President J. L. Moran
c/o Oakwood Junior College
Huntsville, Alabama

Dear Brother Moran:

Your letter of February 9 has been received. Replying to your letter I wish to thank you for giving me more detailed information concerning the conference which you had with Professor Morrison and the other college presidents. As you know, I was not present at that meeting but conferred with you privately and if I understood you correctly, the matters were as represented in my letter to Miss Harris.

I regret that according to your statement this does not represent the situation in its entirety. Perhaps I took too much for granted in the conversation I had with you. I wish you to know however that there has been no intention on my part to misrepresent any statements that you have made to me with regard to educational problems.

The circumstances as I recall them in Battle Creek were these: I approached you with a question concerning the number of young people who were being admitted to this institution and asked you for your reaction to the proposal of establishing a separate dormitory for colored students if the number should increase appreciably above the number now being admitted. In response to my inquiry you indicated that such a proposal would not meet with the approval of our colored people and it was then that you stated to me that a conference of the college presidents had been held which you attended and if I understood correctly, it was suggested that each of the colleges would take a quota of you graduates as might be arranged between the receiving institution and yourself.

It is unfortunate that certain agitators should have seen fit to betray the interests of the colored people in this matter of education because the problem has thereby been made many fold more difficult of solution than would have otherwise have been the case. The fact is that this year we have taken in quite the largest number of colored students over [sic] enrolled in this institution, and this has been done pursuant to the policy in which I have believed that our colored young people should enjoy the same educational privileges as are assured to our white young people. It is unfortunate that my desire to make adequate provision for the educational needs of our colored youth should have been made the occasion for such gross betrayal of the interests of the colored people themselves.

I can only assume that this does not represent the best thinking that is being done by the more substantial class of colored people and can therefore only regard this injustice to the colored race as an aberrant case of irresponsible judgment. I regret that my reference to our conversation in Battle Creek should have become in any way a matter of embarrassment to you. I have confidence in your leadership and wish you to know that you have my sincere support in the difficult situation in which you are placed.

With every good wish, I am

Very cordially yours,
H. J. Klooster
President

# APPENDIX 11

## SHALL THE FOUR FREEDOMS FUNCTION AMONG SEVENTH-DAY ADVENTISTS?

> Those who slight a brother because of his color are slighting Jesus.
> *Southern Work*, p. 9.

I.  Result of neglect of the colored people—the curse of sin on the church.
    *Southern Work*, p. 12.

II. Estimate of the colored people as being

   A. Brethren. *Southern Work*, p. 4.
   B. Men capable of attaining eternal life as the white man. *Ibid.*, p. 27.
   C. Travellers [sic] to the same heaven to sit down at the same table as the whites. *Ibid.*, p. 10.
   D. Worshippers of the same God as the whites. *Ibid.*, p. 6.

III. Capabilities of the colored people: talent, T 9:202; ability, 9:202; quick perception and bright minds, T 7:229; reasoning power. *Southern Work*, p. 27.

IV. Duty of the white Adventists

   A. To repair as far as in their power past injury done to the colored people, 7:230.
   B. To show "exact and impartial" justice to the Negro race.
   C. To increase the force of colored workers, T 9:207.
   D. To throw their influence against the customs and practices of the world.
      *Southern Work*.

V. Solution: the love of Jesus a "dissipater" of hereditary and cultivated prejudices.
   *Ibid.*, p. 14.

# THE OBSERVATIONS OF THE COMMITTEE FOR THE ADVANCEMENT OF WORLD-WIDE WORK AMONG COLORED SEVENTH-DAY ADVENTISTS

THESIS: The present policy of the white Adventists in responsible positions will not stand the acid test of the Judgment.

I. The policy in the educational and medical work is discriminatory and un-Christ-like.

   A. Colored people are not admitted generally to our institutions as patients, students, and nurses.

      1. The Washington Sanitarium refuses to admit colored people: The Byard case,* Gaither case, Walker case, the Clark case.

\* Mrs. Byard of New York, after being brought to the Sanitarium from the train as a sick patient, was refused admittance and sent to one of the city hospitals, where she later died.

      2. Colored girls are denied admittance to the Washington Sanitarium School of Nursing and some other schools open to the whites. As a result, they are forced to travel long distances to such schools as will accept them or undergo inconveniences at the risk of their souls at non-Adventist schools.

   B. No academies like the Shenandoah Academy are available in the East for our colored youth.
   C. Academies that might accept colored students are not easily accessible.
   D. There is no standard satisfactory creditable academy for our colored youth.
   E. A notorious example of injustice was the policy of Emmanuel Missionary College.

      1. Colored students were assigned to the rear seat during worship at chapel.

2. Colored students were subjected to an unwarranted and humiliating form of segregation in having to wait for their meals until there might be a "quota" of colored students to fill a table.

F. The "quota" policy of our institutions of higher learning with its limitations of equal opportunities for our colored youth to obtain a Christian education is indefensible.

G. There is inadequate supervision of our educational work by those who should be interested.

H. In contrast to the policy of the Adventists, many non-Adventist institutions admit colored applicants.
   1. A S. D. A. colored girl is pursuing nursing at Bellevue in New York City with no discrimination.
   2. Catholic University accepts colored students.

I. There are no Negroes so far as we know on staffs of Adventist institutions. In contrast:
   1. City College of New York City employs a fulltime Negro psychologist, who is a director of the Evening School.
   2. Hunter College of New York City employs a fulltime Negro professor.
   3. The University of Chicago employs at least five fulltime Negro professors as well as visiting professors.
   4. Harvard, Boston, Northwestern, New York, De Pauw and Toledo employ Negro instructors.

J. There is a policy of evasion and futile appeasement relative to our work.
   1. It is said, for example, that it is against public policy to have Negro and white patients in the Washington Sanitarium.
   2. It is said that colored patients would be objectionable to white patients, especially those from the Southern States.
   3. Non-Adventist institutions in Maryland use no such subterfuges.

> > a. Johns Hopkins Hospital in Maryland accepts Negro patients.
> > b. Sandy Spring Hospital in Maryland accepts Negro patients.
>
> II. The policy in the administrative sphere is discriminatory and un-Christ-like.
>
> > A. Negroes do not have adequate representation on committees at all levels—local, union, and general conferences.
> >
> > > 1. The Potomac Conference Legal Association (as well as the Union and General Associations) has no representation for the 16,000 colored constituents of Seventh-day Adventists.
> > > 2. Deeds of churches and other properties are held by the Conference Legal Association—deeds to institutions occupied by colored Adventists, yet no colored Adventist is a member of these associations.
> > > 3. Appropriations made by many committees are proportionally inadequate to the needs of the colored work.
> > > 4. There is not even one General Conference office filled by a colored person.
> > > 5. Even the General Conference stationery (there may be another type) "unwittingly" shows discrimination in that the caption about the Colored Department and its Secretary is shunted down to the bottom of the letterhead and to the left. "Left" and "bottom" often have sinister connotations.
> > > 6. The fact that there is a colored constituency should entitle it to at least one general conference administrative officer and colored supervisory officers with proper office personnel, equipment, and power.
> > > 7. The financial contributions of the colored constituency warrants the carrying out of the statement under "6" above.
> > > 8. The present disinterestedness on the part of the General Conference Committee as a unit calls for

the presence of a General Conference officer who can sympathize with the plight of 16,000 colored Adventists.

B. Funds are allocated so that moneys from the colored constituency finance institutions where we derive no *direct* financial and economic benefits; in other words, our money is not used enough for our advancement.

1. There is an over-emphasis and dramatization of "deficits" in the colored work.
2. The reports of these continual deficits in the colored work are too vague and lacking in detailed information for unqualified acceptance on the part of the colored laity.

C. We have no representative connected with the disbursement of funds from the colored constituency.

D. The office of the Secretary of the Colored Department does not carry with it enough administrative authority, jurisdiction, and equipment. In the eyes of the laity, it seems to be in matters pertaining to the impartial progress of the colored group powerless to function adequately.

E. There is no definite, detailed report of Negro funds and their disbursement.

1. The colored people know nothing of the business, organization, loss, profits, and expenses connected with the *Message Magazine*.
2. There are no colored editor, circulation manager, and business manager of the only Adventist periodical devoted exclusively to the interest of the 13,000,000 colored people in the United States.

F. The personnel in the administration of the colored work is not proportionate to the needs, demands, and interest of such work. For example, the colored work at large consists of evangelizing, teaching, and selling books.

III. The policy in the field of employment is unfair, partial and un-Christ-like.

## Appendix 11

- A. Negroes are not employed as: stenographers, in all divisions of work: local, union, and general; printers, linotype setters; shipping clerks; camp directors, secretaries over such departments as Missionary Volunteer Department, Army, etc., editors and members of editorial staffs.
- B. Negroes are not encouraged to find employment in the "work".

IV. The policy in spiritual matters is too one-sided and narrow.
- A. Conference officials (general, union, and local) neglect to lay plans for the improvement of the colored Adventists as a group.
- B. Conference officials do not initiate, encourage, and foster dignified programs for the up-lift of the colored constituency.
- C. Conference officials visiting colored churches on the Sabbath preach sermons fostering conference objectives, e.g., Harvest Ingathering, Sabbath School, Big Week, etc.
- D. Conference officials foster only institutes which have to do with bringing in money to the general treasury.
    1. Colporteurs enrich the treasury. (We admit they help to save souls).
    2. Lay workers' institutes emphasize the bringing in of souls, but these souls will bring in more tithes, more Harvest Ingathering funds, etc.
- E. No dignified programs are offered, suggested, encouraged, or emphasized for the improvement of our only sanitarium and college, or for the building of new academies, sanitariums, or colleges.
- F. There are according to our knowledge no recreational camps for our many boys and girls.
- G. Whites and colored do not worship together, although:
    1. The Bahais worship together.
    2. The Friends have a common meeting place.
- H. Since white and colored eat without friction daily in the cafeterias of the Library of Congress, Union Station,

National Art Gallery, Interior Department, and other government buildings, it is illegal to segregate the Secretary of the Colored Department for his meals.

V. These unfair practices embarrass the colored laity, form a definite obstacle to the spread of the message among colored people in the highways and byways, and also if we may paraphrase 2 Samuel 12:14 give occasion to the enemies of the Lord to blaspheme.

*Recommendations:*

*Educational and Medical*

1. That Seventh-day Adventist sanitariums, hospitals, and educational institutions discontinue the un-Christian policy of discrimination towards colored people.
2. That the "quota" policy of our institutions of higher learning be discontinued.
3. That a standard satisfactory academy be opened for our colored youth.
4. That qualified colored people be given opportunity to serve on faculties of our institutions of learning.

*Administrative and Supervisory*

1. That colored people be given adequate representation on committees at all levels—local, union, and general.
2. That adequate appropriations be made to meet the demands and needs of the colored people.
3. That at least one General Conference Office be filled by a colored person.
4. That funds from the colored constituency be allocated so that the colored people may derive direct financial and economic benefit.
5. That colored people be appointed to supervise various phases of the work.
6. That conference officials encourage our ministers and workers to be frank in declaring the needs of their own people. Otherwise, those who should

be like Elijah, Esther, and Moses will become craven cowards.
7. That the office of the Secretary of the Colored Department be given administrative authority, jurisdiction, and equipment.
8. That the colored people be given detailed reports of the colored funds and their disbursement.
9. That there be appointed a colored editor of the *Message Magazine*, with associate editors of either group, plus a business manager so the colored people can be informed of the profits or losses of this magazine.

*Occupational*

1. That the number of colored people employed by the conferences be determined by some fixed ratio in all types of positions.
2. That colored secretaries be appointed to foster the educational, social, and welfare work in all departments.
3. That colored people be appointed as editors and on editorial staffs of Adventist periodicals.

*Spiritual*

1. That there are no intimidations of our colored clergymen and workers supported by the conferences when they attempt to better the conditions of their brethren.
2. That the conference officials encourage our ministers and workers to be frank in declaring the needs of their own people. Otherwise, those who should be like Elijah, Esther, and Moses will be mere sycophants and craven cowards.
3. That conference officials be elected who through their knowledge of and interest in colored people can foster programs in their behalf.
4. That campaigns for colored work be given the prominence and dignity that are given to all other phases of the work.

5. That new and adequate academies and educational institutions of higher learning be erected for the Christian education of colored youth.

Copyright April, 1944

Joseph T. Dodson, Chairman
A. V. Pinkney, Co-Chairman
Valarie Justiss Vance, Secertary
Alan A. Anderson
Willie A. Dodson
Eva B. Dykes
Helen R. Sugland
Myrtle G. Murphy

# APPENDIX 12

## ARNA BONTEMPS LETTER TO LANGSTON HUGHES

Oakwood Junior College  
Huntsville, Alabama  
[Summer 1934]

Dear Lang,

What has happened to you out there in California? I have been hearing reports of your triumphs and, of course, I am very anxious that you should love the place. How long will you be there? How did the tour turn out from a business angle? Etc? Etc?

I have just written to the GOLDEN STAR PRESS for a copy of the *Scottsboro Limited*. Did you see the dummy of *Popo and Fifina*? [Juvenile by Hughes and Bontemps] And how did you like it? I was pleasantly surprised. I like the style of the drawings—those that I have seen. But I will not be too joyful unless you are too. When will the *Dream Keeper* be off? and who is the illustrator?

I notice that Wallie has another novel, a collaboration entitled *The Intern*. He is writing books faster than I can afford to buy them, but I will try to get this one anyhow.

The boys here in school were successful in getting Tucker out. The board voted it last week, but they also voted to send the leaders in the strike home. So Herman Murphy, Allan Anderson, Earnest Moseley and Rashford and Fordham are gone (you may remember some) and the place is dreary as a result. I was also pointed out as being favorable to the revolution and, as a result, may not be rehired. I am not really bumped, but the faculty is to cut in half (due to depression) and I may not be on the new slate. If not, I shall come to California and go to U.S.C. next winter—that is really what I want to do. Then I could spend time in Mexico, write more children's books, finish a long delayed novel, etc. etc.

Made the long trip through Mississippi last week. They talked about you at Tougaloo, LeMoyne, Greenville, etc. It was a great trip.

So long,  
Arna

# APPENDIX 13

## F. W. HALE LETTER TO F. L. PETERSON

May 3, 1961

Elder F. L. Peterson
General Conference of Seventh-day Adventists
6840 Eastern Avenue, N. E.
Takoma Park, Washington 12 D. C.

Dear Elder Peterson:

You must know the surge of overwhelming emotions which gripped the strings of my heart as I read the letter from the gentleman, who, just 10 years before, had started me on my career as a teacher in higher education. Elder Peterson, I will always have the highest regard for your qualities as a man, for the source of inspiration which you have personally been to me, and for your counsel though the years. And your sincere concern for the church of God and also my personal welfare at this moment only deepens my admiration and respect for you as an individual.

However, I must not equivocate on the matter at hand.

That I am considered the principal in a "confederacy against the church of God" is a matter of astonishment and chagrin.

It is no exception that the eye of one who introduces reforms is met with angry flashes, but his heart may well beat lighter when he is promoting a just cause.

It is well to know that there is a "better way and a better plan;" yet great streams are not easily turned from channels, worn deep in the course of ages. Likewise the difficulties which must be overcome to remedy the racial problems which are among us can not be taken lightly as they are by no means slight.

Elder Peterson, you are aware that I have been an Adventist since a child, and I plan to be, God helping me, until I die. I have accepted the doctrines and teachings of the Adventist Church much as I accept the Constitution of the United States. I do not debate either. Although the Constitution has been explicit in its emphasis upon the rights of the individual, it has just been recently that all men have begun to benefit by its proclamation. So too, does the doctrine of the church embrace truths which would make it possible for blacks and whites to live and work harmoniously together if we all adopted a serious attitude toward our teachings.

It is for this reason that I cannot accept the statement that the current laymen's movement is a "confederacy against God's church." *The laymen's movement is not an anti-church movement*; it is anti-segregation and anti-discrimination. Would you not agree that the anti-segregation and discrimination movement among us will cease, when our leaders will assume a positive position instead of a negative one towards the movement?

Are all Seventh-day Adventists members to be forever bound to hear but *one* side and *that* side being the side of the oppressors? Elder, it is a most unfortunate thing when those who sit in the seats of justice are bound in deciding racial issues, to listen to the most conservative viewpoints. And when I project such a statement, it is not a matter of indicting the church organization. But I speak of many of its most eloquent leaders who have shamelessly given the sanction of the Bible and the Spirit of Prophecy to endorse the whole treacherous system. These leaders make the principles which we practice in the areas of race relations a cold, heartless thing. It is *not* "…easy to be entreated, full of mercy and good fruits and without partiality. …"

Now, to your point of our bringing the church into disrepute. Nothing could be farther from our imagination. In a sense you are saying, "Spare the denomination; spare her leaders." Elder Peterson, the very nature of the statement suggests an impasse which none of us can afford to admit. Spare them from what? The implication suggests that any laymen's movement designed to improve race relations will be met on the threshold by the church and its leaders to do battle against it. I have never entertained the thought of such a struggle. We want to give a whole-hearted support to the newly established Race Relations Committee of the General Conference.

We want to serve as one channel for assisting the General Conference in pinpointing certain areas of sensitivity among us. We want to assume that our leaders will appreciate and solicit a "grass roots" reaction from those who make helpful and constructive suggestions in the area of race relations. If there are leaders who would suppress such actions by challenging the efforts of those who would snatch truth from the dust, how our brethren could conceive of such men as being stalwart representatives of Jesus Christ is a mystery which I leave all of us to penetrate.

But your major concern is method, and I have attempted to answer that by assuring you that we accept the establishment of the Race Relations Committee as a forward step. And we should like to weld the laymen into an organization that will serve as an effective adjunct to the work which many of our ministers have already begun.

And permit me to make myself clear on my reaction to the Seventh-day Adventist ministry. In my Chicago speech I alluded to the fact that many Seventh-day Adventist workers have been too reticent in their reactions to the condition of Negroes in our denomination for fear they might have jeopardized their personal positions and ambitions. *This cannot be denied.* Yet I recognize there are numerous exceptions, and I thank God that there are. I understand that Elders G. E. Peters, J. H. Wagner, W. W. Fordham and W. S. Lee, among others, have been particularly dutiful in attempting to elevate and improve the conditions of the regional constituents.

Friend, you give me no other choice but to take exception to the word "hero," and I accept your caution in the right spirit. I must confess, however, that if I were pursuing this program for personal gain or prestige, I'm afraid that the potential liabilities would outweigh the assets. I am aware that this action (1) will cause some to consider me as a "heretic rebel and a flaunt"; (2) will cause others in key positions "to pull the shade" on my career as far as my future service to the denomination is concerned; and (3) will cause still others to even challenge my motives and sincerity of purpose.

So I have no doubt about what personal damage could result; however, I can no longer "hide my light under a bushel" in these matters. I recall the words of Sister White in *The Southern Work*: "I know that that which I now speak will bring me into conflict."

*I maintain that there is no circle in the church that could sustain segregation and discrimination for one moment, if it were not sustained in the circle of leadership.*

If the General Conference, the Union Conference, the local Conferences, the publishing houses, the evangelists, the ministers, the missionaries, and the educational and medical institutions would all combine their powers to erase the smudge of racial segregation and discrimination among us, the whole system would crack and crumble overnight.

Such a challenge is for us the living! I have no other plans but to accept the challenge.

We think of you and Sister Peterson so often; we will never be able to repay you for your many kindnesses. Special greetings to Sister Peterson.

Very sincerely yours,

F. W. Hale
FWH/me

# APPENDIX 14

## RANDY STAFFORD LETTER TO OBIE CLARK

December 8, 1981

Mr. Obie Clark
President NAACP
P. O. Box 1986
Meridian, Mississippi 39301

Dear Obie,

On my recent trip to Meridian, I attempted to contact you, but you were out dealing for the people as usual. I did see Charles Johnson and told him to give you my highest regards.

Obie, the reason I am writing you has to do with the legal action that we were proceeding with against the Adventist Church concerning their discriminating policies in the local church school. If you recall, we were challenging the tax status of the Alabama-Mississippi Conference of Seventh-Day Adventist, their association, the Southern Union conference of Seventh-Day Adventist, and their association, the General Conference of Seventh-Day Adventists. I received a letter of support from the NAACP expressing a willingness to join in this process. Although our case never reached a point of litigation, it precipitated a major race-relations policy in the Seventh-Day Adventist Church. Until recently, I possessed a copy of your letter to me, but in December, a fire in my home destroyed all my records. Your letter was dated mid August 1970 and I am wondering if you have a duplicate of that letter. At this time a very popular writer within the Adventist Church is in the process of including this action in a book on the history of the Seventh-Day Adventist Church and he wishes to include that letter in this book that is to be published in the very near future. If you have a copy of that letter, please send me a copy as soon as possible. Hope to hear from you soon.

God bless,

Randy Stafford
Cc: Dr. C. B. Rock

# APPENDIX 15

## C. B. ROCK TELEGRAM TO R. H. PIERSON AND H. M. S. RICHARDS, JR.

Telegram
Dec. 31,
Elders   R. H. Pierson                6840 Eastern Ave. N. W.
         Neal Wilson                  Washington, D. C.

The use of Gov. Wallace in connection with the Voice of Prophecy "New Year-Bible Reading Marathon" casts a very unfavorable light upon the church and reveals a continuing insensitivity within our ranks to the social issues of our day. While I am sure this is not intentional it is nevertheless damaging to our image and will raise doubts in the minds of the public and our members. Perhaps some words from you to appropriate individuals will preclude this happening again.

Very sincerely,
C. B. Rock

---

Telegram
Dec. 31,
Elder    H. M. S. Richards Jr.        1500 Chevy Chase Blvd.
                                      Glendale, Calif.

According to the Birmingham Post Herald, Dec. 25, you are using Gov. Wallace as one of the readers in the New Year Bible Reading Marathon. Assuming that this is a fact, I wish to point out that the publicity involved in using Gov. Wallace's name in the press as well as on the air is most damaging to the image of brotherly love and concern which the church is striving to attain. We are happy that the Gov. likes to read the Bible, but we feel it ironic and discouraging that one who literally "stood in the way" of Black children seeking an education in Alabama, and who is still walking in the counsel of reactionary conservatism and racial prejudice should read Psalm 1, in public, under the banner of Adventism. We hope you can appreciate the delicacy of this matter and will work with your staff to avoid this type of unintentional but nevertheless unfortunate publicity.

# APPENDIX 16

## CONCERNED BLACK CLERGYMEN LETTER TO R. H. PIERSON

December 3, 1969

Elder R. H. Pierson, President
General Conference of S. D. A.
6840 Eastern Avenue, N. W.
Washington, D. C. 20012

Dear Elder Pierson:

On December 3, 1969, a group of concerned black Seventh-day Adventist clergymen from all the Regional Conferences assembled to discuss some of the urgent problems confronting them in their continuing effort to serve particularly the black community. It should be early and clearly stated that this gathering is not to be interpreted as ignoring and/or showing disrespect for our Regional leadership; on the contrary, our expressed concern is a natural outgrowth of the concepts enunciated during the Regional Quadrennial Session in Miami, April, 1969.

It was the unqualified concensus [sic] of the participating pastors that in view of the mood of the black population both within and without the church, the effectiveness of our ministry mandates the administrative accommodation termed "Black Unions."

Black Unions, it was resolved, would advance the work of the church by providing:

1. Meaningful programs responsive to the black community.
2. Priorities appropriately suited to the needs of the black community.
3. Broader outlets for the utilization of administrative and evangelistic abilities and talents among black workers.
4. The placement of black able men in policy-making positions so that the consideration of black needs, especially needs of the community, be no longer an afterthought.

5. The procurement of more funds for the advancement of the work in the black society.

Let us hasten to add that the preceding provisions are by no means exhaustive either in enumeration or explanation.

In a subsequent letter to Elder H. D. Singleton, Secretary of the Regional Department of the General Conference of S. D. A., a meeting will be respectfully requested at which session details regarding Black Unions will be discussed.

Yours in the hope of advancing the gospel,

cc: Elder Neal C. Wilson
Elder F. L. Bland
Elder H. D. Singleton
Elder W. W. Fordham
Elder E. E. Cleveland
Regional Conference Presidents
Elder Norman Simons
Dr. Frank Hale, Jr.

# APPENDIX 17

## REGIONAL CONFERENCES AND HUMAN RELATIONS

1. Seventh-day Adventist Churches open their doors to any would-be worshipper or prospective member regardless of race or color and welcome such with brotherly love and concern. Where it is felt that this principle is violated it is the duty of the next higher organization to investigate and recommend effective measure to correct.

2. The following additions to the baptismal vow and Church Manual are being recommended to the General Conference Session (1970):

    6) All who enter the kingdom of heaven must have experienced conversion, or new birth, through which man receives a new heart and becomes a new creature. *Thus, regardless of ethnic or social background, he becomes a member of 'the whole family in heaven and earth.'* Matt. 18:3; Jno. 3:3; II Cor. 5:17; Eze. 36:26, 27; Heb. 8:10–12; I Peter 1:23, 24; Eph. 3:15; Acts 17:26.

    13) Do you believe that the Seventh-day Adventist Church is the remnant church of prophecy into which people of every nation, race and language are invited and accepted, and do you desire membership in its fellowship?

    At an appropriate time during this session a forthright statement should be made by the leadership of the church dealing with and giving support to the position of the church on Race Relations.

3. Conferences selecting 'qualified' spiritual leaders as pastors shall not be limited by race or color. Should some black pastors be appointed to white churches and some white pastors to black churches, a very desirable example of church fellowship and understanding would result; therefore, programs to this end should be undertaken with the support and guidance of unions.

4. In order to make our public ministry more effective and to help members and potential members realize the importance of this

*Appendix 17* 273

brotherhood, conference administrators are urged to make clear to pastors and evangelists that it is their duty to teach these principles as a part of the gospel and our special message for the world. We further recommend that prospective members be so instructed either in the baptismal class or in personal Bible studies.

5. Special emphasis should be given to Human Relations Workshops to implement resolutions which unless carried out, are useless. These workshops should include all workers—field, educational and institutional, and leading laymen from both black and white conferences and churches. It is recommended that union and/or conference-wide Human Relation Workshops be conducted in every union in North America before the 1971 Autumn Council.

6. Where normal entrance requirements are met, all Seventh-day Adventist Schools from the elementary to the university level shall admit Seventh-day Adventist Youth to the school of their choice without regard to race or color. Where a church supported school fails to follow the counsel of the Church as stated on this point, it is the duty of the next higher organization to investigate and recommend corrective measures.

7. A BiRacial Commission of not more than seven (7) members shall be appointed in the North American Division to deal with complaints of discrimination or exclusion and other problems that arise in the area of Race Relations that they may be appealed to it for help. This Commission in co-operation and in counsel with the union conferences and/or the local conference and/or the institution shall have authority to act immediately, making a thorough investigation and seeking solutions to these problems.

8. On the Union Conference Level positive steps should be taken to open doors in the area of administration and departmental leadership for those who have 'demonstrated their ability and qualifications' to serve all segments of the church. In unions where there are Regional Conferences or where there is an organized Regional Department, the administrative officer level should include Black leadership.

9. Black personnel shall be selected to serve in our Publishing Houses, Hospitals, Academies, Colleges, Universities and other Denominational Institutions on the staff and/or Administrative

levels. Where it seems advisable, institutions should 'institute training programs' for the development of Black personnel in technical and administrative skills.

10. There is a missionary magazine dedicated to the Black community in North America. The circulation of this journal is primarily the responsibility of the Regional Conferences. The Autumn Council of 1967 voted to help finance a Black circulation manager for Message Magazine. We re-affirm that recommendation on the basis of the 1967 agreement on union participation and ask that this be implemented in the immediate future.

11. At the time of the Annual North American Union Conference Presidents' Meeting one or more Black administrators on the union level will be invited to participate as well as representation from the Regional Department of the General Conference.

12. In order to provide opportunity for the presidents of Regional Conferences (Including the secretary of the Regional Department of the Pacific Union) to consult together regarding problems distinctive to their work, Autumn Councils will schedule two meetings of this group each year, under North American Division leadership, in conjunction with other regularly called meetings. When additional meetings are required such would be arranged by the North American Division Administration.

13. The next edition of the Ministers' Manual should include as a part of the ministerial candidate examination before ordination questions regarding the candidate's attitude toward Human Relations.

14. We recommend that the General Conference lay plans to provide literature that would be useful in operating Human Relations Workshops, setting forth standards, guidelines and procedures in this area.

15. We recommend that the General Conference officers develop some plan whereby reports of progress in Human Relations may be publicized throughout the constituency in North America on local as well as general levels.

16. We recommend that the adoption in principle of the following plan of financial relationships involving Regional Work;

## THE GENERAL PLAN

It is suggested that in addition to funds provided by existing policies and union appropriations for Regional Work, a new fund be set up by the General Conference which would be reverted to the unions, who in turn would allocate amounts to the Regional Work to be used only for capital improvements and denominational scholarships. The amounts reverted to the unions would be in proportion to tithe income received by the General Conference for each union. The fund would be known as 'Regional Capital Reversion Fund.' This plan is to be reviewed at the end of three years. The General Conference protion [sic] of these funds will remain with the General Conference to be distributed by N A D C A upon recommendation by the union conference presidents at the time of their annual meeting.

This fund would be made up from sources of non-tithe income calculated on the following basis:

1. From the Unions—20% of the union share of tithe received from the Regional Conferences and the Regional Churches.

2. From the General Conference—6% of the General Conference share of tithe received from the Regional Conferences or Regional Churches.

Based on 1969 figures, this would result in a fund total as follows:

| Union | Union Share of Tithe | 20% | % of Total |
|---|---|---|---|
| Atlantic | $210,781.11 | $42,156.22 | 24.54 |
| Central | 31,478.04 | 6,295.61 | 3.6 |
| Columbia | 187,666.00 | 37,533.22 | 21.85 |
| Lake | 103,023.90 | 20,604.78 | 12.00 |
| North Pacific | 7,001.24 | 1,400.25 | .82 |
| Northern | 2,427.25 | 485.45 | .28 |
| Pacific | 124,676.44 | 24,935.29 | 14.52 |
| Southern | 151,768.45 | 30,353.69 | 17.67 |
| Southwestern | 39,957.91 | 7,991.58 | 4.67 |
|  | $858,780.42 | $171,756.09 | 100.00 |
| General Conference Share of fund |  | 108,206.27 |  |
|  |  | **$279,962.36** |  |

## IMPLEMENTATION

This plan could be effective as from January 1, 1971. (If approved by the Autumn Council of 1970)

Unions would remit amounts to the General Conference monthly along with their regular report.

Then, beginning with the close of April, 1971, the amounts would be reverted to the unions following the close of each quarter. This would keep the reversions to the unions quite current and result in four regular remittances each year. The unions could then be flexible in relation to the Regional conferences and local churches according to the allocations or needs as they arise. Distribution of the General Conference share through the unions to be designated projects would be done on an annual basis after the total for the first year had been credited to the fund.

# APPENDIX 18

## C. E. BRADFORD LETTER TO PASTORS, ELDERS, LAY ADVISORY MEMBERS

April 19, 1970

Pastors
Church Elders
Lay Advisory Committee Members

Dear Brethren and Sisters:

You have known that for some time the matter of regional unions has been under discussion. The discussion got under way at the quadrennial advisory meeting of the General Conference Regional Department held in Miami, Florida, April 7–10, 1969. The delegates to this meeting sent a resolution to the General Conference requesting that study be given to the idea of this administrative accommodation.

In response to the Miami request the North American Division Committee set up a commission composed of ministers and laymen from every conference, as well as, a number of General Conference, union and institutional representatives. The ratio of the committee is 47 from the field and 42 from the General Conference, unions and institutions. The purpose of this commission was to ear both sides of the question and send on a recommendation to the General Conference committee.

The first meeting of the commission was called for January 13, 1970 at the General Conference office. The group spent some 15 hours together. A motion was made that the General Conference immediately take steps to organize two new unions. An amendment to the motion was made requesting that alternatives be studied. The entire motion was laid on the table.

Meanwhile, the General Conference officers prepared a document to present to the commission setting forth the alternative to black unions. This alternative proposal is enclosed in this letter. It was thoroughly discussed at the recent meeting of the commission, (April 16) also at the General Conference office. A motion was made to proceed to form regional unions, at the same time accepting the spirit of the document. This motion was made at 9:45 a.m. Debate went on until 9:00 p.m., at which time the motion was defeated 41 to 28.

I have prepared an analysis of the vote based on private interrogation of as many delegates as possible:

| Total number of delegates voting | 69 |
| Total number voting "Yes" (to form unions) | 28 |
| Total number voting "No" | 41 |
| Number of field men voting (local conference workers, laymen) | 36 |
| Number of non-field men voting (GC, union, institutions) | 33 |
| Possible number of field men voting "Yes" | 23 or 64% |
| Possible number of field men voting "No" | 13 or 36% |
| Possible number of non-field men voting "Yes" | 5 or 15% |
| Possible number of non-field men voting "No" | 28 or 85% |
| Ten large city pastors voted. Eight (8) voted "Yes", two (2) voted "No". | |
| Approximate membership of pastors voting "Yes" | 8,500 |
| Approximate membership of pastors voting "No" | 1,500 |

If my analysis is correct, and I believe it is, the representatives from the field voted decisively in favor of black unions. The General Conference, union and institutional delegates voted overwhelmingly against black unions.

I am led to conclude therefore that the men who serve the people, who are closer to the rank and file, were outvoted by men who are twice removed from the field. It is regrettable that the voice of the delegates from the field was drowned out by the non-field segment.

The brethren agreed to try the proposals set forth as an alternative to black union for a year and then reconvene the commission. At that time the determination will be made as to which approach is best for the work among the black people of North America.

I solicit your prayers on behalf of the commission.

Sincerely yours,

/s C. E. Bradford, President
CEB: eb
Enclosure

# APPENDIX 19

## BLACK PRESIDENTS LETTER TO R. H. PIERSON AND MEMBERS OF PREXAD

October 19, 1977

Elder R. H. Pierson and
Members of PREXAD

Dear Brethren:

We cannot conscientiously support the decision on 'Regional Unions' that was read to us at the time of the PREXAD meeting held on Thursday, October 13, 1977.

We share the common burden of the leaders of the church to work for 'a finished work now' and to hasten our Lord's soon return; therefore, we feel that the "Regional Union" concept is still the only organizational structure that can best meet the needs of advancing the Black work in the United States of America.

Very sincerely yours,

H. L. Cleveland, President
ALLEGHENY WEST
CONFERENCE

W. C. Jones, President
SOUTHWEST REGION
CONFERENCE

G. R. Earle, President
NORTHEASTERN CONFERENCE

C. D. Joseph, President
LAKE REGION CONFERENCE

C. E. Dudley, President
SOUTH CENTRAL
CONFERENCE

R. L. Woodfork, President
SOUTH ATLANTIC
CONFERENCE

S. D. Meyers, President
CENTRAL STATES
CONFERENCE

L. R. PALMER, President
ALLEGHENY EAST
CONFERENCE

cc: N. C. Wilson
C. E. Bradford
W. W. Fordham

# APPENDIX 20

## R. H. PIERSON LETTER TO BLACK LEADERS

November 2, 1977

Regional Conference Presidents
North American Division

Dear Brethren:

Before me today is your letter dated October 19, in which you pass along to me some rather disappointing news. During the course of the past 11 years my contacts with you men have led me to have a great deal of Christian love in my heart for each one of you. We are not unmindful that you have some real problems in your sphere of leadership, but my contacts with our black work in North America have led me to believe that the Lord has been with you and you have much for which to be thankful.

I had hoped that after our meeting just prior to Annual Council that we might move ahead unitedly in a good strong thrust to get the work finished. You brethren requested PREXAD to study the matter of black unions in depth and give you our mature consideration as to the best direction for our black work in North America to take.

We spent hours, yes days listening, reading, discussing, studying, praying over the matter from all angles. We did not pass over the matter lightly for we felt you fellow leaders deserved our best attention. We feel the consensus conveyed to you is the best in the interest of God's work—for us to stay together and shoulder to shoulder under the blessing of God to move the work ahead to a speedy finish.

I trust that as all of you pray over this matter in the quietness of your own homes and as you speak with the Lord concerning the needs of your field, that He will lay such a burden upon your heart for souls that this will be the uppermost thrust of your administration, despite any disappointments you may have had regarding the mode of administration you felt best.

You may be sure that we wish to continue to stay close together with our Black leaders here in North America, working and praying together and I am sure that the Lord will lead for the future. In the meantime, may God bless each one of you as you give strong leadership in your respective conferences.

Cordially yours,

Robert H. Pierson

Dictated: 10/21/77
Cc: N. C. Wilson, C. E. Bradford, W. W. Fodham

# APPENDIX 21

## BLACK CONFERENCE PRESIDENTS LETTER TO N. C. WILSON

October 16, 1978

Elder N. C. Wilson, Vice-President
North American Division—General Conference
6840 Eastern Avenue, NW
Washington, D. C. 20012

Dear Elder Wilson:

Black leadership deems it necessary to state that the recent Autumn Council proceedings demonstrate, once again, the impossibility of fair and candid treatment of their request for Black Unions or any request, for that matter, which is opposed by Church leadership. The reasons as we see it are as follows:

> PROBLEM #1  *Lack of a Tangible Parliamentary Code*
> When asked at the inception of our October 12, 1978 discussion to pinpoint the parliamentary code that guides at our councils, the Chair replied that there are no adopted guidelines; rather, that we are a church and, as such, choose to be led by a general spirit of cooperation, not specific procedures. We view this as a huge disadvantage to any minority, especially one opposed by the Chair. For it is quite evident that when the chairman is aggressively involved in defeating a proposition, the petitioners can be overruled, outflanked and silenced at any point at which the Chair exerts its authority. It is also self-evident that appeals to the floor for help are futile when the majority is fully aligned with the Chair and depending upon him to be chairman and parliamentarian, as well, and at the same time retain a healthy respect for his leadership.

## Appendix 21

PROBLEM #2   *Overt Partisanship on the Part of the Chair*

Although the Chair, early in the proceedings, announced that the Council could not be bound by a specific code of parliamentary procedure, he did, once or twice, read from Roberts Rules of Order when seeking to clarify actions. One of the rules made most clear in Roberts and all other codes which govern debates and discussion is that the Chair must remain neutral when a motion is before the house. Roberts Rules of Order, Page 240 reads,

> "If the Chairman has even the appearance of being a partisan, he loses much of his ability to control those who are on the opposite side of the question. There is nothing to justify the unfortunate habits some chairmen have of constantly speaking on questions before the assembly, even interrupting the member who has the floor. One who expects to take an active part in debate should never accept the Chair, or at least should not resume the chair, after having made his speech, until after the pending question is disposed of. The presiding officer of a large assembly should never be chosen for any reason except his ability to preside."

Another source which we wish to quote is Sturgis Standard Code of Parliamentary Procedure, Page 8.

> "The presiding officer can best serve the interests of an organization by being strictly impartial toward members or groups of the organization. He should assist the organization in reaching its decision and be guided by those decisions. He should not participate in controversies. He serves as the honored but impartial servant of the assembly.
>
> The presiding officer should not be a partisan in debate. If there is information which the assembly needs, he may call upon some other member to present it. If no other member has the information, the presiding officer may present it from the chair. If the presiding officer considers that it is essential to argue any question he has the right to do so; but his right should be used very sparingly. He leaves his position as presiding officer and calls upon the Vice Chairman to preside while he speaks from the floor."

And also page 104 from the same book:

> "A President's success as a presiding officer depends upon his ability to remain impartial and to keep business moving steadily ahead. The presiding officer acts as a judge not as a partisan advocate. Any tinges of partisanship or favoritism will soon destroy the respect of members for their President. The presiding officer's duty is to carry out the will of the assembly and not to force or coerce the assembly into carrying out his will, the will of any group or faction, or even the will of the assembly as he personally interprets it."

We recognize that any pastor or President may, at times, have promotional materials or plans that he wishes to sell to his organization. But if it is true, as the Chairman stated on Thursday, October 12, that the matter of the Black Union request is a moral question, we affirm that he had no parliamentary or ethical right to become an antagonist in the debate and that the question, (the moral issue as he put it) of whether or not there should be Black Unions, should have been discussed without the weight of his office being thrown into the controversy.

It should be noted that at the recent October 12 debate that the Chair was not only partisan, he, in fact, made the major address against the proposition. The fact that he was also speaking for PREXAD does not mitigate the inequity when one recalls that he made clear that *he* wrote the deposition against the minority. For as noted above, acceptable parliamentary rules require that when the Chair feels he must declare himself, he should appoint a Chairman pro tem and does not resume the Chair until the matter is fully decided. However, the pattern of having declared antagonists chair discussions of the Black Union request is well established. In fact it has never been any other way:

  a. The Chairman of the first commission for discussion, in 1969–1971, was openly opposed to Black Unions.
  b. The Chairman of the Regional Advisory, which was later asked to carry the request to PREXAD in 1976, was openly opposed.
  c. The Chairman of the Commission which PREXAD appointed to study the matter in 1976–1977, was vocally opposed to the concept.

      d. The Chairman of PREXAD, who studied the Commissions report was openly opposed.
      e. The General Conference, in discussion in the Spring Council of 1978, was chaired by one who was actively opposed.
      f. The Chairman of the recent Autumn Council was, again, vocally, openly and energetically opposed.

It is thus established that at every level of presentation we have been denied fair and equitable hearing.

PROBLEM #3    *Structuring Responses for Maximum Effect*

In each of the votes taken: (a) the Commission vote of 1970–1971, (b) the Spring Council vote of 1977, (c) the Autumn Council vote of 1978, the Chairman has closed debate with a statement, or statements, from the General Conference President. His statement always precedes the ballot. We do not think that the General Conference President (if he is not in the Chair) need remain nonpartisan. He should certainly express himself; however, we see the Chairman's consistent positioning of remarks (negative to the request) at the end of the debate as a deliberate attempt, by a partisan Chair, to influence the vote by making the final impressions those of the most beloved and respected leader of our people. Of course there are other elements of concern.

    We cannot understand how or why the majority refuses to address the *real* issues we advance. We talk about the need of isolated Black presidents to be brought together under a common umbrella for relevant counsel and planning. They talk about their childhoods when Blacks were their best friends and how they loved us.

    We talk about the impossibility of a White Union president to relate to and understand much of the problems and personalities and psychology involved at Black conference sessions. They talk about the power of the Holy Spirit to translate our problems for them and how much they love us.

    We talk about the administrative bottleneck which prevents Blacks from having lateral and vertical mobility in the system, and they tell us we should not worry—that all things are in the Lord's hands and how much they love us.

It may be that some of the persons involved in the debate actually cannot conceive the problem enunciated. We can understand how some Blacks, who have spent considerable time overseas, are still hopeful of full integration in American and willing to suffer and wait. We know that there is a general time-lag that they must overcome. That it will probably take considerable dealing with reality to awaken them. We also understand how some Blacks who reside in areas where there is no self-determination, might be happy with their status of limited or quasi assimilation. We can understand how some liberal whites, who honestly wish that our Church would function as one culturally and functionally, would still hold onto their dreams. We can understand that some paternalistic Whites, who think they know what's best for Blacks, cannot trust our leadership and would be reluctant to see it happen. But we do not understand, nor do we believe, that the top administrative leadership of our division or of our Church, fail to get the point. We think they do understand. We think that the Local Conference Presidents, the Union Conference and General Conference personnel and leadership to understand our position and that the real issue with them is not the danger of a separate Church, or world opinion, but *money* and *power*! We believe that the *real* reason we have not had them support this idea, is that they (especially the Union Presidents) fear what will happen when Black money is no longer funneled to them. We think the real problem is that without Northeastern, the Atlantic Union will have to restructure its staff and without Allegheny East and West, the Columbia Union will have to reorganize, etc. Of course, the above conclusion is not ours alone. Several of our White friends in leadership in local and Union and General Conference positions have come by night to tell us so.

And this brings us back to where we began. Even though the ballot is secret, as long as our discussions and votes must be conducted in an arena, where the judge is also prosecuting attorney, parliamentarian and Chairman of the jury, justice cannot be had—impartiality is impossibility. Actually if it were possible, the matter should be reconsidered in an appropriate and fair arena. But since in the nature of our structure and tradition,

*Appendix 21*

this is impossible, we suspect that the issue will never be voted until the judge, himself, decides to recommend it. We would not take exception if after fair treatment we the minority were told by the majority "hitherto shalt thou come and no further" (to use the analogy employed by the Chair October 12, 1978).

To be told that under the circumstances outlined above raises serious questions in our minds as to who is doing the restricting—the Lord who has promised to speak through the council when it is functioning properly or His servants, who are stymied by unawareness, lack of sensitivity, distrust of Black leadership, fear of loss of Black money and baptismal reports? It is distressing to know that (even in 1978) not only has Black leadership not the power or the option to chart its destiny along the legitimate, philosophical and structural lines of Church administration, but it is denied a proper arena within which to debate its needs.

Sincerely yours,

s/ G. R. Earle, President
NORTHEASTERN
CONFERENCE

s/ L. R. Palmer, President
ALLEGHENY EAST
CONFERENCE

s/ H. L. Cleveland, President
ALLEGHENY WEST
CONFERENCE

s/ C. E. Dudley, President
SOUTH CENTRAL
CONFERENCE

s/ C. B. Rock, President
OAKWOOD COLLEGE

s/ C. D. Joseph, President
LAKE REGION CONFERENCE

s/ R. L. Woodfork, President
SOUTH ATLANTIC
CONFERENCE

s/ S.D. Meyers, President
CENTRAL STATES
CONFERENCE

s/ W. C. Jones, President
SOUTHWEST REGION CONFERENCE

# APPENDIX 22

## SOUTHERN UNION CONFERENCE HUMAN RELATIONS COMMITTEE GUIDELINES

September 3, 1968
1:30 p.m.—Union Office

MEMBERS PRESENT:
H. H. Schmidt, J. H. Whitehead, W. S. Banfield, W. O. Coe, C. E. Dudley, E. L. Marley, E. S. Reile, Donald Welch, C. B. Rock, W. D. Wampler.

GUESTS: George Babcock, R. B. Hariston, H. R. Trout.

PRAYER: W. O. Coe

WHEREAS, There are many forces in the world seeking to disrupt the unity of the Seventh-day Adventist Church, and

WHEREAS, There should be present in these last days in the church the spirit enunciated by Christ in His prayer for His disciples that we should all be one as He and the Father are one, and in harmony with His teaching that we should love our neighbor as ourselves and do unto others as we would have others do unto us,

WE RECOMMEND, That stronger efforts toward unity and brotherhood be made in the conferences of the Southern Union and in the churches.

WE RECOMMEND ALSO, That in achieving this aim, special study be given to ways of developing effective means of communication and a greater spirit of cooperation and fuller and freer association of all workers and laymen throughout the Southern Union.

VOTED, To recommend that the union committee give consideration to the following actions:

1. That all pastors and church members in our union extend a cordial welcome to all visitors to their churches regardless of race or color.

2. That an educational program be promoted and conducted among our workers and laymen preparing the way for acceptance into membership of our churches of all ethnic groups.

3. That when a city-wide evangelistic program or campaign is being planned by any conference, all pastors in the given area, regardless of color, be invited to study the plans and be kept informed as to the progress of the campaign, and all developed interests desiring church fellowship be baptized and accepted into membership by those conducting the evangelistic program. The member may transfer his letter of membership to another church if he so desires.

4. That where space is available in our white conference church schools, admission be granted Negro students living in the area upon application if they meet all financial and scholastic requirements.

5. That where union-wide or inter-conference meetings are being held, open housing arrangements be made.

6. That joint workers' meetings of the Regional conferences and neighboring white conferences be planned and conducted periodically.

7. That we invite, specifically, the Kentucky-Tennessee and the South Central Conferences to have a joint workers' meeting for the express purpose of discussing social relationships among workers and laymen—this to serve as a pilot to future such meetings of other conferences.

8. That one Sabbath a year be considered Brotherhood Day, and a sermon outline be prepared which may be used in all churches of the Southern Union.

9. That we encourage integrated youth teams to participate in various evangelistic projects as may be authorized, planned, and executed.

10. That local conference presidents work together in selecting locations where pulpit exchange meetings can be conducted on Sabbath or in special meetings.

11. That we encourage the departmental heads of the Southern Union to have periodic meetings specifically with the departmental heads of the two Regional conferences, thus developing a better spirit of understanding and cooperation as relates to the departmental activities of the union.

12. That conference administrators of the Southern Union be alert to any spirit of racism or intolerance manifested on the part of any worker and take steps to eradicate this spirit in a kindly but firm manner.

13. That our educational superintendent be encouraged to include in the school curriculum a study of the hisotry [sic] of the Negro race and its contribution to the church and society.

14. That at our teachers' institutes the topic of human relations be discussed so the teachers will understand fully the denominational position.

VOTED, To recommend to the General Conference that the position of the organization be clearly stated and that the actions of the Spring Council of 1965, as they relate to human relations, be considered by Autumn Council and become denominational policy.

VOTED, That the actions of the Spring Council of 1965 dealing with human relations, and as outlined in the pamphlet "Guiding Principles in Race Relations," be recognized and implemented in the Southern Union.

VOTED, That the Human Relations Committee of the Southern Union meet twice a year, with special meetings to be called as needed.

VOTED, That we recommend to the union committee that the chairman of the union committee be authorized to appoint an appropriate committee to study the implementation of those recommendations that are approved by the union committee.

PRAYER: W. S. Banfied

H. H. Schmidt, Chairman

J. Henson Whitehead, Secretary

# APPENDIX 23

## CONCERNED CHRISTIAN COUNCIL GUIDELINES

Revised April 21, '69

| | |
|---|---|
| *Name* | The name of this organization, formerly identified as the Human Relations Forum, shall be the Concerned Christian Council. |
| *Purpose* | The purpose of the Concerned Christian Council is to promote understanding and foster Christian fellowship among all segments of the Seventh-day Adventist Church, and to assist in the implementation of the Human Relations Guidelines as spelled out in the Bible and Spirit of Prophecy and formally adopted by the Seventh-day Adventist Church. It is the Council's desire to do this by legitimate and Christ-like means. |
| *Membership* | Membership in this Council is open to all members of the Seventh-day Adventist Church. Associate membership, without dues, is open to other men of good will who are in agreement with the stated purpose of the Council. |
| *Voting* | All decisions shall be by majority vote of the regular members present. A quorum shall consist of five regular members. |
| *Officers* | Regular members shall be chosen for the following offices: President, Vice-president, Secretary, Treasurer, and Chaplain. |
| *Term of Office* | Officers shall be elected to serve for a period of one year. |
| *Funds* | Funds shall be obtained from voluntary contributions, fund-raising projects sponsored by the Council, and from membership dues in the amount of 50¢ per month or $5.00 per year. |
| *Guideline Changes* | Changes in the guidelines shall require a two-thirds majority vote. All members shall be notified of proposed changes at least one week in advance. |

| | |
|---|---|
| *Dissolution of the Council* | Dissolution of the Council shall be by majority vote of members present at the last called meeting. Notification of such a meeting shall be given at least one week in advance of the meeting. |
| | Upon the dissolution of the Council, any funds remaining in the treasury shall be contributed to the Human Relations Committee of the Southern Union Conference of Seventh-day Adventists. |

## GUIDELINES COMMITTEE

**Co-Chairmen:** Dunbar Henri and Tom Carter

| | |
|---|---|
| Fern Babcock | Denyce Follette |
| Calvin Brown | Earl Richards |
| William Davis | Emily Thompson |

(Note: This committee disbanded 3-11-1969 until further notice)

## EDUCATION COMMITTEE

**Co-Chairmen:** Warren Banfield and George Babcock

| | |
|---|---|
| Calvin Brown | Thesba Johnston |
| Elder Carter | Bertha Mills |
| Myrtice Dye | Clara Rock |
| Dunbar Henri | Emily Thompson |
| Lorraine Henri | Joyce Zytkoskee |

## ACTION COMMITTEE

**Co-Chairmen:** Calvin Rock and Adrian Zytkoskee

| | |
|---|---|
| Fern Babcock | Denyce Follette |
| Geraldine Banfield | Lyle Follette |
| Delorise Davis | Harold Johnston |
| William Davis | Ann Richards |
| Malcolm Dean | Earl Richards |
| Frank Rice | |

## *SOCIAL COMMITTEE*

**Co-Chairmen:** Ann Richards and Fern Babcock

   Denyce Follette

### OFFICERS

**President:** Thesba Johnston     **Secretary:** Fern Babcock

**Vice-President:** Lyle Follette     **Treasurer:** Earl Richards

**Chaplain:** Harold Johnston

# APPENDIX 24

## FRANK HALE JR. LETTER TO RAYMOND F. COTTRELL

"A Response to an Editorial of October 17, 1963, in *The Review and Herald*"

Elder Raymond F. Cottrell
Review and Herald Publishing Association
Takoma Park, Washington 12, D.C.

Dear Elder Cottrell:

In an editorial ("Rendering to Caesar What Belongs to God") of October 17, you justify the Seventh-day Adventist position for not supporting the "March on Washington" by citing as support an editorial in the *U.S. News and World Report*.

My brother, I cannot abandon my conscience by not recording my protest against what appears to be a subtle, yet cynical, disregard for the principle of human freedom as it affects the Negro in particular.

For years the American Negro has smarted under a continuous train of almost unprecedented abuse and venomous prejudice at the hands of David Lawrence. More recently, his editorials of June 10, June 17, July 1, August 5, August 19, September 9, September 16 in addition to his comment of September 23 to which you referredfirmly [sic] expose all the impertinencies of which Lawrence is capable in order to keep the Negro at "arms length" and beyond the circle of human brotherhood.

How shall we ever convince the world of our sincere concern for human equality, while we openly join hands and ally ourselves with those who make their livelihood by generating and fertilizing the prejudices of men?

You indicate that the church should not "enforce its opinion" in legislative matters. Bu do not Adventists seek legislative support and influence public opinion for their position in the areas of temperance, Sunday laws, and health reform?

Furthermore, the "March on Washington" was far more than an appeal for favorable legislation in the area of civil rights. It was a symbol of the involvement of men "in all walks of life" who were expressing their discontent over the plight of the dispossessed. It was a uniting of men and organizations—with the church strongly included—who were responding to the incredible patience that the Negro's discipline of non-violence has exhibited.

The redemptive role of the church discovers its challenge in eliminating those barriers which frustrate, thwart, and degrade life. Racial exclusiveness is one of those barriers which has diluted the concept of the Christian ethic because it alienates man from man as well as man from God. If the church is not prepared to bridge this gap, to whom shall we turn for the promulgation of the Great Commandment?

Sincerely yours,

Frank W. Hale, Jr., Ph.D., Chairman
Layman's Leadership Conference

# APPENDIX 25

## COMMITTEE OF TEN LETTER TO W. S. BANFIELD

December 4, 1978

Elder W. S. Banfield, Director
Office of Ethnic Relations
General Conference of Seventh-day Adventists
6840 Eastern Avenue, N. W.
Washington, D. C. 20012

Dear Elder Banfield:

Thank you for your recent letter attesting to your interest and concern for the total program of the Church. We wish you well and believe that the department of "Ethnic Relations" can be helpful in building inter-group understandings.

What we do not like about your letter is the inference in the final paragraph that we allowed a mere difference of opinion to rupture relations and interfere with a healthy working climate. If, in fact, relationships have been affected in the current debate, it is not that you differ, but in our opinion, you were unethical and discourteous in the use of your office. To disagree is one thing but to publically exert oneself in hopes of defeating the efforts of the very people you are paid to represent and advise, is quite something else.

Please do not mistake our disenchantment of such conduct with the inability to be disagreed with; it is, rather, the unwillingness to allow those who supposedly represent us to undermine and combat our objectives.

Very sincerely,

| G. R. Earle, President | L. R. Palmer, President | H. L. Cleveland, President |
| NORTHEASTERN CONFERENCE | ALLEGHENY EAST CONFERENCE | ALLEGHENY WEST CONFERENCE |

C. B. Rock, President
OAKWOOD
COLLEGE

R. L. Woodfork, President
SOUTH ATLANTIC
CONFERENCE

W. C. Jones, President
SOUTHWEST REGION
CONFERENCE

C. E. Dudley, President
SOUTH CENTRAL
CONFERENCE

C. D. Joseph, President
LAKE REGION
CONFERENCE

S. D. Meyers, President
CENTRAL STATES
CONFERENCE

# APPENDIX 26

## PROPOSED BLACK UNION TERRITORIAL ARRANGEMENT

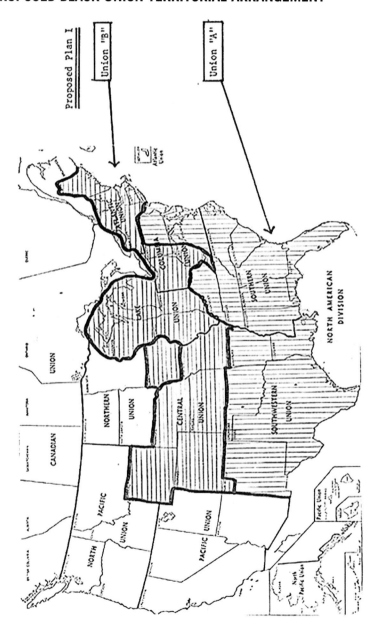

# APPENDIX 27

## C. E. DUDLEY LETTER TO PASTORS

October 28, 1979

S. H. COX, C. D. JOSEPH, R. L. WOODFORK,
G. R. EARLE, H. L. CLEVELAND, W. C. JONES,
C. E. Dudley, E. E. CLEVELAND, L. R. PALMER,
C. B. ROCK

Dear Brethren:

As per our conversations during the Annual Council, I am listing the membership mixes of the territorial councils that are scheduled to meet on Monday, December 3, 1979 at 10:00 a.m. at Oakwood College.

The suggestion is that there will be two (2) territorial councils with the following groupings:

| | |
|---|---|
| Territorial Council No. 1: | Northeastern Conference |
| | Allegheny West Conference |
| | Lake Region Conference |
| | Central States Conference |
| Territorial Council No. 2: | South Atlantic Conference |
| | South Central Conference |
| | Southwest Region Conference |
| | Allegheny East Conference |

| | |
|---|---|
| Each conference is to have the following number of persons from its area to serve as members of the council: | 1 President |
| | 1 Secretary |
| | 1 Treasurer |
| | 2 Pastors |
| | 2 Laymen |
| | 1 Institutional Worker |

The first general meeting of both councils is to be held on December 3. From this meeting the two councils will meet separately to elect the officers for each group. The councils are to meet quarterly to give study to advancing the work in our areas.

You should bring the persons who have been elected to serve from your conference to the first meeting on December 3. Would you please send a list of the persons to me when you have them in hand? Thank you kindly.

Very sincerely,

/s C. E. Dudley
President

# APPENDIX 28

## C. E. BRADFORD LETTER TO CONFERENCE PRESIDENTS

January 9, 1980

| | |
|---|---|
| H. L. Cleveland | W. C. Jones |
| S. H. Cox | C. D. Joseph |
| C. E. Dudley | L. R. Palmer |
| G. R. Earle | R. L. Woodfork |

Dear Brethren:

During the past twelve months I have tried to give leadership to the North American field and in a special way to be your "coach in the stands." It was my hope that the office which the brethren have asked me to take up could be used in ways beneficial to your fields. This, I felt, could best be done in particular through the Regional Presidents' Council, the Strengthening the Black Work in NAD Committee, and generally through the various boards and committees on which I sit from PREXAD to NADCA.

I had also hoped to enlist the support and good offices of the president of the General Conference. At the same time it was my determination to be available for personal counsel and assistance to you in less formal ways, as a group and man-to-man. (All of us are, after all, longstanding friends—some going back 35 years.) Elder Wilson and the union presidents are, of course, concerned. But I, above all the rest, sense a deep concern because all that I had hoped to be to you and your fields is on the line.

This preamble could go on, but I will spare you. The point is, all the above seems to have been, in your judgment, completely inadequate. This was made clear in a recent letter addressed to the union presidents which states that the Oakwood meeting and the territorial councils were authorized by the "Presidents' Council." You apparently feel that all the other available channels, including the authorized semi-annual meetings of the Regional Presidents' Council and the Strengthening the Black Work in NAD Committee, cannot serve your needs. In all of this my counsel was not sought, although we have had a number of meetings with ample opportunity for discussion.

Please allow me to make an assessment:

1. The regional conferences are still a part of their respective unions. You are, as I have often expressed it, wed to each other.
2. Provision has been made for the special needs of the black work through the Presidents' Council and the Strengthening the Black Work Committee.
3. Regional conference presidents are elected to serve their constituencies and have within our present organizational structure no direct administrative lines to other local conferences.
4. Regional conferences address mutual problems through their Presidents' Council, their respective unions, and any other committees and commissions set up by NADCA.
5. Inter-union meetings of local conference administrators or departmental personnel and workers are convened by NADCA, or on an intra-union basis by the union of which they are a part.
6. Inter-union workers' meetings and councils should be authorized by NADCA.

The Oakwood meeting was fine, but it could just as easily have been cleared through the Presidents' Council and NADCA.

The territorial councils may be the way to go, but we should have talked this through together and arrived at a consensus. Responsible leaders should not be afraid to test their ideas on their brethren and to openly state their case.

To sum up, in light of the December 26 letter, which lays the whole issue on the line before the union presidents, the General Conference president, and the North American Division leadership, I feel to ask you to cancel the January 14 meetings. Then, let's get together and look at this again. Maybe the union presidents, the North American Division officers, and the regional presidents could spend a day together. (Union presidents have sometimes felt left out of our discussions, and they may have a point.)

My greatest desire is to bring about the very happiest and most satisfactory relationships among all organizations and entities in North America. I have been asked to do this, and I take my responsibilities seriously. Granted, there are some things you may have felt compelled to do in the exigencies of the moment, but this cannot become a way of life. This kind of "adhocracy" will ultimately self-destruct. Others whom we lead are looking on, and we are training future leaders. We all need courage, stamina and patience to lead God's church in times like these. Our Lord has promised to supply these in abundance.

Blessings on you, and I do hope to hear from you soon.

Sincerely yours,

Brad
C. E. Bradford

# APPENDIX 29

## C. E. DUDLEY LETTER TO D. A. WALKER, I. J. JOHNSON, ARTHUR SANDERS, P. E. VINCENT, W. MURRAIN, W. E. COOPWOOD, J. E. MERIDETH, C. B. ROCK, E. E. CLEVELAND

South Central Conference of Seventh-day Adventists
Post Office Box 24936 715 Youngs Lane (615)226–6500
Nashville, Tennessee 37202

Office of the President

21 January 1980

D. A. Walker, I. J. Johnson, Arthur Sanders,
P. E. Vincent, W. Murrain, W. E. Coopwood,
J. E. Merideth, C. B. Rock, E. E. Cleveland

Dear fellow-workers:     Re: Territorial Councils Meeting—Atlanta

It was surprisingly interesting to observe the joyous enthusiasm demonstrated by a large number persons [sic] when they learned of the plans that had been laid to hold the Regional Territorial Councils in Atlanta on January 14, 1980. This meeting was to have brought the administrators of the Regional Conferences, departmental directors, pastors and laymen together for once in the history of the church to exchange ideas and to give input as to how the total Black membership at all levels could move harmoniously for a finished work among our people as well as others ere the end of the age catches us.

You were elected by the workers of the conference to represent our field at this meeting because of your love, dedication and interest in seeing the fulfillment of the gospel commission. We were happy that you graciously accepted the responsibility to serve with this lovely group of church members

I am mindful that all of you had made arrangements to attend the meeting even at the loss of personal income from your various professions. Disturbing inquiries have come from some of you as to the reason for the postponement of the meeting a few hours before it was to be held. On January 9 the Regional Conference presidents received a telegram from the vice president of the North American Division which stated: "Because of the intensity of the discussion occasioned by the decision to set up territorial councils, I feel that January 14 meeting should be cancelled. Letter of explanation is in mail."

In his letter to us, the vice president stated: "Elder Wilson and the union presidents are, of course, concerned. But I, above all the rest, sense a deep concern because all that I had hoped to be to you and your fields is on the line." Some of the brethren have learned, so I am told, that the Regional Conference presidents have been credited with Elder R. H. Pierson's early retirement and failing health, with the early retirement of Elder W. W. Fordham from the G. C., with the closing of the office of Regional Affairs in the G. C., with planning the dismissal of Elder L. B. Reynolds from the editorship of the Message Magazine and now with the possibility of the vice president's dismissal from his job. These charges are not true; however, some of the leaders felt that if the Atlanta meeting was to place the vice president's position in jeopardy with his brethren on the union and general levels, it would be best to honor his request that we cancel the meeting on January 14.

Thank you very much for your interest and willingness to be used by God in helping to carry out the divine commission. Let us pray for His Spirit to ever guide us in all things as we face the challenges that lie before us as a church and a people with God's last words of hope for a perishing world.

Very sincerely yours,

C. E. Dudley, President

# NAME INDEX

## A

Adams, Roy, 196
Allen, Gregory J., 198
Allison, Thomas H., 30–32, 37–39
Anderson, Allan (*also* Alan), 64, 108, 262–263
Aquinas, Thomas, 193
Aristotle, 193
Augustine of Hippo, 189, 193

## B

Babcock, Fern, 292–293
Babcock, George, 288, 292
Baker, Benjamin, xx
Baker, Delbert, xx, 197
Banfield, Geraldine, 292
Banfield, Warren S., xviii, 106, 116–119, 130–133, 136, 138, 140–141, 288, 292, 296
Banks, G. N., 237
Banks, Rosa, xx
Barnett, Claude, 35–40, 42, 47
Bates, Joseph, 3, 184
Bates, Ruby, 65
Bauman, Herman, 76
Bediako, Matthew, xviii
Berry, Halle, 170
Blackmon, Alma, 201
Blair, Mardian J., 153
Blake, David E., 22
Bland, L. H., 46, 51
Blunden, H. M., 54
Bock, Lowell, 111–112
Bond, Samuel L., 87–88
Bonhoeffer, Dietrich, 218
Bontemps, Arna, 38, 46, 61–62, 64–66, 69, 232, 263
Borg, Martha E., 246
Bradford, Charles E., xiv, 75, 105, 111–113, 122–124, 133–136, 143, 196, 201, 277–279, 281, 301, 303
Bradford, Etta Littlejohn, xiii
Bradford, Robert Lafayette, xiv
Bradford, Robert Lee, xiii–xiv, 30–31
Bradford-Rock, Eva, xiv–xv, 75–76
Branch, T. H., 21
Branson, W. H., 6, 234–238
Broeckel, Herbert H., 76
Brooks, Charles D., 196, 204
Brown, Calvin, 292
Brown, R. C., 107
Bryant, Alex, 155
Burgess, M. A., 51
Burton, Keith, 196–197
Butler, J. L., 103, 271
Byard, James, 43–44
Byard, Lucille (*also* Lucy), 42–47, 49, 222, 255
Byington, John, 2–3

## C

Campbell, J. M., 32
Canson, Earl A., Sr., 72–73, 75, 78, 118–119, 130–131, 133, 136, 139
Carter, Tom, 292
Cherry, S. O., 52
Christian, J. W., 22
Christian, L. H., 49
Clark, Obie, 268
Cleveland, Earl E., xx, 107, 113, 124–127, 133–136, 196–197, 217, 271, 299, 304
Cleveland, Harold L., 103, 106–107, 271, 279, 287, 296, 299, 301
Cobb, Leon, 63–64
Coe, W. O., 288
Collins, John E., 73
Coopwood, W. E., 304
Cottrell, Raymond F., 120, 294

Cox, Jeter E., Sr., 42–43
Cox, Lula Bell, 46
Crowder, Donald, 103, 106, 271

**D**

Daniells, A. G., 17, 19–20, 60–61
Dart, G. Charles, 77
Dasent, J. Gershom, 31–32, 46, 51, 53
Davis, Delrose, 292
Davis, William, 292
Dean, Malcolm, 292
Dennison, Timothy, Sr., 197
DeShay, William L., 103, 271
Dick, E. D., 49
Dillett, E. S., 50, 53
Diop, Ganoune, 197
Dobbins, H. D., 53
Dodson, Joseph T., 8, 262
Dodson, Willie A., 46, 262
Doggette, James Richard, Sr., 200
Donkor, Kwabena, 196
Douglas, Robert, xiv
Douglas, Walter B. T., 198
Du Bois, W. E. Burghardt, 8, 30, 174–175
Dudley, Charles E., Sr., 107, 128–130, 133, 135–136, 138, 141, 143, 151, 227, 279, 287–288, 297, 299–301, 304–305
Dulan, Garland, xx
Dye, Myrtice, 292
Dykes, Eva B., xx, 46–47, 227, 262

**E**

Earle, George R., 107, 279, 287, 296, 299, 301
Emerson, Ralph Waldo, 170, 203

**F**

Felder, William D., 73
Figuhr, R. R., 6–7, 238
Folkenberg, Robert S., xviii, 104
Follette, Denyce, 292–293
Follette, Lyle, 292–293
Fordham, W. W., xx, 63–64, 138, 140–141, 143, 263, 266, 271, 279, 305
Fountain, T. M., 50, 53

**G**

Gifford, L. Stephen, 76
Goldwater, Barry, 98
Grant, Lorenzo H., 197
Graybill, Ronald D., 126
Green, W. H., 20–26, 71
Greene, Elmira B., 60

**H**

Hale, Frank W., Jr., 9, 68–69, 99–103, 120–122, 130–133, 136, 197, 264, 267, 271, 294–295
Hare, Robert, 43
Harris, Georgia R., xx, 37–39, 247, 250–252
Harvey, Paul, 98–99
Haskell, S. N., 13
Hayes, Rutherford B., 4
Haynes, Carlyle B., 40
Haysmer, A. J., 22
Hector, Winsley Benjamin, 198
Henri, Dunbar, 292
Henri, Lorraine, 292
Hobdy, Cleveland, III, 78
Hodges, Clarence, 197
Holness, Baryl, 246
Hooper, Samuel, 51
Horton, Helen, 82
Howard, James H., 18–19, 46
Huenergardt, J. F., 31
Hughes, Langston, 62, 64–65, 233, 263
Humphrey, J. K., 20, 22, 25, 30, 32, 37, 57–59, 69, 71
Hutchins, S. A., 103, 271
Hyer, Marjorie, 108

**J**

James, David L., 86
Jervis, J. E., 245

Jeter, Derek, 170
Johnson, Lyndon, 98
Johnston, Harold, 292–293
Johnston, I. J., 304
Johnston, Thesba, 292–293
Jones, A. T., 17
Jones, Dan T., 14
Jones, R. Clifford, 223
Jones, William C., 107, 279, 287, 297, 299, 301
Joseph, Charles D., 107, 279, 287, 297, 299, 301
Justiss, Jacob, xx, 30, 45, 197
Justiss-Vance, Valerie, xx, 8, 46, 262

## K

Kay, Thompson, xx
Kellogg, John Harvey, 16–17
Kennedy, John, 7
Kennedy, Robert, 7
Kibble, Alvin, xx, 149, 153, 155
Kilgore, R. M., 239
King, Martin Luther, Jr., xviii, 7, 79, 115, 123, 133, 168, 203
Kinney, Andrew, 13
Kinney, Charles Marshall, 13–19, 23, 221, 227, 239
Kinney, Lucy, 13
Kloos, Karina, 171
Klooster, H. J., 36–39, 247, 249–250, 252–253
Knight, George, 16
Kubo, Sakae, 206
Kung, Hans, 218

## L

Lawrence, David, 120, 294
Lee, Willie S., xx, 266
Lewis, James, xx
Lincoln, Abraham, 3, 52
Livesay, Don, 222–223
London, Samuel G., Jr., 197

Loughborough, J. N., 13
Louis, Joe, xv
Luther, Martin, xviii, 194–195
Luxton, Andrea, 223

## M

Makapela, Alven, 197
Mallery, Lynn, 83
Manns, Charles, 59
Manns, John W., 59
Marley, E. L., 288
Marshall, Thurgood, 202–203
Martin, Mylas, 9
Marx, Gary P., 183
Maxwell, Randy, 196
Maynard-Reid, Pedrito, 196, 198, 201
McAdam, Doug, 171
McCoy, Joseph, 149, 151, 153
McElhany, J. L., 6, 40, 43–45, 48–51, 53, 55, 103, 157, 221, 227
McLeod, Norman, 70
Melbourne, Bertram, 197–199
Merideth, J. E., 304
Meyers, Samuel D., 107, 279, 287, 297
Miles, Norman K., 153
Mills, Bertha, 292
Monk, Paul, 106
Montgomery, James O., 45
Moran, J. L., xx, 37–39, 64, 248–250, 252
Morgan, Douglas, 16–17, 61
Morgan, Irene, 48
Morrison, Harvey A., 245, 252
Moseley, Calvin E., 6, 234–235, 238
Mosely, Earnest, 263
Mostert, Thomas, Jr., 76, 79, 82
Mouzon, Hector, 103, 271
Murphy, Herman R., 51, 64, 263
Murphy, Myrtle G., 262
Murrain, W., 304
Murray, Gilbert, 185
Musvosvi, Joel, 196

## N

Nelson, W. E., 43
Nethery, J. J., 53
Niebuhr, Reinhold, 178, 194–195, 210
Nipson, Herb, 65
Nixon, Richard, 171
Nixon, Timothy P., 73, 79
Nunez, Maitland G., 58, 69, 71

## O

Obama, Barak, 170–171, 221
Ochs, D. A., 64
Oldham, J. H., 210
Osterman, Eurydice V., 200

## P

Palmer, Luther R., Jr., 103, 106–107, 271, 279, 287, 296, 299, 301
Panton, Vera, 75
Partridge, Gaines, 74–75
Paschal, Anthony, 75, 81, 84, 87
Paulsen, Jan, xviii, 104, 153–154
Perry, Clara, 66
Peters, George E., Jr., 25, 32–34, 43, 50, 54–57, 67, 227, 237, 266
Peterson, Frank Loris, xx, 31, 33, 39, 55, 63, 68, 70–71, 101–103, 154, 197, 237–238, 264–265, 267
Pierson, Robert H., 7, 99, 102, 107, 111, 127, 143, 269–270, 279–281, 305
Pinkney, A. V., 262
Piper-Mandy, Erylene, 82
Plantak, Zdravko, 190
Platner, C. Elwyn, 80, 82
Pollard, C. Leslie, xx, 204
Powell, Adam Clayton, Jr., 7
Prime, Peter J., 201
Prosser, Gabriel, 8

## R

Ramsey, Paul, 210
Randolph, A. Phillip, 34
Rebok, Denton, 234, 237–238
Reid, Bert B., 90
Reid, D. B., 90
Reile, E. S., 288
Retzer, Darold J., 77
Reynolds, Louis B., 143, 196–197, 237, 305
Rice, Frank, 292
Richards, Ann, 292–293
Richards, Earl, 292–293
Richards, H. M. S., Jr., 99, 269
Robinson, Eugene, 163, 177
Robinson, Jackie, 97
Rock, Calvin B., xx, 196, 198, 201, 268–269, 287–288, 292, 297, 299, 304
Rock, Clara, ix, 292
Rock, Emily Bovell, xiv
Rock, George Benjamin, xiv
Rogers, P. G., 32
Roosevelt, Franklin D., 34, 182
Rowe, T. M., 51

## S

Sandefur, Cree, 111–112
Sanders, Arthur, 304
Schmidt, H. H., 288, 290
Schneider, Don C., 77
Scott, Alma J., 46
Scott, Francis R., 67
Scott, Sydney, 21
Sheafe, Joseph, 16
Sheafe, Lewis C., 16–17, 59–61, 69, 71
Sheafe, Louise, 16
Simmons, Ella, xviii, xx, 154–155
Singleton, Harold D., xx, 51, 102, 271
Smith, Uriah, 2
Spalding, A. W., 24, 67
Spicer, W. A., 53
Stafford, Randolph, 69, 268
Stephenson, C. B., 22
Stoddard, Errol T., 200
Sugland, Helen, 46, 262
Swan, L. Alex, 197

*Name Index*     311

## T

Thomas, J. G., xx, 51, 69
Thompson, Emily, 292
Thompson, Helvius, 73
Thompson, John, 198
Tolbert, Emory J., 197
Torkelson, Max, 111–113
Trout, H. R., 288
Troy, Owen A., Jr., 66
Troy, Owen A., Sr., xx, 6, 36, 38, 46, 50, 66, 70, 196, 237–238, 250
Truman, Harry, 97
Tubman, Harriet, 202
Tucker, J. A., 63–64, 263
Turner, Nat, 8
Turner, W. G., 45–46

## V

Vesey, Denmark, 8
Vincent, P. E., 304

## W

Wagner, Jessie R., 103, 106, 271
Wagner, John H., Sr., xx, 51–53, 103, 266
Walker, D. A., 255, 304
Wallace, George, 99, 269
Wampler, W. D., 288
Warren, Mervyn A., 201
Washburn, J. S., 17, 61
Washington, Leroy B., 88–90
Webb, A. E., 25
Welch, Donald, 288
Wellington, Clarke A., 49, 51
Weniger, Charles E., 61–62
Wernick, Francis, 111–112
White, Darrell, 79, 84
White, Edson, xiii
White, Ellen G., xiii, 2–5, 13–14, 17–18, 23–24, 60–61, 67, 72, 123, 125–128, 130–131, 134, 164, 182, 186, 198, 200–201, 204–208, 210–211, 218
White, James, xiii, 2–4
White, Major C., 72, 84, 119
White, Walter, 34
Whitehead, J. H., 288, 290
Williams, J. H., 51
Williams, Richard, 197
Willis, Robert L., 103, 271
Wilson, Jessie, 81
Wilson, Neal C., xviii, 7, 104, 106, 108–114, 140, 143, 163, 269, 271, 279, 281–282, 301, 305
Wilson, Ted, 157
Wilson, Thaddeus, 151
Woodfork, Robert, 107, 279, 287, 297, 299, 301

## Y

Young, M. M., 105, 271

## Z

Zytkoskee, Adrian, 292
Zytkoskee, Joyce, 292

# SUBJECT INDEX

## A

Abolition, 2–3, 14, 66, 97, 184, 198, 203
*Adventist Review* (*Review and Herald*), 2–3, 10, 25, 55, 100, 107, 120, 123, 139, 164, 197, 294
Adventist War Service Commission, 40
Alabama-Mississippi Conference, 69, 268
Allegheny Conference (East and West), 9, 46, 51, 56, 107, 121, 279, 286–287, 296, 299
Amalgamation, 126, 168, 219
*Amsterdam News* (see *New York Amsterdam News*)
"An Appeal in Behalf of the Work among Colored People" (Ellen White), 19
Andrews University (*see also* Emmanuel Missionary College), 36, 106, 156, 196, 197, 206, 223
Anti-Lynching Bill, 30, 41, 97
Arizona Conference, 70, 76, 87–88
Assimilation, 110, 122, 167–169, 172, 178, 286
Associated Negro Press, xvi, 35
Atlantic Union Conference, 56, 114, 286
Autumn Council, 32–34, 48, 110, 234, 237, 242, 273–274, 276, 282, 285, 290, 309

## B

Battle of Manassas (Bull Run), 182
Beaumont, Texas, 233
Berean Church (Los Angeles), 61
Bethel Church of Free Seventh-day Adventists (Savannah), 42, 59
Beverly Road Seventh-day Adventist Church (Washington, D.C.), 40
Biscayne Terrace Hotel, 102
Black Caucus, 75, 139, 154–155
Black worship style, 181, 199

Black President's Council, 149
Black Theology, 199–200, 202–204, 207
Black union conferences, 1, 88, 97–147, 149, 153, 163–164, 175, 270–271, 277–278, 280, 282, 284, 298
Blacks for Correction and Improvement without Separation, 75, 77–78
Breath of Life, 176
Busing, 169

## C

Catholic Church, 35, 42, 256
Celebratory worship, 199–201
Central California Conference, 76
Central State University, 68
Central Union, 70
Chicago Historical Society, 35
*The Church Manual*, xix, 206, 272
Church of the Brethren, 42
City Temple Church (Detroit), 103
Civil Rights Act, 98, 205
Civil Rights Movement, 6, 48, 98–99, 115, 121, 137, 169, 183–184, 197, 204, 226
Civil War, 4, 182, 186, 204
Claremont School of Theology, 198, 200
College of Medical Evangelists (*see* Loma Linda University)
Color Blind, 76, 165, 170, 172
Color Line, xvi, 17, 60, 67, 127, 186
Colored Department (*see also* Negro Department), 43, 71, 157, 257–258, 260–261
Columbia Union Conference, 42, 56, 111, 114, 163, 286
Commission on Negro Work, 32
Committee for the Advancement of the World-wide Work among Colored Seventh-day Adventists, 47
Committee of Ten, 107, 110, 114, 141, 296

314   *Protest & Progress*

Concerned Christian Council, 117, 291
Confederate South, 4
Congress of Racial Equality (C.O.R.E), 34
Council for Colored Workers, 31
Cultural Pluralism, 131, 133–134, 167, 170

**D**

Desegregation, 79, 97, 99, 121–122, 167–169
Diet of Spires, 211
Disciples of Christ, 35, 42
*Disintegration: The Splintering of Black America*, 163
Dodson's Bookstore, 46

**E**

*Ebony* magazine, 65
Ecclesiology, 182, 186
Edgefield Junction, 19, 128
Ellen G. White Estate (*also* White Estate), 3–4, 126, 130, 204
Emancipation, xiv, 2, 9, 13, 52
Emancipation Proclamation (*see also* Emancipation), 52, 238
Emmanuel Missionary College (*see also* Andrews University), 36, 247, 252, 255
Ephesus Church (New York), xv, 56–57, 103
Ephesus Church (Washington, D.C.), 45
Ephesus Church (Los Angeles), 82
Ephesus Church (Columbus), 121
Eschatology, 182, 185
Ethnic Solidarity, 172, 174
Ethnocentrism, 204
Ethnorelativism, 204
Evangelical United Brethren, 42
Extensive Free Will, 182–184

**F**

Fair Employment Practices Committee, 34, 97–98

Fisk University, 62
Formal Integration, 168, 177
Four Freedoms, 47, 254
Free Seventh-day Adventists, 59, 61
Freedman's Hospital, 43–44
Fugitive Slave Law, 211

**G**

General Conference Committee, 20, 26, 31, 48, 54, 70, 113, 132, 242, 257, 277
General Conference of Seventh-day Adventists, xviii, 7, 15, 20, 23, 26, 30–33, 45, 48–49, 54–55, 58, 60, 63, 86, 99–102, 104–105, 107, 112, 114, 125, 134, 137–138, 140, 154, 156–157, 186–187, 235, 237, 241, 243, 257, 260, 265–266, 268, 272, 274–278
General Conference Office of Ethnic Relations, 117, 296
General Conference Regional Department, 102, 140–141, 157, 271, 274, 277
Great Depression, xv, 30
Greater New York Conference, 40, 213

**H**

Harambee House, 138, 140
Harlem Academy, xv, 62, 64
Harlem Renaissance, xv, 62
Healdsburg College, 13
Historically Black Colleges and Universities (HBCU), 128
Homogenization, 167, 170
Howard University, 46, 197
Human Relations Council, 140
Human Relations Department, 116, 141

**I**

Informal integration, 168, 177
*Informant, The,* 140
Integration, 18, 35, 46, 48, 60, 72–73, 97, 101, 110, 115, 117, 119, 121–122, 132–133, 167–169, 234, 236, 286

## Subject Index 315

Integrationists, 115–122, 130–133, 137–139, 168, 177
Interracial, xxi, 114, 118, 170, 178
Involuntary desegregation, 169

## J

Jack Tar Hotel, 101
Jim Crow, 37–38, 195, 233

## K

Kansas Avenue Church (Riverside), 81
Ku Klux Klan, xvi, 233

## L

Lake Region Conference, 9, 56, 103, 105, 122, 153, 222–223
Lake Union Conference, 53, 56, 114, 222
Latin America, 164, 173
Latter rain, 165
Layman's Leadership Conference, 9, 99–101, 120, 137, 295
*Layman's Voice, The,* 74
Leadership Conference on Civil Rights, 98
Loma Linda University, xix, 74, 156, 246
Lutheran Church-Missouri Synod, 42
Lynching, 29–30, 41, 97
Lynwood Academy, 213

## M

Meharry Medical College, 66
Melrose Sanitarium, xiii
Melting Pot, 8, 169, 177–178, 203
*Message Magazine,* 52, 56, 140, 143, 197, 258, 261, 274, 305
Methodist Church, 35, 42, 68, 180
Miracle motif, 182, 184–185
Mid-America Union, 114
Middle axiom, 210
*Ministry Magazine,* 197
Mission particularity, 181
*Morgan v. Virginia,* 48

Morning Star Boat, xiii, 128
Munich accord, 37–38, 91
Mutual of America, 153

## N

National Association for the Advancement of Colored People (NAACP), 29, 98, 116, 268
National Association for the Advancement of World-Wide Work among Colored Seventh-day Adventists, 8, 19, 46
Nazi, 91, 190–191, 214
Neighborhood House, 99
Negro Department (*see also* Colored Department), 6, 20–23, 26, 33–34, 39, 51, 60, 174, 243
Nevada-Utah Conference, 74, 77
New Deal coalition, 98
*The New York Amsterdam News,* 37, 58
*New York Times,* 101
North American Division, xviii, xxi, 6, 45, 74–75, 98, 104, 109, 111, 114, 122, 124, 127, 144, 149, 152, 156, 164–165, 175, 180, 221, 273–274, 280, 302
*North American Informant* (see also *The Informant*), 138, 140
*North American Regional Voice,* 125, 176
Northeastern Conference, 9–10, 107, 122, 286
Northern California Conference, 73, 77

## O

*Oakland Tribune,* 101
Oakwood University (Junior College, College), xiii, xvii–xx, 36–39, 46, 52, 56, 62–65, 71, 73–74, 102–103, 107–108, 120–121, 124, 127–128, 152, 155–157, 172, 174, 176, 178, 200, 248, 252, 263, 287, 297, 299, 301–302
Office for Regional Conference Ministry, xx, 138, 155, 176, 213

Office of Human Relations (*see also* General Conference Office of Ethnic Relations), 116–118, 132, 141, 296
"Onward Christian Soldiers," xvii, xviii
"Our Duty to the Colored People," 15

**P**

Pacific Union College, 13, 61, 63, 65, 73, 164
Pacific Union Conference, 70, 76, 79–82
"The Pacific Union Conference Regional Department: Facts and Figures," 119
*Pacific Union Conference Regional News*, 72
*Pacific Union Recorder*, 80
Pacific Union Regional Department, 72
Pastoral Evangelism and Leadership Council (PELC), 176
People's Seventh-day Adventist Church (Washington, D.C.), 60
Pine Forge Academy, 39, 103, 173
Pledge of Allegiance, xvii–xviii
Poll Tax, 97
Post-racial, 170–171
Praise Worship, 200
Presbyterian Church, 35, 42
President's Executive Group on Administration (PREXAD), 106–107, 279–280, 284–285, 301
Principle of Policy, 24, 67
Private Integration, 169
Protestant ethic, 189
Protestant theology, 189, 203

**R**

Racial Bias, 113, 225
Racism, xix, 15, 30, 62, 138, 164, 177–178, 186, 204, 212, 221, 223, 225, 290
Radical determinism, 182
"Recommendation from the Council with Colored Workers," 32

Reconciliation, 198, 221–223
Red Summer, 29
Regional Advisory Committee, 102
Regional Affairs, 72, 118, 143, 305
"Regional Conferences and Human Relations" (*see also* "Sixteen Points, The"), 105, 272
Regional Department, 75, 102, 116, 119, 140–141, 157, 180, 271, 273–274, 277
Regional Fellowship, 87
*Regional News*, 72–73
Regional Territories, 141–142
Regional Territories' Council, 141–142
Regional Voice, 125, 176
Reparations, 136, 169, 207
Retirement system, 150–159, 176
*Review and Herald* (see *Adventist Review*)
Righteousness of God, 182, 187–192
*Riverside Press Enterprise*, 81
Riverside Sanitarium, 56
Rules of Order, 114, 283

**S**

Sacralization, 225
San Fernando Valley Academy, 61
*San Francisco Chronicle*, 101
*San Francisco Call-Bulletin*, 101
Scottsboro Boys, 64–65, 263
Self-determination, 1, 85, 110, 115
Self-determinationists, 115, 121–130, 133, 137–139, 178–179
Separate but Equal, xvii, 3, 5–6, 48, 98, 157, 165, 186
Sharon Seventh-day Adventist Church (Jamaica, New York), 45
Shiloh Academy, 62, 250
"Sixteen Points, The" (*see also* "Regional Conferences and Human Relations"), 106, 114
Slavery, xiv, xx, 2–4, 8–9, 52, 123, 139, 174, 184, 190, 195, 198, 204, 207–208, 210

Social conservatism, 4, 10
Social injustice, 183, 186, 189–191, 206
South American Division, 40
South Atlantic Conference, 51, 116, 279, 299
South Central Conference, 51, 69, 128–129, 149, 151, 287, 289, 299, 304
Southeastern California Conference, 74–76, 79–80, 82–86
Southeastern California Conference Black Caucus (SECBC), 75, 79–80, 84–87
Southern California Conference, 61, 74, 77
Southern Christian Leadership Conference, 79
*Southern Tidings*, 98
Southern Union Conference, xviii, 14, 32, 52, 98, 114, 116–117, 151, 235, 268, 288–290, 292
Southern Union Conference Human Relations Committee, 288
*Southern Work, The*, 126, 266
Structural Accommodation, 1, 23, 26, 31, 90, 167, 180–181, 192, 219, 225

**T**

Territorial Councils, 142–143, 299, 301–302, 304–305
*Thousand Oaks News Chronicle*, 81
*Together for a Finished Work*, 107
Types modality, 202, 206–207

**U**

Underground Railroad, 8, 198, 226
Union of American Hebrew Congregations, 42

Union Presidents' Council, 104
United Church of Christ, 42
United Sabbath-day Adventist Conference, 57
Unity, iii, 54, 86, 106, 117, 119, 130, 134, 136, 139, 165, 180, 188, 218–219, 239, 288
Unity in Diversity, 135, 227
University of Chicago, 36, 62
University of Illinois, 62
*U.S. News and World Report*, 120, 294

**V**

*Ventura County News*, 81
Voice of Prophecy, 99–100, 269
Voluntary Integration, 169
Voting Rights Act, 5

**W**

Washington Adventist University, 45, 190
Washington Conference, 80, 89
*Washington Post*, 108
Washington Missionary College, 45
Washington Sanitarium, 42–45, 255–256
West Coast Exceptionalism, 71
Western Lay-Persons for a Regional Conference (WLPRC), 86–87
Westerners United for a Regional Conference (WURC), 74–75, 77–80, 82, 84–87
"White flight," 136, 177, 179
World War I, 29, 34, 62, 233
World War II, xvi, 34, 191, 233

**Y**

Yale University, 62

# OTHER TITLES BY CALVIN B. ROCK

- *Our God Is Able* (Review and Herald, 1970)
- *Maranatha: The Lord Is Coming* (Review and Herald, 1976)
- *Church Leadership: A Call to Virtue* (Pacific Press, 1990)
- *The Love of Christ* (Pacific Press, 1991)
- *Go On! Vital Messages for Today's Christian* (Review and Herald, 1994)
- *Seeing Christ: Windows on His Saving Grace* (Review and Herald, 1994)
- *Perspectives: Black Seventh-day Adventists Face the Twenty-first Century* (Review and Herald, 1996)
- *Ellen White and Saving Perfection: A Compilation with Scripture and Commentary* (self-published, 2013)
- *Something Better: God's Gracious Provisions for Our Daily Decisions* (Review and Herald, 2014)
- *Faith Alive* (Outskirts Press, 2015)